/*Continued from front flap*

With this solid background of documenta-
tion, Fr. Winter's fresh conclusions on the
questions of divine or human institution of the
Papacy, the right of Peter to be called the first
Pope, and the position of Rome as the seat of
the Papacy, are a significant contribution to the
history of the early Church. Throughout, his
style is reasonable, thought-provoking, and
thoroughly scientific. For the historian, theologian, or student of Christianity, his book will
offer incomparable aid in solving the problem
of what really happened in the first centuries
of the Church.

Saint Peter and the Popes

SAINT PETER
AND THE POPES

MICHAEL M. WINTER

Formerly lecturer in Fundamental Theology at St. John's Seminary,
Wonersh

HELICON PRESS   DARTON, LONGMAN & TODD

BALTIMORE   LONDON

DARTON, LONGMAN & TODD LTD
29a GLOUCESTER ROAD
LONDON, SW7

HELICON PRESS
5305 EAST DRIVE, BALTIMORE 27, MD

First published 1960

PRINTED BY W. & J. MACKAY & CO. LTD., CHATHAM. NIHIL OBSTAT ADRIANUS VAN VLIET, S.T.D.
CENSOR DEPUTATUS. IMPRIMATUR E. MORROGH BERNARD, VIC.GEN. WESTMONASTERII, DIE 16A JANU-
ARII, 1960. THE NIHIL OBSTAT AND IMPRIMATUR ARE A DECLARATION THAT A BOOK OR PAMPHLET IS
CONSIDERED TO BE FREE FROM DOCTRINAL OR MORAL ERROR. IT IS NOT IMPLIED THAT THOSE WHO
HAVE GRANTED THE NIHIL OBSTAT AND IMPRIMATUR AGREE WITH THE CONTENTS, OPINIONS OR
STATEMENTS EXPRESSED.

PREFACE

OF the various Englishmen who have been associated with the papacy, it is not Nicholas Brakespeare, who actually became Pope, but Cardinal Reginald Pole who has made the greatest mark on papal history. He spent many years in the service of the Roman Curia, presided over the opening of the Council of Trent, together with Cardinals del Monte and Cervini, and in the conclave of 1549–50 he failed to gain the two-thirds majority by only one vote. It is somewhat startling to realize how tardily this man came to appreciate the divine origin of the papacy. In his early years he adhered to the view that the rule of the Pope was no more than a human convenience of government, and it was only after Bishop Fisher and Sir Thomas More had been executed for their fidelity to Rome that he changed his opinion.

The uncertainties of one so close to the papacy as Pole indicate the measure of obscurity which has shrouded this doctrine at various times. For an understanding of it, the Greek fathers are unhelpful, being pre-occupied with other matters; the Reformation polemics did much to obscure its true delineaments, and it was not until the last century that the doctrine began to receive methodical investigation. Newman's theory of doctrinal development, combined with the historical researches of others, particularly those of Batiffol, produced a new understanding of the early papacy.

Since the war a new impetus has been given to this much-studied matter by the publication of the findings of the Vatican excavations, and the important studies of Cullmann, Ludwig, and others. At the same time many of the classical studies on the papacy have long since been out of print, while encyclopedias and theological reviews which contain information on this subject are not accessible to the reader who does not have at his disposal an extensive theological library. It has therefore been my intention to present to the English reader a comprehensive account of all the important aspects of the early papacy, as revealed by modern scholarship, without attempting to exhaust any one of them, since this would be impossible in one volume.

My objective has been to supply an answer to the question 'Is the papacy to be ascribed to Christ, or is it merely a human instrument of

v

government invented by the church?' In answering that question one has the opportunity of demonstrating, constructively, how the early papacy developed. With such an objective in view the limits of the inquiry are fairly clear. The starting-point must be an examination of St. Peter's role in the infant church. For the term of the inquiry I have chosen the pontificate of St. Leo the Great. Nowadays it is almost universally agreed that he was a pope in substantially the same sense as, for instance Pius XII. The establishment of the papacy was achieved in the years between Peter and Leo. In attempting to decide how it was established inevitably one must enter the arena of controversy and pronounce for or against the papal claims. When faced with the same situation, Dr. Cullmann, in the preface to his book on St. Peter, expressed his unwillingness to aggravate the bitterness of denominational differences. That sentiment I wish to make my own. I shall be well contented if these pages may present a contribution to the irenical study of the papacy, an attempt to show that our attitude to the Roman primacy is perhaps not as unreasonable as might have been imagined.

In conclusion I wish to express my gratitude for having been accorded the use of the libraries at St. Basil's House, the London Oratory, and Worth Priory.

MICHAEL M. WINTER

Crawley, Sussex.
The Feast of S. S. Cornelius and Cyprian, 1958.

ACKNOWLEDGMENTS

We are indebted to His Eminence the Cardinal Archbishop of Westminster, Burns & Oates Ltd., and Sheed & Ward Inc., New York for extracts from the late Monsignor R. A. Knox's translation of the Bible, copyright 1944, 1948 and 1950 Sheed & Ward, Inc.; Longmans Green & Co. Ltd., and The Newman Press for material from Volume 25 in the series *Ancient Christian Writers* and The Society for Promoting Christian Knowledge for material from *Apocalypse of Baruch*, XI, 1 and 2 ed. R. H. Charles.

CONTENTS

LIST OF ABBREVIATIONS

A.	Acts of the Apostles.
C.S.E.L.	Corpus Scriptorum Ecclesiasticorum Latinorum, Vienna.
D.A.C.L.	Dictionnaire d'Archaéologie Chrétienne et de Liturgie, Paris.
D.T.C.	Dictionnaire de Théologie Catholique, Paris.
G.C.S.	Die Griechischen Christlichen Schriftsteller, Leipzig.
Hefele	Hefele-Leclerq, Histoire des Conciles, Paris.
J.	Gospel according to St. John.
J.T.S.	*Journal of Theological Studies.*
Jaffé	Jaffé—Wattenbach, Regesta Romanorum Pontificum. Leipzig, 1885.
L.	Gospel according to St. Luke.
M.	Gospel according to St. Matthew.
m.	Gospel according to St. Mark.
Mansi	Mansi, Sacrorum Conciliorum Collectio (ed. of 1901–27), Paris.
M.P.G.	Migne, Patrologia Graeca, Paris.
M.P.L.	Migne, Patrologia Latina, Paris.

I

ST. PETER IN THE GOSPELS

CERTAIN of the documents emanating from the Pope terminate with the quaint formula *Sub anulo Piscatoris* (Under the seal of the Fisherman). Nobody imagines for a moment that St. Peter had a ring with which to seal his correspondence, but the reference to the Apostle is characteristic, and is, of course, quite deliberate. Ever since the time when their authority was first seriously challenged the bishops of Rome have appealed to the power of St. Peter. In fact, they have claimed to inherit nothing more and nothing less than the authority which St. Peter had as the head of the Church. The nature of this claim decides in advance the nature of a study of the papacy. In order to appreciate, or justify, the position of the Pope, it is necessary first of all, to examine the position of St. Peter in the Apostolic group and in the early church. Unless a study of the papacy is firmly rooted in these historical sources, and the history of the primitive church, it will be no more than a creation of speculative theology.

Such an inquiry is helped considerably by the fact that the gospels give ample information about St. Peter. In fact, the very quantity of the matter is a preliminary indication that the man in question is differentiated from the rest of the Apostles. The famous Russian convert Vladimir Soloviev observed the singular fact that the name of Peter occurs with a frequency that cannot be ascribed to chance. A statistical analysis of the Gospels and the Acts shows that among the Twelve the name of Peter occurs no less than 195 times, whereas the rest of the Apostles together can muster only 130 nominations. This proportion is further enhanced by the fact that the Apostle who comes next in prominence is St. John, with only 29 references to his name.[1]

From this abundant information it is possible to reconstruct a comparatively full picture of St. Peter. He was a native of Bethsaida (J. 1:44), a fishing port on the northern shore of the Sea of Galilee. His

[1]McNabb, V., *New Testament Witnesses to St. Peter*, London, 1928, p. 136. In the latter part of Acts, Paul (named sometimes Saul) is mentioned approximately 150 times. Since, however, he is studied there in virtual isolation, its value as an indication of his status relative to the other apostles is negligible.

father's name was Jona or John (J. 1:42), and one brother is mentioned, Andrew. His own name Simon (Σίμων) is not Hebrew but Greek,[1] as is that of his brother Andrew ('Ανδρέας).[2] The possession of Greek names by a family living in a region where Greek was the language of commerce renders it probable that St. Peter himself spoke a little Greek, in addition to his native Aramaic. Concerning the rest of his education the gospels are silent. In the Acts (4:13) Peter and John are described by the priests and elders, as being 'without learning', a designation which does not mean complete illiteracy. Much the same expression was used of Christ (J. 7:15) and it is certain that he knew how to read. It did mean, however, that they had not passed through the rabbinic schools, and did not therefore belong to the intelligentsia of the nation. Some knowledge of reading and writing was not uncommon among the men at that date, and it is not improbable that St. Peter, too, enjoyed this accomplishment. His trade was that of a fisherman, and in this occupation he and his brother were in partnership with the sons of Zebedee (L. 5:10). It is clear from the gospels that he was married, and he was perhaps in early middle-age during the public life of Christ, since at that time his mother-in-law was still alive. Of his wife nothing is told, and the accounts of her martyrdom together with those of her children are purely legendary in character. It is clear from the data available that he did not possess the greatness of St. Paul nor the charm of St. John, but the principal trait which emerges in his character is that of un-questioning fidelity to the person of Christ, summed up in the words: 'Lord, to whom should we go? Thy words are the words of eternal life.'[3]

These details give a fair amount of information about the person of Peter, but much more information can be gleaned about his position in the group of the Apostles. In order to do this it is necessary to read between the lines to a certain extent. It must be emphasized constantly that the gospels were not written to prove anything about church government. They were a simple biography of Christ, and when they are used to substantiate such a matter as the precise position of St. Peter one cannot expect to find proofs of a juridical type. They will yield information about his position in an unselfconscious way, which from many points of view is all the more convincing. Their account of St.

---

[1]Cullmann, Oscar, *Saint Pierre*, Neuchatel and Paris, 1952, p. 13. And Zorrell, F, *Lexicon Graecum Novi Testamenti*, Paris, 1931, col. 1202.
[2]Zorrell, op. cit., col. 110.
[3]J. 6: 68.

Peter is, moreover, unaffected, consistent, and in complete harmony with the general tenor of the gospel narrative.

St. Peter is introduced at the very threshold of the public life, at the point where Christ is solemnly acclaimed by St. John the Baptist. At that period a number of St. John's disciples transfer their allegiance to Christ, and among them, though not the first to be invited, is St. Peter (J. 1:40). Later on the members of this small group receive their definitive vocation, and in this incident, with its miracle of the draught of fish, St. Peter is clearly the central figure (L. 5:10). In the pages of the New Testament various lists of the Apostles are given; some of them are just random groupings of the names, but four of them are of special interest.[1] These are the only lists which give the names of all the twelve, and they are drawn up on an artificial scheme; in short, they are the official catalogues, and each one starts with the name of Peter. A small point it is true, but one which is deliberate, and which is emphasized by St. Matthew: 'These are the names of the twelve Apostles: First ($\pi\rho\hat{\omega}\tau\sigma$) Simon also called Peter.' The use of the word 'first' before the name which occurs first in the list must indicate some kind of pre-eminence, or else it is a meaningless tautology.[2] Singled out thus at the head of the Apostolic group, Peter henceforth enjoys a general prominence in a variety of circumstances. On several occasions the group of disciples is called 'Simon and his companions' (m. 1:36).[3] When Christ walks on the waters towards the boat of the terrified Apostles it is Peter who shares in the miracle and also walks upon the sea (M. 14:29). At the feast of the Pasch which was the prelude to Christ's arrest it is Peter and John who are chosen to make the preparations, conceivably to preserve the knowledge of the rendezvous from Judas (L. 22:8).

A rather more significant series of events is the group of important incidents from which the majority of the Apostles are deliberately excluded by Christ. At each of these St. Peter is present and indeed plays the leading role. The first of these incidents is the miraculous healing of the daughter of the ruler of the synagogue (L. 8:51). More significant, though, is the Transfiguration (L. 9:18), where St. Peter alone speaks with Christ, leaving the sons of Zebedee to look on as silent witnesses. In the Garden of Gethsemane Peter is once more in the inner circle

---

[1] M. 10:2; m. 3:16; L. 6:14; A. 1:13.
[2] Lagrange, M. J., *L'Évangile selon S. Matthieu*, Paris, 1948 (7th ed.), p. 195.
[3] $\Sigma\acute{\iota}\mu\omega\nu$ $\varkappa\alpha\grave{\iota}$ $o\acute{\iota}$ $\mu\varepsilon\tau$' $\alpha\grave{\upsilon}\tauo\hat{\upsilon}$.

(m. 14:33), and he alone draws a sword to defend the Master at the arrest (J. 18:10).

Most revealing of all are the numerous occasions on which St. Peter is seen to be the spokesman of the Apostolic group. He voices the questions which are in the minds of all. He is approached by outsiders as the representative of the group, and he even receives the reprimands which are destined to correct the faults of them all. When Christ asks the Apostles 'Whom do men say that I am?' it seems quite natural that St. Peter should reply for them all (m. 8:29). With the same easy confidence he endeavours to rectify Christ's hard words about the sufferings of the Messiah, and thus he receives the rebuke which they all deserved (m. 8:32, 33). This attitude to St. Peter is not confined to the disciples alone. When the collectors of the Temple tax approach they single out St. Peter and say to him: 'Does not your (plural) Master pay the Temple pence)' (M. 17:24). The Master does in fact pay it and commissions St. Peter to do so for him. After the sermon on the Bread of Life, many of the disciples departed and walked no more in Jesus' company. Wishing to make sure of the loyalty of the twelve, Christ asks them: 'Would you, too, go away?' (J. 6:68, 69). The answer is voiced by St. Peter: 'Lord to whom should we go? Thy words are the words of eternal life.' Within the group of the Apostles, it is St. Peter who asks the questions which are common to them all. He inquires about the duty of forgiveness (M. 18:21), and about the reward which will compensate those who have given up all for Christ's sake (m. 10:28). In the dramatic scenes of the Last Supper, St. Peter is the one who protests against having his feet washed by Christ (J. 13:6), and he takes the lead in declaring his fidelity to the Lord, who is then seen to be in danger (m. 14:29). Of especial significance is the announcement of the resurrection, when the angel says: 'Go and tell Peter and the rest of his disciples that he is going before you into Galilee' (m. 16:7). Various other examples could be quoted, but their tenor is the same. Quite naturally and unselfconsciously the gospels show that St. Peter is in a place apart, and this is apparent without reference to the most important Petrine texts. The value of these incidents lies, too, in the fact that they show how the principal Petrine texts are in conformity with the general tone of the gospel, and indeed they demand the promises made in these greater texts as an explanation of how one Apostle could have emerged to preeminence in a group so sensitive about seniority.

This prominence which is accorded to St. Peter is not confined to any one of the gospels. That the synoptics are unanimous in their verdict on St. Peter is now agreed by the majority of Protestant scholars,[1] and consistently it has been taught by the Catholics. As for the fourth gospel, there is not quite the same agreement. Catholics are unanimous in upholding its historical character, and seeing in it a picture of St. Peter which is the same as that of the synoptics. For a long time Protestants have been reluctant to grant so much to St. John, but the tide is now flowing more strongly in his favour. It is significant to see that Cullmann[2] accords him a very large measure of agreement with the synoptic gospels.

In searching for an adequate reason to explain how St. Peter could have stolen so much of the limelight from his rather sensitive companions one would naturally expect to find some intervention on the part of Christ. Such an intervention is, in fact, foretold very early in the public life, when Our Lord promises to Peter a change of name (J. 1:42). The incident may not appear important to a reader of the twentieth century, but for the ancients it had a peculiar significance, and even more so for the Jews. Names for them were closely bound up with the person's role in life, and the imposition of a name by God denoted the conferring of a special divine mission. The best-known example is probably that of Abraham. Prior to his special vocation he was called Abram, but when called to be the father of the chosen race, God spoke to him saying: 'No longer shall thy name be Abram, thou shalt be called Abraham, the father of a throng' (Gen. 17:5). The name Abram[3] means literally 'exalted father', and Abraham[4] is rendered as 'chief of a multitude.' The change of his name not only showed that God was calling him to a special task, but it also gave a clear indication of the nature of his destiny.

In St. John's account of the first meeting of Christ and St. Peter the new name is already foretold: 'Thou art Simon the Son of Jona; thou shalt be called Cephas (which means the same as Peter)' (J. 1:42). When it was actually conferred is not so easy to determine. When St. Mark is narrating the call of the twelve he says quite simply: 'To Simon he gave the fresh name of Peter' (m. 3:16). It is possible that the change

[1] Cullmann, op. cit., p. 21.
[2] Cullmann, op. cit., p. 22.
[3] אַבְרָם.

[4] אַבְרָהָם. Thus the popular play on words. The strict etymology is somewhat more complicated. Cf. J. Chaine, *Le Livre de la Genèse*, Paris, 1951, p. 228.

of name took place then, but the Greek text does not demand it absolutely. It could refer to a change which took place at some time in the
public life and which St. Mark notes here for the sake of convenience.
The most obvious occasion for the change to have been made is the
famous confession of St. Peter recorded by St. Matthew: 'Thou art
Peter and upon this rock I will build my church.' As will be seen below,
this incident shows clearly why the enigmatic name 'Rock' should have
been chosen, and it also makes St. Peter's role in the church quite clear.
No more reasonable occasion could be found to make the change and it
is very probably to be traced to this time. It must be emphasized that it
was a solemn act and not just a nickname. Other Apostles were given
nicknames. The sons of Zebedee were called 'Boanerges' (sons of
thunder) (m. 3:17), and St. Thomas was called Didymus (J. 11:16),
but none of these names persisted. Simon's new name was in a different
category, and it was closely bound up with his role in the church.

The name Peter is so familiar in the present day that it is hard to
realize that as a name it was unknown to the ancients. Attempts have
been made to show that it was derived from the Latin *Petronius*, but
the theory is now abandoned.[1] The Latin name *Petrus*, from which the
English version is transliterated, was itself a transliteration from the
Greek πέτρος (*petros*, a rock). This was how the New Testament
authors translated the Aramaic word *kepha* which Christ must have
used. *Kepha* means quite simply a rock; like its Greek equivalent *petros*,
it was never used as a proper name,[2] and its sense is clearly shown in the
illustration of the 'wise man who built his house on a rock' (M. 7:24).
When translating the words of Christ into Greek, the better word for
the Evangelist to use was *petra* (πέτρα, a mass of rock), as indeed
occurs in the sentence 'Upon this rock I will build my church' (M.
16:18). When the word was to be used as a man's name it was quite
natural to use the masculine noun *petros* (πέτρος). This latter denotes
primarily an individual rock, but the nuance is slight, and does not
affect the real signification.[3]

In the famous passage of St. Matthew[4] the play upon words is deliberate and it leaves no doubt as to the reason why Simon's name was

[1]Cullmann, op. cit., p. 14. Also Tricot, A., in art. 'Saint Pierre', in D.T.C.,
Vol. XII (ii), col. 1747.
[2]Cullmann, O., art. 'Πέτρος' in Kittel-Friedrich, *Theologisches Wörterbuch
zum Neuen Testament*, Vol. VI, p. 100.
[3]Cullmann, *St. Pierre*, p. 14.
[4]M. 16:18.

changed: 'Thou art Rock and upon this rock I will build my church.'
Before proceeding to a full examination of St. Matthew's famous text in
the sixteenth chapter of his gospel, it should be remembered that Peter's
change of name is itself an important event and already gives some
explanation of his coming to the forefront. It shows that Christ had
singled him out for a special position, and in its turn it requires further
explanation; in a sense, it demands as its background the text of
Matthew 16:18.

There can be few passages of the New Testament which are better
known than this. When the Pope is carried into St. Peter's on the *sedia
gestatoria* for the celebration of a solemn high Mass the choir greets his
entry with the triumphant chant of '*Tu es Petrus . . .*' (Thou art
Peter . . .). In the pages of theological polemics the text is likewise
echoed and re-echoed, so that there can be few texts of scripture which
have caused so much ink to flow. The importance of the passage and the
controversy which has raged over it has tended to isolate it in the popular imagination. It must be emphasized, though, that the passage is in
complete harmony with the whole of the gospel picture of St. Peter,
serving as an explanation and itself being explained by the overall predominance of St. Peter in the Apostolic group.

The words of St. Matthew's sixteenth chapter are so important that
they deserve to be quoted in full:

16. Then Simon Peter answered, Thou art the Christ, the Son of the living God.

ἀποκριθεὶς δὲ Σίμων Πέτρος εἶπεν· σὺ εἶ ὁ Χριστὸς ὁ υἱὸς τοῦ Θεοῦ τοῦ ζῶντος.

17. And Jesus answered him, Blessed art thou Simon son of Jona; it is not flesh and blood, it is my Father in heaven that has revealed this to thee.

ἀποκριθεὶς δὲ ὁ Ἰησοῦς εἶπεν αὐτῷ· Μακάριος εἶ, Σίμων Βαριωνᾶ, ὅτι σὰρξ καὶ αἷμα οὐκ ἀπεκάλυψέν σοι ἀλλ' ὁ πατήρ μου ὁ ἐν τοῖς οὐρανοῖς.

18. And I tell thee this in my turn, that thou art Peter, and it is upon this rock that I will build my church; and the gates of hell shall not prevail against it; and I will give to thee the keys of the kingdom of heaven; and whatever thou shalt bind on earth shall be bound in heaven; and whatever thou shalt loose on earth shall be loosed in heaven.

κἀγὼ δέ σοι λέγω ὅτι σὺ εἶ Πέτρος, καὶ ἐπὶ ταύτῃ τῇ Πέτρᾳ οἰκοδομήσω μου τὴν ἐκκλησίαν, καὶ πύλαι ᾅδου οὐ κατισχύσουσιν αὐτῆς. καὶ δώσω σοι τὰς κλεῖδας τῆς βασιλείας τῶν οὐρανῶν, καὶ ὃ ἐὰν δήσῃς ἐπὶ τῆς γῆς ἔσται δεδεμένον ἐν τοῖς οὐρανοῖς, καὶ ὃ ἐὰν λύσῃς ἐπὶ τῆς γῆς ἔσται λελυμένον ἐν τοῖς οὐρανοῖς.

During the sixteenth and seventeenth centuries an attack was directed against the meaning of the passage. It was, for instance, denied that it referred to St. Peter himself, or that it included any idea of authority in the church.

Towards the end of the nineteenth century the hostility became more extreme and many critical scholars, particularly in Germany, denied the authenticity of the text. The principal arguments adduced were the absence of the passage from the parallel sections in St. Mark and St. Luke, and the occurrence of the rare word *ekklesia*, which is found in only one other place in the gospels. To the scientific considerations there was sometimes, at least implicitly, present the idea summed up in the well-known adage *Is fecit cui prodest*. It was alleged that all or part of the text was introduced into the gospels by those who wished to reinforce the authority of the bishop of Rome. For instance, A. Resch[1] excluded the whole of verse 18 and would admit the inclusion of verse 19 only if it were addressed to all the Apostles in the plural. H. J. Holtzmann[2] declared that the passage assumed its present form only at the end of the second century, and that it revealed the background of the church of Rome becoming aware of its position. The progress of critical scripture studies forced such critics to modify their views, and the last serious attack upon the integrity of this text was that of the distinguished scholar A. Harnack[3] in 1918. The basic principle of Harnack's position was the assumption that the 'gates of hell' could mean only the death of an individual (in this particular context of course it would be immunity from death), and the text must therefore refer the attack of the gates to Peter's person. Accordingly Harnack emended the text to an alleged original as follows: 'Thou art Peter and the gates of hell (i.e. death) will not prevail against thee; and I will give to thee . . . etc. 'Having decided on the original form of the text he sought to produce evidence in favour of it in the writings of the early church. In several passages of his writings St. Ephraim of Syria has the phrases: 'Blessed art thou, Simon . . . and the barriers of hell will not prevail against THEE' (Sermons on Isaias, 54:17), and 'Blessed art thou, Simon, and the gates of hell shall not conquer THEE' (*Evangelii Concordantis Expositio*).[4] It is known that St. Ephraim was commenting

---

[1] *Ausscanonische Parralleltexte zu den Evangelien*, II, p. 185.

[2] *Handkommentar*, Freiburg im Breisgau, 1889, I, p. 193.

[3] In *Sitznbungsberichte der königlisch preussischen Akademie der Wissenshaften*, 1918, p. 637 ff. cf. Jalland, T. G., *The Church and the Papacy*, London, 1944, pp. 94, 95.

[4] *Evangelii Concordantis Expositio*, ed. J. B. Aucher and G. Mösinger, Venice, 1876, p. 153.

on Tatian's compilation of the four gospels called the Diatesseron, which was composed towards the end of the second century. Harnack therefore considered that the Diatesseron knew nothing of the longer text as it is read today. He also adduced in favour of the shorter version, passages from Macarius Magnes, Ambrose, Epiphanius, and Jerome. By contrast he declared that the first writer to use the longer form as it now stands was Tertullian, about the year 200.

The argument is impressive at first sight, but its premises are not as well established as was once imagined. If indeed the primitive text was the shorter version preferred by Harnack, it is difficult to understand how the longer one has survived in all the important manuscripts and versions. Closer examination of Harnack's premises reveals certain weaknesses. The key phrase, 'the gates of hell', will be examined fully farther on, but for the moment let it suffice to say that it is inaccurate to restrict its meaning solely to the death of an individual. The first assumption does not, in fact, enjoy the decisiveness which Harnack attributed to it. The second principle is likewise insecure. It is true that St. Ephraim was quoting from the Diatesseron, but it is open to question whether he was quoting every word. More recent research has made it clear that the text of the Diatesseron contained the Petrine promise as it is read in the Bible today. Indeed, the passage of the *Evangelii Concordantis Expositio* quoted above is preceded almost immediately by the words: 'When the Lord built his church, he built a tower whose foundations were able to support all that was later to be built on to it.' Clearly, the copy of the Diatesseron which St. Ephraim had in front of him must have contained the Petrine promise in its long form.[1]

In the period between the two world wars the case in favour of the authenticity of the text became still stronger. In particular the strongly Semitic tone of the passage has ruled out the possibility of its originating anywhere but Palestine, and the early date which must be ascribed to the gospel of St. Matthew brings the time of composition back to the middle of the first century. Under such conditions it is difficult to postulate interpolations into the gospel text, and now scholars of all persuasions are almost unanimous in declaring that the Petrine promise was present in the original gospel in the form that is printed out above.

The absence of the Petrine promise from the parallel passages in

---

[1] cf. Ephraim's use of M. 16:16–18, quoted in C. Burkitt, *Saint Ephraim's Quotations from the Gospels*, Cambridge, 1901, p. 30.

Mark and Luke[1] is no longer alleged as an argument against the authenticity of Matthew's version, but it does merit some explanation. It is a strange enigma that two of the synoptics should follow the third in all the details of an incident, using at times the very same words, and then stop short at a point which appears to be the climax of the particular section. To argue from the absence in the parallels to the non-authenticity of the text would indeed be rash, and if one were consistent in following such a principle one should reject the majority of the Sermon on the Mount, only small portions of which are to be found outside St. Matthew.[2] In other words it would lead to a Biblical *reductio ad absurdum*. It must be remembered furthermore that both John and Luke have strongly pro-Petrine passages which are absent from Matthew.[3] Mark alone is without any such passage, but when it is remembered that the gospel of St. Mark was based on the catechesis of St. Peter himself, the omission is not surprising. The same gospel also omits several other incidents recorded by Matthew and Luke, seemingly because they accord prominence to St. Peter. They are the miracle of the coin in the fish's mouth, the miraculous draught of fish, Peter's walking upon the waters, and the appearance of the risen Christ to St. Peter. The realization of the editorial work of the evangelists has provided a principle which may elucidate the cause of the omission of the Petrine text from the parallels. It is now generally recognized that the evangelists selected and arranged the details of the life of Christ in a manner which seems unusual to the readers of modern biography where the overriding principle is chronology. For the evangelists it was otherwise, and it appears that they chose matter from very varied periods in the career of Christ to amalgamate into the long discourses and other subject-groupings. Concerning the text in question, it has been suggested[4] that St. Matthew is here amalgamating two incidents, the confession of St. Peter and Christ's promise to him. The latter may have been transposed from another place. The absence of an incident from the parallel places in the synoptics may well indicate the transference of a text, but not its interpolation. The opinion of the Protestant scholar K. L. Schmidt[5] is a fitting conclusion to the examination of the authenticity of the text. He

[1] m. 8:29; L. 9:20.
[2] Cullmann, op. cit., p. 154.
[3] J. 21:15–17; L. 22:31–32.
[4] Lagrange, M. J., *S. Marc*, Paris, 1911, p. 218.
[5] Art. 'Καλέω', Kittel, *Theologisches Wörterbuch*, Vol. III, pp. 502–39. More accessible to English readers in the series *Bible Key Words*, Vol. *The Church*, trans. J. Coates, especially p. 36.

says categorically that the text is above suspicion on manuscript evidence, but remarks that the persistence of a reluctant attitude is due principally to a desire to banish the *locus classicus* for the papal primacy.

The agreement which is now almost universal as to the authenticity of the Petrine text does not quite solve all the difficulties, for there are some who push their doubts further. Certain critics (notably the Form critics) ask whether the authentic gospels are a true record of the sayings of Christ. In other words, although these words are in the original gospel, did the original gospel report the words of Christ or did it contain a large quantity of the opinions which the early church attributed to Christ?

Strictly speaking, the defence of the reliability of the gospels as historical records lies outside the scope of this book. Excellent works have been written for this purpose.[1] A word, however, must be said about the attitude of the Form critics, since their most famous representative, R. Bultmann, has denied consistently that the words of Matthew 16:16–18 were spoken by Christ.

Originally the exponents of this school of thought set out to examine the method by which the oral teaching came to be formed into the written gospel. It was almost inevitable that they should, in fact, pass judgements on the reliability of the written text. Their premises and methods are open to many criticisms, and in particular Christ's teaching is unlikely to have been changed, as suggested by these critics, in the short space of time available between the death of Christ and the writing of the gospels.[2] It is rather unrealistic to imagine that the eye-witnesses, many of whom were still alive when the gospels were written, would have allowed any tampering with the sacred memory of the Master, and his exact words and deeds. The presence of the rare word *ekklesia* has been used before by those who wished to impugn the text in question, and it has been used more recently by Bultmann and others of the Form critics' school[3] in their attempts to remove the passage from the teaching of Christ himself. Such a word could not have been on the

---

[1]Cf. Arendzen, *The Gospels, Fact, Myth, or Legend?*; Batiffol, *The Credibility of the Gospels*; Chaine, J., *Valeur Historique des Évangiles*, Paris, 1944. Also the archaeological studies of Ramsay and Kenyon. A useful study of the actual process by which the words of Christ were preserved in the oral catechesis and thence transferred to the written sources is Cerfaux, L., *La Voix Vivante de l'Évangile au début de l'Église*, English translation, Darton, Longman & Todd.

[2]Redlich, E. B., *Form Criticism*, London, 1939, p. 78.

[3]cf. Bultmann, R., *Geschichte der Synoptischen Tradition*, Gottingen, 1921, pp. 147–50; *Theologie des Neuen Testaments*, Tübingen, 1953, pp. 8, 49, 60. The Modernists, too, used much the same arguments. Cf. Loisy, A., *Les Évangiles Synoptiques*, Ceffonds, 1907, 8, II, p. 815.

lips of Jesus, so they declare, since the thought of a church was utterly alien to his preaching. The only explanation of its presence is the editorial work of the early church; done in all sincerity, one is led to hope! Confirmatory evidence is also adduced from the fact that the word *ekklesia* is found in only one other passage in the gospels (M. 18:17).

The argument from word statistics is rather fragile and needs no lengthy refutation. The same apparent difficulty could be alleged in the Epistle to the Romans. The word 'cross' occurs only once, but the idea of a redemptive death is fundamental to the whole letter. Similarly the idea of the church permeates the whole of the First Epistle of St. Peter, but the word does not occur at all.[1] What is essential is to examine whether the idea and concept of an *ekklesia* is consistent with the teaching of Christ.

For the writers of classical Greek, *ekklesia* denoted the legislative assembly of the citizens called together by a herald. This word was chosen quite deliberately to translate a Hebrew expression in the preparation of the Septuagint translation of the Old Testament. In the opinion of these translators the word *ekklesia* was the most accurate way to render the Hebrew *qahal*,[2] which also denoted an assembly. Although this word is used for all kinds of assemblies, for wars, religious feasts, and so on, its meaning *par excellence* is that of the chosen people called together by God and assembled before Sinai for the covenant which would then constitute them as the privileged race allied to God. In this sense it occurs frequently in the book of Deuteronomy. It is therefore relevant to the problem in hand, to see whether the idea of an assembly of people is consistent with the thought of Christ.

Once expressed in these terms, an affirmative answer seems to be likely. The frequent references to the Kingdom of Heaven are the first indications that Christ is forming some kind of group around himself. The Kingdom was an element of his preaching from the very start of the public life, and his subsequent teaching and activity gradually clarified the notion. The calling of the Apostles gave the group stability and a governing body. The parables in Matthew's thirteenth chapter reveal many of the characteristics of the group; notably that it will not have to wait until the second coming of Christ before it is constituted.

[1]Cullmann, op. cit., p. 169 (following Oepke); Lowe, J., *Saint Peter*, Oxford, 1956, p. 50.
[2]Cf. Zorrell, op. cit., col. 398.

Details of the life and practices of the community are indicated by the numerous rules given to them and by the sacraments and institutions which will be theirs. It is then a determinate group which Christ refers to as his 'little flock' (L. 12:32). One of the most reliable ways of interpreting the mind of Christ is to examine how the Apostolic church understood his words. On this particular question their conduct is an eloquent testimony to their understanding of the intention of Christ. They display no hesitations. From the very start, their behaviour shows their awareness of their nature as a society, and nearly every chapter of the Acts of the Apostles could be cited to justify this judgement. One short passage is of particular value:

'They persevered in the teaching of the Apostles, and in the fellowship, in the breaking of bread and the prayers.'[1]

Thus far it is apparent that Christ had the intention of gathering round himself a group which corresponds well with the notion of an assembly or *ekklesia*. However, a deeper inspection of the matter shows that Christ's group was not just any assembly, but in fact the Messianic assembly, expected since Old Testament times.[2]

The fact that Jesus was the promised Messiah is a truth which needs no justification here. What is often forgotten, though, is the fact that in the Jewish understanding of the Messiah he was intimately connected with the Messianic people. The assembly which Jesus gathered round himself had, in fact, all the characteristics of that Messianic people. That the group of the Apostles should number exactly twelve is a clear imitation of the twelve tribes, and prepares the ground for seeing the church as the new Israel which the Messiah will constitute as the perfection of the Israel of the Old Covenant. When these Apostles are sent on their preliminary mission, the tasks which they are instructed to perform are specifically Messianic works (M. 10:6–10).[3] The 'little flock' spoken of by Jesus on various occasions (L. 12:32 and M. 26:31) is in fact the Messianic 'remnant'[4] which is the true Israel. More clearly still does the Messianic nature of the group appear when the institution of the Eucharist is examined. All the accounts of the institution agree that Christ declared the chalice to be his blood of the Covenant (in fact, the New Covenant, in the accounts of St. Luke and St. Paul). The implied

---

[1]A. 2:42. A literal translation of the critically established Greek text, whose nuances are not rendered in the standard translations.
[2]The idea is admirably developed by Cullmann, op. cit., p. 170.
[3]Lowe, op. cit., p. 53.
[4]Cullmann, op. cit., p. 172.

reference to the inauguration of the Old Covenant on Sinai is obvious; there is a clear parallel between the two incidents, showing that Christ is setting up the new People of God. The consciousness of being the assembly of God is still more marked in the life of the Apostolic church.[1] In the eyes of the Jewish converts particularly, the events of the Jerusalem community in its early days are the re-enactment of the events in the desert of Sinai when the Old Covenant was established. The Christians looked upon themselves as the new people of God, bound to Him by a New Covenant.

In other words, the idea embodied in the Christian community as envisaged by Christ corresponds perfectly with the idea underlying the word *ekklesia*. If, then, the idea was present to the mind of Christ there is no reasonable ground for doubting that he spoke the word which connotes it. The solution of this difficulty removes the latest of the relevant problems connected with the Petrine text. It is indeed an anomaly that such dispute should have arisen, for the evidence of even this last defence of the text was appreciated half a century ago by the Jewish convert Alfred Edersheim.[2]

Although defence of the text of the Petrine promise may be lengthy, the sense of the passage itself is not unduly complex. First, however, some attempt must be made to situate the incident in its historical setting.

If the evangelist has amalgamated two incidents here, then it is difficult to say exactly where the Petrine promise was made. If, as is possible, the Petrine promise followed directly after the famous confession, then the location is fairly certain, since this latter event took place in the vicinity of Caesarea Philippi. The precise spot is usually taken to be a large rock to the south of the site of the town, which suggests so eloquently the metaphor of the 'rock'.[3] At the base of this rock is a grotto, out of which flows a stream which is the principal source of the Jordan. The beauty and solemnity of the place had always commended it as a religious shrine, first of all dedicated to Baal and Astaroth, and later under Greek influence to the woodland god Pan. This accounts for the original name Panaeus which has been modified to the modern Arabic name of Baniyas.

---

[1]cf. The excellent study of Cerfaux, L., *La Théologie de l'Église suivant S. Paul*, Paris, 1948 (2nd ed.), pp. 3–111. English translation.

[2]Edersheim, A., *The Life and Times of Jesus the Messiah*, London, 1907, II, p. 84.

[3]Prat, F., *Jésus Christ*, Paris, 1952 (21st ed.), I, p. 428; Smith, C. A., *Historical Geography of the Holy Land*, p. 474.

The first words which Christ addressed to St. Peter, 'Blessed art thou', are (by reason of their inversion) an indication of the Semitic character of the speech. In fact, the passage is so impregnated with Aramaic metaphors and constructions that it could have had no other origin but Palestine. This fact has been admitted even by Bultmann, who, though unwilling to attribute the words to Christ, is prepared to give them a Palestinian origin. The next phrase bears the same imprint. The inability of 'flesh and blood' to make known the nature of Christ means simply the limitations of human powers in such profound religious truths.[1] The Aramaic word behind Peter (rock) has already been discussed, and it can be seen that the play upon words is most obvious in the original: 'Thou art *Kepha,* and upon this *Kepha* . . .' When the Aramaic pun is thus appreciated it is clear that the subsequent promise is addressed to St. Peter in person. This particular point did, however, give rise to much dispute at the time of the Reformation, when many Protestant theologians, following Luther, declared that it referred to St. Peter's faith, or Christ, or even the rock at Panaeus.[2] Quite recently the two Jewish scholars Strack and Billerbeck[3] have returned to the same idea, in suggesting that the Greek version of Matthew is a false translation of an Aramaic original which was possibly 'I say to thee, Peter: On this rock I will build my church . . .' The assumption is quite gratuitous, and it must be remembered that in the absence of the Aramaic original of Matthew there is no justification for challenging the reliability of the Greek text. It is indeed an axiom that all New Testament exegesis must start from the Greek text as it is preserved in the best manuscripts. This opinion of Strack and Billerbeck is an isolated case; in fact, Catholics and Protestants alike take it for granted now that the promise was made to St. Peter in person.[4] Having thus designated the person, Christ comes right to the pith of his promise with the words 'Upon this rock I will build my church'. St. Peter is here singled out as the one who will be the head of the infant church and, humanly speaking, its founder. This line of thought may seem a little unfamiliar to the reader of the present day but to the Jews the metaphors involved no difficulties. In a general way the Bible speaks of God

[1]cf. Gal. 1:16.
[2]cf. Cullmann, op. cit., p. 147.
[3]Strack and Billerbeck, *Kommentar zum Neuen Testament aus Talmud und Midrasch,* Munich, 1922–8, Vol. I, pp. 722 ff.
[4]For instance among Protestants, Jalland, op. cit., p. 55; Lowe, op. cit., p. 56; Cullmann, *Theol. Wörterbuch,* art. cit., Vol. VI, p. 108.

as the rock of Israel, denoting its source of strength and security, but in a more precise sense the idea of a building upon a rock denoted the relationship between the founder and a human society. There is an interesting comparison in the Midrash Jalqut,[1] where Abraham the father of the chosen race is spoken of as the rock. 'When God looked upon Abraham who was to arise, he said, Behold I have found a rock on which I can build and found the world, Therefore He called Abraham a Rock . . .' The society which St. Peter will govern is the church, or the assembly of those called by God. The discussions above about the word *ekklesia* show how Christ conceived of his church, namely as the people of the New Covenant, corresponding to the people of the Old Covenant of Sinai.[2] This idea would present no obstacle to the understanding of the Apostles, since they were by then aware of the Messianic character of Jesus.

Having enunciated the main promise, Christ proceeds to elucidate certain particular aspects of it. The first of these is the promise that the 'gates of hell will not prevail against it'. This particular sentence has occasioned a certain amount of discussion and it is not altogether free from difficulties. The metaphor of the gates is taken directly from the Old Testament. The need of fortifying the gate, and the central position that it occupied in the cities of the ancients made it the natural focus of the town, the place of the law courts and a symbol of the city itself.[3] The prevalence of this idea in the Oriental tradition explains the use of the title 'Sublime Porte' in the Ottoman Empire. The city in question is called *hades* (hell). This was the Greek word for the underworld of their mythology and religion, and the Greek translator of St. Matthew saw no harm in using it to denote the underworld of Jewish religious thought. The obvious question now arises, precisely who or what is the 'it' which will survive the onslaught of the power of the underworld? Grammatical considerations would indicate the nearest feminine noun as being that which is represented by the word *autes* (it). The word thus indicated is *ekklesia* (church) and not *petra* (rock). The precise nature of

[1]Strack and Billerbeck, op. cit., Vol. I, pp. 732–8, quoted by Lowe, op. cit., pp. 56, 57.

[2]If Christ had used a Hebrew word, it would probably have been קָהָל rather than עֵדָה. Had he used an Aramaic expression it could have been קְהָלָא, צִבּוּרָא, or כְּנִישְׁתָּא. The latter is regarded as possible by Lagrange (op. cit., p. 324), and highly probable by Schmidt (art. cit., pp. 46–48).

[3]cf. Gen. 22:17; Deut. 16:5; III K. 8:37.

the onslaught to be survived is the matter which has caused the debate. The most obvious meaning to attribute to the expression is that of death, since it is most frequently used in this sense in the Old Testament.[1] However, it must be noted that the use of the expression as denoting death is always in the sense of somebody going down to the underworld. The idea of the gates of the underworld being actively engaged is not found in this sense, and in the present instance the active use is the first indication that another meaning is to be sought. With the progress of Jewish theology they acquired more precise ideas about the nature of the underworld. In particular the notion of punishment after death introduced them to the idea of the underworld as a place of evil and the source of the power of evil. This later meaning is to be found in the religious books immediately prior to the time of Christ and in the canonical New Testament.[2] This latter meaning of the expression is more suitable to the idea of an active onslaught such as is envisaged in the passage in question, and although some writers have applied the idea of immortality to the survival of the church, it seems preferable to see it as a promise of triumph over evil.[3]

The remainder of the passage serves to clarify the nature of the power which is to be entrusted to St. Peter. The image of the keys is one of the most picturesque and probably the clearest in the present text. In the ancient Oriental court the keybearer was next in rank to the sovereign, and the metaphor is well known from Isaias, who uses it when speaking of the replacement of Sobna by Eliacim: 'I will give him the key of David's house to bear upon his shoulders; none may shut when he opens, none open when he shuts' (Is. 22:22).[4] The reference to the shoulder is literally true, as the key in the early period was very elementary, being rather like a crowbar and having a device on the end so that the bolt could be operated, through a hole, from the outside of the door.

The power to bind and loose is the final clarification of the authority which the keybearer could be presumed to have. The terms 'bind and loose' are taken from the rabbinical jurisprudence of that period: to bind was to declare that a law obliged the fulfilment of a duty, and to loose

---

[1]cf. I K. 2:6; Job 38:17; Ps. 9:14.
[2]M. 11:23; L. 16:23; Apoc. 1:18; 20:23; cf. Zorrell, op. cit., col. 25, who cites the two meanings of 'gates of hell', and Lagrange, *S. Matthieu*, p. 325, who quotes several apocryphal uses of it in the sense of evil.
[3]Lagrange, op. cit., p. 326; Prat, op. cit., I, p. 436.
[4]cf. also Apoc. 1:17, 18; 3:11.

was to declare a person free of obligation. As far as the rabbis were concerned the initiative rested with the written law, of which they were only the interpreters. For St. Peter the order of events is reversed; he will make the decisions and his decision will be given ratification in the heavens (the plural form of which is another of the unselfconscious Aramaisms of the passage). The scope of this power is wide, and bears no evident restriction in this context. After the sacrament of penance had been instituted, it was realized that the forgiveness of sins came within its scope, but such a notion was unfamiliar to the rabbis. It must be insisted upon that the basic and obvious meaning of the metaphor is that of imposing rules and obligations at the human and external level, not that of judging in the realm of God and the conscience. This point was clearly recognized by Edersheim,[1] but strangly enough it has been overlooked by certain later writers.[2]

Once the Hebrew figures of speech have been understood, the text has no real difficulties. Far from it. St. Peter is here promised the supreme authority in the church in such clear terms, that it is hard to see how the idea could have been expressed with greater force or precision.

The problem of successors is one which has caused some doubts in the minds of non-Catholic writers. In the first place it must be remembered that the Gospel is not a legal document expressing the juridical constitution of the church. It is the biography of Christ, and a too precise legal definition of the church would be an anomaly in such a book. No one else in the New Testament is told by Christ to appoint a successor, but they understood the need quite naturally.[3] The Apostles elected St. Matthias to their number, and later on St. Paul had no scruples in ordaining clergy in all his churches. When the matter had been disputed the early church was quite certain that it was the intention of Christ that there should be successors to the various hierarchs, though the gospels do not record his instructions. St. Clement of Rome states the principle of succession explicitly in the letter which he sent to Corinth about the year 96.[4]

[1]Edersheim, op. cit. II, p. 85.
[2]Cullmann, *S. Pierre*, p. 185; Lowe, op. cit., p. 59.
[3]Editorial in *Istina*, 1955, pp. 377–8. Another question which must be borne in mind is that of the two necessary distinctions. The first, between the Apostolic succession in general and the primacy of Peter's succession. The second, between the extraordinary powers of the Apostles as founders and their ordinary powers as rulers of the church. cf. R. Beaupere, art. 'Dialogue Oecumenique autour du "S. Pierre" de M. Oscar Cullmann', in *Istina*, 1955, pp. 359, 360.
[4]Clement of Rome, Letter to the Corinthians, chs. 42 and 44.

Cullmann goes so far as to say[1] that since St. Peter is made the foundation of the church he could not have a successor, since there can be only one foundation. This statement needs some qualification. A man can be spoken of as a foundation or founder in two senses, that of the originator whose function is never again repeated (as for instance Abraham as the father of the Jewish race), or secondly as the first of a series. In this latter sense all the creators of empires and dynasties have been looked upon as their foundations or founders. In this sense William I is spoken of as the founder of the Norman dynasty, since he was the first of a line of kings. However, this did not rule out a successor for him. His powers passed to his sons, who in their turn occupied the supreme position after their father. From the text in question it can be seen that St. Peter is promised the normal juridical power in a stable and permanent society which indicates that he is the founder in the sense of William I. In this way the presumption of a successor is implied, and in fact that is just how one would expect the gospels to present the matter. In the sense of a progenitor, Christ alone is the founder of the church, and that role cannot be repeated. This quasi-presumption of a successor is now being realized by certain Protestants and has been expressed in the remarkable manifesto of the German Lutheran group known as 'Die Sammlung'.[2]

Although this text of Matthew is rightly regarded as the *locus classicus* for the matter of the Petrine authority and the papal claims, it is by no means the only important passage relevant to the matter. For the sake of completeness one must take into account the famous passages of St. Luke and St. John.

The Last Supper is the scene of Luke's testimony, but it is not altogether easy to say exactly when it was spoken, since the events of that evening are difficult to assemble in chronological order. It seems probable, though, that the text of St. Luke 22:31–32 should be inserted after the meal and immediately before the warning to St. Peter that he would thrice deny the Lord. The words of Christ are so impressive that they could easily have provoked St. Peter to his extravagant boast that he would follow the Lord to prison and to death: 'Simon Simon behold Satan has claimed power over YOU all, so that he can sift YOU like wheat; but I have prayed for THEE, that THY faith may not fail; when, after a while, THOU hast come back to me, it is for THEE to be the support of

[1]Cullmann, op. cit., p. 188.
[2]Printed in *Unitas*, 1957, p. 195. Much the same conclusion was reached by Soloviev. cf. *La Russie et l'Église Universelle*, p. 131. Quoted by C. Journet: *La Primauté de Pierre*, Paris, 1953, pp. 123, 124.

THY brethren.'[1] On hearing such words as these it is not surprising that St. Peter should be stimulated to the extent of offering to follow the Lord to martyrdom; only to be cautioned by Jesus that he would in fact deny him.

The request of Satan is, of course, the trial of the Apostles' courage at the time of the arrest of Jesus, and as the sequel shows, it was a partially successful request. The fact that St. Peter in particular will betray him is implied in the words 'when after a while thou hast come back to me', and that of the other Apostles can be inferred from their need of being supported. The contrast between the singular 'thou' and the plural 'you' is so obvious that it must have been quite deliberate. This singling out of St. Peter in the present instance is emphasized, too, by the fact that in St. John's account of the last supper Christ prayed for all the Apostles collectively (J. 17:19). It indicates that St. Peter is being selected for some special responsibility, which is made explicit in the command 'It is for thee to be the support of thy brethren'.

The general import of the text is quite clear, but the precise signification has occasioned some disagreement. The presence of the straightforward command has induced some to see here a grant of authority in fulfilment of the promise in St. Matthew 16:18. Yet it must be remarked that the circumstances do not altogether favour such an interpretation. In the actual context St. Peter's denial is foreseen, and humanly speaking he is perhaps the least suitable to confirm the brethren in that instance. The faithful St. John would surely have been the most obvious choice. Nevertheless Peter alone is chosen despite his anticipated lapse; thus it appears preferable to subscribe to the opinion of Lagrange, that St. Peter is designated because of his authority which is here presupposed rather than constituted.[2] This view gives a more natural explanation of his designation for confirming the brethren when, other things being equal, he is the least suitable. The text should then be understood as a witness to St. Peter's authority, rather than the constitution of it.

Turning now to the Petrine text in St. John, it must be borne in mind that the authority of the fourth gospel as an historical source has been denied in the past by the majority of non-Catholic scholars. The climate of opinion is now more favourable to it, but its testimony is only accepted rather reservedly. As has been stated before, the scope of the

---

[1]Knox's translation is an excellent rendering of the sense of the Greek. The text is critically established beyond cavil; the suggested variant ἐπιστρέψον in place of ἐπιστρέψας is negligible.

[2]Lagrange, M. J., *S. Luc*, Paris, 1921, p. 552.

present book does not permit of a lengthy discussion of the matter. It should, however, be remembered that this distrust of St. John does not always spring from purely scientific reasons, and some of those who cast doubts on the historical character of this gospel do not hesitate to use it as evidence for an alleged demotion of St. Peter! St. John's style and approach are quite different from that of the synoptics, but the topographical and other details which he gives receive constant confirmation from archaeological research. Discoveries such as the five arches of the pool at the Sheep gate mentioned in the fifth chapter give consistent vindication of his historical accuracy.

The last chapter which contains the dialogue between St. Peter and the risen Christ is clearly a postscript to the gospel which was designed to end with chapter 20. Nevertheless its presence in all the manuscripts and versions rules out the possibility of its having been forged. The meeting in question is set on the shore of the Sea of Galilee in the early morning. After they had eaten, Jesus said to St. Peter: 'Simon, son of John, dost thou care for me more than these others? Yes, Lord, he told him, thou knowest well that I love thee. And he said to him, Feed my lambs. And again, a second time, he asked him, Simon, son of John, dost thou care for me? Yes, Lord, he told him, thou knowest well that I love thee. He said to him, Tend my shearlings. Then he asked him a third question, Simon, son of John, dost thou love me? Peter was deeply moved when he was asked a third time, Dost thou love me? and said to him, Lord, thou knowest all things; thou canst tell that I love thee. Jesus said to him, Feed my sheep' (John 21:15–18).[1]

In St. Matthew's famous Petrine confession it was theological faith which prompted Christ to make the promise to St. Peter; here it is the virtue of charity. The initial question, 'Dost thou care for me more than these others?' is ambiguous even in the Greek. However, the context makes it clear that it means St. Peter's love of Christ compared with the other Apostles' love of him. Christ's insistence on having a threefold affirmation of it is a delicate allusion to the denial. St. Peter understands this and he is deeply moved. This consideration has led some to declare that the dialogue represents no more than a reinstatement of St. Peter to the position of a disciple which he had forfeited by his denial of Christ.

---

[1] Two words are used for 'love': ἀγαπάω and φιλέω. The former denotes the more deliberate love of the will, while the latter expresses the more impulsive love of the emotions. The nuance is slight in the present instance, and Christ uses them both with no apparent distinction of meaning.

Such an interpretation does not do justice to the passage.[1] The idea that
personal sin or holiness had a direct connexion with the loss or gain of
ecclesiastical office is alien to the mind of the New Testament, and was
only adopted by the Donatists at the end of the third century. Moreover,
it can hardly be doubted that St. Peter's forgiveness was granted when
he had his first apparition of the risen Christ. The meaning of this text
is very much deeper. St. Peter is here constituted as the shepherd of the
flock of Christ. This manner of speaking was well known to the ancients,
both Jews and Greeks. In Homer the princes of the people are called
shepherds, and the same idea is found in the Old Testament.[2] The
image is more striking when seen in its New Testament setting. In the
tenth chapter of St. John, Christ speaks of himself as the good shepherd
in terms which are a fitting prelude to the present text. The meaning
behind the image is not only that of Christ's giving to St. Peter the
supreme power in the infant church, but more precisely he is installing
him in the position which he himself has occupied. This passage in St.
John, then, is the culmination of the preparation of St. Peter for his task.
The change of name and the promise of the keys had led up to it. Then
on the eve of Christ's return to the Father, he places St. Peter in the
position which he himself had occupied in the infant church.[3]

The separate consideration of these three texts about St. Peter has
the incidental advantage that it allows them to show quite naturally how
consistent is their picture of the Apostle. This in its turn confirms their
obvious meaning and is perhaps the best way to forearm the mind
against the more radical difficulties of the Schools of the Modernists
and Form critics. It is no longer possible to challenge the authenticity
of the texts as they appear in modern critical editions, but there is a
tendency on the part of some to declare that the religious life of the early
church fashioned the narratives even before they reached the written
gospels. It is alleged that in the interest of preaching, liturgy and so on,
the original narratives were changed to suit particular needs, so that the
primitive content was lost under a mass of additions long before it was
consigned to the written records.

In the present case it has sometimes been alleged that the authority
of St. Peter is to be traced to an appearance of the risen Christ or to a

[1]Recognized by Protestants; cf. Cullmann, op. cit., p. 24.
[2]cf. Ezechiel 34:23; II K. 5:2; Mich. 5:4, etc.
[3]The natural interpretation is so straightforward that it is difficult to subscribe to Bultmann's interpreting it as the transference of authority from Peter
to John. cf. *Das Evangelium des Joannes*, Gottingen, 1950, p. 555.

commission of power after the resurrection. This simple situation was then embellished by the imagination of the early church, and in particular the event was projected back into the period of the public life of Christ, by rearrangement, or creation if necessary, of incidents to substantiate the desired picture.[1]

One is tempted to rebut these allegations by the observation '*Quod gratis assertur gratis negatur*'. This rejection of the obvious and literal meaning of the text is hard to justify, and does violence to the normally accepted rules of interpretation. What is more significant is the failure to do justice to what is known of the process of transferring the events of a life, such as that of Christ into the oral catechesis and thence to the written gospel. The dominant characteristic of this process is one of simplification, and not multiplication of incidents. For instance, in the records of the resurrection the salient feature that the neophyte had to appreciate was the fact that Christ rose again. Various resurrection appearances would supply him with the evidence, but once the fact was appreciated he would retain in the memory only a few of the appearances and neglect the rest. Thus in the most condensed of all statements emanating from the catechesis of the early church, the Apostles' Creed, only the conclusion is retained: 'The third day he rose again from the dead.' A potentially richer conclusion is recorded in Acts 1:3: 'He had shewn them by many proofs that he was still alive after his passion; throughout the course of forty days he had been appearing to them . . .' However, the normal catechesis was somewhat fuller. A passage of it has been recorded in I Cor. 15:3–8: 'The chief message I handed on to you, as it was handed on to me, was that Christ, as the scriptures had foretold, died for our sins; that he was buried, and then, as the scriptures had foretold, rose again on the third day. That he was seen by Cephas, then by the eleven apostles, and afterwards by more than five hundred of the brethren at once, most of whom are alive at this day, though some have gone to their rest. Then he was seen by James, then by all the apostles.' This is a classical example of the oral catechesis being consigned directly to the written records, but even this is a simplification of the reality. The passage of St. Paul's catechesis makes no mention of the apparitions to the women, nor of the appearance on the shore of the Sea of Galilee (J. 21).

Finally it must be remembered that the famous reduplications of the Old Testament (where the same incident is reported twice), do not

[1]Various views are discussed by Cullmann, op. cit., pp. 50–55.

provide the key to understanding these passages relating to St. Peter. Each incident is so different in circumstances that it must be independent of the others. Moreover the time-lag between the event and the written account of it is too short for divergent traditions to have become established. Cullmann himself, it is interesting to note, maintains that the particular prominence of St. Peter was established before the death of Christ.[1]

Perhaps the most extreme theory to be advanced in this type of criticism is that of the Russian Orthodox writer Bishop Cassien.[2] In his opinion the three main texts of Matthew, Luke, and John represent the successive judgements of the early church on St. Peter. The Petrine text of St. Matthew is the expression of St. Peter's status at the head of the Jerusalem community. That of St. Luke is the first witness to his demotion; the power to bind and loose has been omitted deliberately, leaving him with the competence to give only exhortation, which he is supremely well qualified to do in virtue of his experience of sin and repentance. Finally St. John shows the complete demotion of the one-time leader of the Apostolic group when he is made a 'pastor'. This method of exegesis is arbitrary in the extreme. To interpret one passage in the New Testament with reference to others is a valid method of exegesis, but to attempt to find contradictions by the same rule is a complete travesty. In the particular instance it necessitates a renewal of the long since vanished quarrels about seniority within the Apostolic group. The alleged significant omission of the power to bind and loose from St. Luke's account is similarly valueless; there is no question of their both relating the same incident, so there can be no thought of a deliberate omission. Last of all, the relegation of St. Peter to the role of a pastor is perhaps the most serious error of all. Nowhere in the twenty-first chapter of St. John is the title of 'pastor' applied to St. Peter. The functions of a shepherd can rightly be inferred from the words of Christ, but they refer to the tenth chapter of the fourth gospel itself. Far from being demoted, St. Peter is being put into the position of Christ the Good Shepherd.

This last commission by Christ is the climax of the gospel picture of St. Peter. It represents the term of a consistent 'build up', which began with the promise of a change of name at the first meeting of Christ and

[1]Cullmann, op. cit., p. 56.
[2]Principal of the Russian Orthodox Theological Academy in Paris; art. 'S. Pierre et l'Église dans le Nouveau Testament: Le Problème de la Primauté', *Istina*, 1955, pp. 257–304.

Peter. From that moment the Apostle moves into a place of prominence the promises of power and authority become more and more definite, until the morning on the shore of the Sea of Galilee when he assumes the place which the Master himself is about to vacate. The implications about a successor for his position are just what one would expect in documents of this kind, and the idea of demotion in the not too distant future is, to say the least, inconsistent with the whole tenor of the gospels.

2

ST. PETER IN THE APOSTOLIC CHURCH

AN inquiry into the intentions and designs of Christ must always take into account the conduct of the Apostolic church, since it is in that community that one may rightly expect to find the most authentic interpretation and understanding of the mind of the Master. An examination of St. Peter's position must therefore turn to the history of the primitive church to ascertain whether the position of prominence indicated by the gospels is indeed the correct interpretation of the provisions of Christ.

Information about the infant church can be gathered from the Epistles of the various Apostles, particularly St. Paul, and above all from the Acts of the Apostles. This second book of St. Luke is specifically designed to show how the work of Christ found permanence in the Christian community, and it provides the earliest surviving historical records of the infant church. The plan of the book is deliberately selective, but the incidents chosen are truly representative, and in the main the chronology is reliable, although that did not mean as much to the ancients as to those who have lived since Descartes and Newton. The sources from which St. Luke derived the earlier sections have been the matter for a fair amount of speculation.[1] It seems fairly certain that he must have used written records of the events of the Jerusalem and Antioch communities for the period before his own conversion. However, his use of these documents, and indeed of all his material, is so masterly that the homogeneity and unity of the work is in no way impaired, still less the historical reliability.[2] The book falls into two logical divisions, the Jewish community of Jerusalem and the mission to the gentiles. These are connected logically and in reality by the conversion of the first uncircumcized pagan, the Centurion Cornelius, whose meeting with St. Peter occupies the whole of the tenth chapter and provides a fitting introduction to the mission to the gentiles. In the first half of the book St. Peter is the dominant figure, in the latter it is

---

[1]Renié, J., *Actes des Apôtres*, Vol. IX of *La Sainte Bible*, Paris, 1949, pp. 20–22.

[2]The matter has been disputed in various schools. Notably that of the Modernists, led by Loisy and others.

St. Paul. Whether St. Luke intended to write a third book and unite these main themes and characters must remain a matter for speculation. Nevertheless the conclusion of the present book of the Acts is a very unsatisfactory anti-climax, leaving many questions unresolved.[1]

The book of the Acts shows the Apostles as a group of men who are considerably more mature in matters spiritual than one would have imagined from their gospel record. The events of the passion and death of Christ had been a severe crisis for them both spiritually and psychologically, and they emerged from it purified and perfected. This perfection received its completion at Pentecost and from then onwards they are seen to be firm and resolute in living up to the ideals of their Master. In particular the Apostles have no doubt about their authority over the infant church and St. Peter's authority over them. From the first he takes the lead and in the absence of Christ the former spokesman of the group becomes quite naturally their director.

When the Apostles have returned to Jerusalem after the ascension of Christ, St. Peter decides that their first task must be the replacement of Judas. The incident is important because the Apostolic vocation could be given only by Christ, and St. Peter's decision in the matter shows that he was counting on a power and authority which was more than human. The qualifications which he demanded were that the candidate should have witnessed the whole of the public life of Christ as well as His resurrection (A. 1:21, 22). In addition there is the matter of the actual call or vocation which could not be given by a man.[2] This was to be decided by the casting of lots, and therein lies the supreme interest of this incident. The confidence with which St. Peter presumes upon the divine intervention in the matter of the lots is an illuminating commentary on the promise 'Whatever thou shalt bind on earth shall be bound in heaven'.

The coming of the Holy Spirit at Pentecost marks the beginning of the public mission of the church and in the selection of events with which St. Luke describes this mission, St. Peter is in the foreground just as he was in the gospels. There is no question of trying to create an impression of his importance, still less to prove that he had authority. The picture which is conveyed is quite natural and unselfconscious. St. Peter is in the lead and his conduct is just what one would expect as a sequel to the gospel promises.

[1]Chapman, J., *The Four Gospels*, London, 1944, p. 28.
[2]Renié, op. cit., pp. 47–49.

The first public preaching at Pentecost is described as 'Peter with the eleven apostles at his side, stood there and raised his voice . . .' (A. 2:14). The sequel to this speech is in the same vein. The crowd was impressed and 'they asked Peter and his fellow apostles, Brethren, what must we do ?'

The first miracle which is recorded is a miracle of St. Peter's doing (A. 3:1–12). It is the cure of the lame man at the Beautiful Gate of the Temple. St. John is there as well, but his role is that of an onlooker,[1] while St. Peter says to the man: 'In the name of Jesus Christ of Nazareth, rise up and walk.' As a result of this miracle and their preaching, the two Apostles were put in prison until the following day, when they had to give an account of themselves. This is the first recorded instance of the church making a public profession of faith before the civil authorities and, as one might have guessed, it is St. Peter who makes it (A. 4:8–12).

The way in which St. Luke selected his matter seems to have been governed by the intention of showing the beginnings of the various Christian usages. The first preaching, the first miracle, and the first imprisonment are all brought to the reader's attention in a careful and deliberate manner. The same is true of the next act in the drama of the early church; the first recorded use of the disciplinary power. Ananias and Sapphira had sold an estate and very laudably gave the money to the Apostles for the use of the Christian community. One stain, however, spoilt the purity of their action; they had deceived the Apostles about the purchase price. Their punishment did not come directly from God as used to happen in similar cases in the Old Testament, but it is only when St. Peter has examined them and pronounced them guilty that they are struck dead (A. 5:3–10). Once again this divine intervention after St. Peter's decision illustrates the working of the power to bind and loose on earth, and in this particular case there is no consultation with the other Apostles.

Many similar incidents could be described, such as the tour of inspection in Samaria (A. 8:14–25) or the profusion of St. Peter's miracles (A. 5:15), but the same lesson is to be derived from them all. One final act of St. Peter does, however, demand special consideration because of its revolutionary character. Although the Apostles had received the command to teach all nations, it was many years before they implemented so drastic an innovation, and the decisive step was accomplished

[1]Lowe, op. cit., p. 15.

by a divine intervention,[1] characteristically, through St. Peter. The conversion of Cornelius and his household which occupies the tenth chapter of the Acts appears as the first occasion when baptism was given to the uncircumcized. The exact chronology of that part of the book is not easy to decide and it is possible that the evangelization of the region of Antioch took place at the same time although recorded in the following chapter. On hearing that gentiles were being admitted to the church at Antioch, the Jerusalem community sent Barnabus to investigate the matter (A. 11:22). He was overjoyed at what he saw and the admission of the gentiles seems to be taken for granted by then. Very different was the reaction to the baptism of Cornelius (A. 11:3). On that occasion St. Peter found it difficult to reassure the horrified Jews, and it was only when the action of God was perfectly clear that they acquiesced. This contrast in the two incidents shows that whatever may be the state of the chronology of chapters 10 and 11, the action of St. Peter was the decisive step in the church's admission of the gentiles.

After this decision has been reached, the book of the Acts leaves the Jerusalem community and relates in detail the mission to the gentiles. It is natural that attention should henceforth centre on St. Paul, but the lesson of the first half of the book is not thereby invalidated. The picture of St. Peter is just the same as that of the gospels. Without any attempt to force the meaning of the text, he is seen in a position of particular authority, and although the precise amplitude of his powers cannot be decided without reference to the gospels he is rightly seen to be the director of the infant church.[2] There is no suggestion here that St. Peter is about to be demoted, and although little more is said about him, no evidence can be found to show that it was the intention of Christ or the infant church that he should relinquish his position of authority.

Before proceeding to a detailed account of the mission to the gentiles, the book of the Acts gives enough information for one to reconstruct the situation in the mother church at Jerusalem. Shortly after the baptism of Cornelius, Herod initiated a persecution which struck even at the Apostles (A. 12:1-3). James (the brother of John) was killed and St. Peter was cast into prison. This persecution should probably be ascribed to the year 44. St. Peter was released miraculously, and before departing elsewhere he sent news of his release to 'James and the rest of the brethren' (A. 12:17). The fact that no other Apostle is named

[1]Renié, op. cit., p. 155.
[2]Cullmann, op. cit., p. 30.

gives a strong presumption that James was the only one still in the city, and it is a first indication that he had been designated as the superior of the Jerusalem community. Later in the Acts (21:18), he is seen surrounded by his presbyters in a position very reminiscent of that of the early monarchical bishops of Asia Minor. Whether the other Apostles were in hiding during the persecution or had actually departed on their missionary journeys is hard to say. They were all reassembled for the council of Jerusalem (A. 15), in the year 49, and that was the last recorded instance of their meeting together. Their final dispersion almost certainly took place after that, leaving James in charge of the church of Jerusalem.

Against this background one must study the position of St. Peter. Cullmann has declared that after the dispersion of the Apostolic college St. Peter underwent demotion and James took charge of the whole church.[1] This opinion commands fairly wide acceptance in Protestant circles, and is based on the information to be found in the Acts and the Epistles. It is alleged that when St. Paul was entrusted with the mission to the gentiles, St. Peter was commissioned to preach to the Jews of the Mediterranean world. The difference between their missions was, among other things, that St. Peter was under close supervision from the Jerusalem community headed by James, whereas St. Paul was in a position of comparative autonomy.

The evidence in support of this theory is not very great, but the silence of the second half of the Acts is brought forward as a first indication of St. Peter's demotion. The almost total silence about the man who once dominated the picture is taken as an indication that he must have forfeited his erstwhile authority. The council of Jerusalem is said to confirm this view, since James is presiding, and the quarrel at Antioch recorded in Galatians 2:11 can be explained adequately only if St. Paul is at least equal to the man whom he reprimands. The same passage of the Epistle to the Galatians seems to suggest that St. Peter's mission to the Jews was conferred upon him by the church, and finally his name no longer heads the lists of Apostles.

This is the sum total of evidence brought forward to sustain the case against the man to whom Christ promised the keys of the Kingdom of Heaven. In the first place it must be remembered that the whole tenor of the promises of Christ is in favour of permanence, and there is no hint that it was his intention that St. Peter should be demoted. The

[1]Cullmann, op. cit., pp. 36–40.

silence of the second part of the Acts is of little value. St. Luke's plan is obviously selective and the choice of the gentile mission for the second half of the book meant inevitably that he would accord prominence only to St. Paul. For the same reason there is also silence about all the other Apostles, with the exception of St. James, yet no one would suggest that the other eleven were demoted after their dispersion.

Of the other matters relevant to this question, the Council of Jerusalem has caused much ink to flow. This has been due to the light which it throws on the respective positions of the Apostles Peter and James. In reality the question of authority was irrelevant to the debate. The question which the Apostles met to decide was the vital matter of admitting the gentiles to baptism without first of all adopting the law of Moses, and in particular, circumcision. To the reader of the present day it seems a small point, but for the infant church it was the most serious crisis which had to be faced. Although the matter was settled to the advantage of the gentiles, echoes of the trouble are to be heard in nearly every one of the Apostles' letters. Not until the city of Jerusalem had been destroyed in the campaign of Vespasian and Titus was the danger of a Judaized Christianity finally removed.

The crisis came to a head after the first missionary journey of St. Paul, when the conversion of large numbers of gentiles revealed all that was implied in the conversion of Cornelius. To settle the matter a meeting was decided upon at Jerusalem between the two missionaries Paul and Barnabus and the convert pharisees, together with the presbyters of Jerusalem and the Apostles who would act as judges in the matter.

The first conclusion which is relevant to the present inquiry is the fact that St. Paul's mission is seen to be dependent upon the whole church, and not an autonomous venture. He had to conform his practice to that of the rest of the church and to that end he was subject to the authority of the whole Apostolic college.

The second matter which concerns the present study is the relationship between St. Peter and St. James. This is the problem which has caused so much dispute, since it is widely, though not universally, held by Protestants that the council shows St. James in a position of authority over St. Peter.[1]

The sources of information about this council are rather fragmentary. They are the fifteenth chapter of the Acts, and probably Galatians

[1] For instance, Gore, C., *Roman Catholic Claims*, London, 6th ed., 1905, p. 83; Cullmann, op. cit., pp. 42, 43.

2:6–10. Whether the deliberations referred to in Galatians are the same as those in the Acts has been debated at considerable length. The most compelling argument in favour of identifying them is the fact that a matter of such importance would hardly have been decided twice over. It is possible that the account in the Acts comprises three meetings; a public inquiry (vv. 4 and 5), the deliberative meeting of the Apostles and Presbyters (v. 6, corresponding to Gal. 2:6–10), and lastly the public session for announcing the decision (v. 7 onwards).

The first matter to be decided is the question of the president of the assembly. Did St. James preside over the deliberations, thereby showing that he was then the supreme ruler of the church? Before examining the evidence for the matter, it must be borne in mind that his being chairman is intrinsically possible, since he appears already to have been designated as the future Bishop of Jerusalem, and the dispersal of the rest of the Apostles is imminent. On the other hand, though, it would be anachronistic to imagine that this council was conducted with all the formality which later attended the synods of the church, and at that date precedence would not be linked closely with seniority. As far as the evidence is concerned, St. Peter spoke first and St. James gives the impression that he was summing up. The actual words which he used 'And so I give my voice . . .' (ἐγὼ κρίνω) (v. 19), do not actually favour the view that he was summing up, or deciding the matter on his own authority. Elsewhere in the Acts[1] the same verb *krino* is used to denote the expression of an opinion and could better be expressed by the phrase 'in my opinion', or 'as for me'. In the present instance, this sense is regarded as possible by the Protestant Kirsopp Lake, and it is accepted as the correct interpretation by Hort and Jalland,[2] as well as by Catholic authors generally.[3]

A careful examination of the position of St. Peter indicates which of the two had the superior authority, thereby elucidating the principal matter under discussion. It is his speech which decides the course of action to be adopted, and when he gives his reasons he makes it clear that the course has been indicated by God *to him*. This speech does not require the approval of the assembly, but rather it puts an end to the discussion.

[1]A. 13:46, 16:15, 26:8.
[2]Kirsopp Lake and Foakes Jackson, *The Beginnings of Christianity*, 1926, IV, p. 177; Hort, F. J., *The Christian Ecclesia*, 1897, pp. 78–80; Jalland, op. cit., p. 62.
[3]cf. Jacquier, *Les Actes des Apôtres*, Paris, 1926, followed by Renié, op. cit., p. 213.

The speech of St. James is of a different character. He acquiesces to what St. Peter had said, although it seems to have been against his personal inclinations, and then puts forward a practical suggestion for the sake of harmony. This suggestion from James receives the approval of the assembly, and it is promulgated in the name of the whole Apostolic college.[1]

There is always a danger of making mountains out of molehills when the documents of the primitive church are examined to see what light they throw on problems with which they were not concerned. This danger is present in the matter in question, yet without forcing the texts it seems most natural to see in this account of the council a further confirmation of the position of authority for St. Peter, rather than his demotion.[2]

The first sequel to the council of Jerusalem was the division of the gentile and Jewish missions. The matter is not recorded in the Acts, but St. Paul speaks about it in the second chapter of Galatians. Since he refers to several of the Apostles, and since it is so close to his account of the decision of that council, it seems natural to conclude that the matter was settled at Jerusalem, soon after the council, if not at the council itself. His actual words are as follows: 'Those who were reputed to be the main support of the Church, James and Cephas and John, saw plainly that I was commissioned to preach to the uncircumcized, as Peter was to the circumcized.' At first sight it might appear that St. Peter and St. Paul were being appointed to their missions by the Apostolic college or at least the 'main support' of it. Yet closer examination reveals that the decision was not one which had been left to the initiative of the church. Of the two of them, St. Paul's missionary vocation is the easier to investigate. There is ample evidence in the New Testament that he was destined to preach to the gentiles by the special command of God, which came to him directly and not through the church. In fact he states this explicitly at the beginning of the Epistle to the Galatians: 'Paul, an apostle not holding his commission from men, not appointed by man's means, but by Jesus Christ, and God the Father who raised him from the dead . . .' This is fully in accord with what is known of the nature of the Apostolic vocation from other sources, so

---

[1]This need of approbation by the assembly holds true even if one subscribes to the view that the regulations about food were decided at a later date, but were inserted here by St. Luke.

[2]This is the conclusion generally subscribed to by Catholic authors, cf. Pope, H., in *The Papacy*, ed. Lattey, Cambridge, 1924, p. 23; and all standard textbooks on the matter.

that when Matthias was designated for the place of Judas, the actual choice was left to God. Since St. Paul makes no difference between his own missionary assignment and that of St. Peter, it is reasonable to deduce that St. Peter also received his commission from God. This is, in fact, the most natural sense of the rest of the passage from Galatians: 'He whose power had enabled Peter to become the apostle of the circumcized, had enabled me to become the apostle of the gentiles.' The role of the Apostles gathered at Jerusalem is not therefore to appoint Peter and Paul to their respective missions, but to acknowledge the dispositions of God. Thus understood, the text can hardly be used in favour of the idea that St. Peter had been demoted and had been commanded by the church at Jerusalem to take up the mission to the Jews of the Mediterranean world.

The second sequel to the council was the dispersion of the Apostolic college. At a date which is not easy to determine they all departed from Jerusalem with the exception of St. James. It is clear from the subsequent narrative in Acts that he was left in charge of the mother church. It would, however, be unwise to infer from this that he acquired authority over the whole church. The early Christian communities had great respect for Jerusalem, but they did not regard it as a superior. Therefore it does not follow that the ruler of the church at Jerusalem was automatically the head of the whole church. When St. Peter was at the head of the Jerusalem community his supreme authority came to him not in view of the city which he occupied, but because at that time Jerusalem was virtually the only Christian community, i.e. in practice the whole church. Later on in the Acts, St. James is seen to be in charge at Jerusalem but he is surrounded by the presbyters, and not by the Apostles as was St. Peter.

The net result of the council was, then, that it settled the matter of the entry of the gentiles into the church; the Apostles departed on their missions, leaving James in charge of Jerusalem, but there is no question of the promotion or demotion of anyone to a status which he did not occupy before the council.

This conclusion is not weakened by the quarrel between Peter and Paul at Antioch which is reported in the next few verses of Galatians. The incident is well known, and the pith of it is expressed succinctly by St. Paul, 'When Cephas came to Antioch, I opposed him openly.' The wording of the text leaves some doubt as to the time of this occurrence.[1]

[1] ὅτε δὲ ἦλθεν Κηφᾶς εἰς Ἀντιόχειαν, Gal. 2:11.

Several authors have suggested that it occurred before the council of Jerusalem and the thesis has been adopted recently by Père Féret.[1] Nevertheless St. Paul seems to be following a chronological plan, and the majority of commentators assign it to the period after the council.[2]

Peter and Paul were both at Antioch, and it appears that they had been happy to sit down at table with convert gentiles; a practice which the Jewish Law would not countenance. This state of affairs lasted until a party of convert Jews arrived from Jerusalem, and then Peter and Barnabus consorted only with the former Jews. It was this conduct which roused St. Paul's anger and drew forth his outspoken protest. The import of this rebuke was greatly exaggerated by the early reformers, but many Protestants still maintain that it reveals St. Peter's loss of authority.[3] It is difficult to see how this incident can be used as a decisive argument against the authority of St. Peter. The most reasonable interpretation of it seems to indicate just the opposite. Since Barnabus had been on the missionary journey with St. Paul, it would appear that he was more deserving of a rebuke than St. Peter. In fact, his indiscretion is ignored and Peter alone receives the protest of St. Paul. Viewed in this way, it can be inferred that the conduct of St. Peter was likely to be the most influential precisely because of his authority, and St. Paul felt that it was imperative to recall St. Peter to the true path lest his conduct should influence others.[4]

The only other recorded meeting between Peter and Paul is that which occurred a few years after St. Paul's conversion.[5] He writes about it in Galatians 1:18: 'Then, when three years had passed, I did go up to Jerusalem, to visit Peter, and I stayed a fortnight there in his company'. The actual verb employed (ἱστορῆσαι) denotes the making of an inquiry, or the ascertaining of information. However, since St. Paul is at pains to point out in that very chapter, that he has learnt of Christianity from God and not from human sources, it seems advisable to diminish the force of the verb somewhat and see in the incident his first official visit to the authorities of the church. What is significant is the fact that such

---

[1]Féret, H. M., *Pierre et Paul à Antioche et à Jérusalem*, Paris, 1955, pp. 47–52, etc.
[2]cf. Lagrange, M. J., *Épître aux Galates*, Paris, 1950, p. 41; Dupont, J., arts. in *Recherches de Science Religieuse*, 1957, pp. 42–60, 225–39.
[3]Cullmann, op. cit., p. 40.
[4]Jalland, op. cit., p. 60. It should be remembered too, that Paul's quarrel with Barnabas indicates no more than a difference of opinions. cf. F. J. Foakes Jackson, *Peter, Prince of the Apostles*, London, 1927, p. 100.
[5]It is almost certain that A. 9:27 and Gal. 1:18 represent the same event.

a visit should have been made to St. Peter. James's name is added merely as an afterthought.

These three incidents are the only recorded occasions when the two Apostles actually met each other. It is rather artificial to examine such meetings to see if they show a demotion of St. Peter, but in so far as they reveal anything, they tend to confirm the impression of Peter's importance and cannot reasonably be adduced in favour of his demotion.

The Pauline Epistles and the remaining books of the New Testament were all written to deal with particular problems, and the problem of the interrelation of the Apostles did not arise. The theological consequences of the admission of the gentiles to the church caused far more trouble than the matter of the hierarchical structure within that church. For this reason it would seem superfluous to pursue the investigations about St. Peter into these remaining books of the New Testament. However, the course to be followed is in a sense predetermined by the fact that practically every phrase in the Scriptures which mentions the name of Peter has been used as evidence for or against his authority. The same applies to the passages which refer in any way to groups of Apostles.

For instance, it is commonly stated[1] that the Epistles teach the equality of the Apostles, who are spoken of as foundations, as St. Peter alone was in Matthew 16:16. It is true that St. Paul told the Ephesians that 'apostles and prophets are the foundation on which you were built' (2:20), and in the Apocalypse the twelve foundation stones of the heavenly Jerusalem represent the twelve Apostles (Apoc. 21:14). Yet these passages cannot be taken to mean that the Apostles are the foundation of the church in an utterly exclusive sense. If that were so, what could be the meaning of I Cor. 3:12, where Christ is spoken of as the foundation? As Jalland has rightly pointed out[2] the metaphor of the foundation is applied in the various places from different points of view. This is a legitimate usage for a writer and it is the theologians' business to be able to discern the different applications. The use of the idea of a foundation to describe the Apostolic role in the church reveals something of the dependence of the later converts on these first ministers. It is inaccurate to use it for the purpose of examining the relationship of one Apostle with another.

Further indications are sought in the lists of names. What is to be

[1]cf. Gore, op. cit., p. 84, and Cullmann, op. cit., p. 195.
[2]Jalland, op. cit., p. 64.

deduced from the fact that St. Paul does not write the name of Peter in the first place? Can it therefore be inferred that St. Peter had been demoted? In the gospels and the Acts the name of Peter occurs with those of the other Apostles on about twenty-five occasions. In every case the name of Peter is written first.[1] As has been stated above, it would be unwise to read too much into this fact, since only four of these collections of names are formal catalogues. The Epistles of St. Paul appear in sharp contrast with this arrangement of Apostolic names. In the First Epistle to the Corinthians he gives them in the order Paul, Apollo, Cephas, Christ.[2] It appears that St. Peter has been relegated to the last place, but St. John Chrysostom declared that the list was written in order of ascending dignity.[3] The same pattern is to be found later in this Epistle (9:4–6), where the persons are: the other apostles, the Lord's brethren, and Cephas. Chrysostom's theory of ascending dignity is perhaps even clearer in this case.[4]

There is only one place in the New Testament where St. Peter's name is not standing in the place of honour and that is in Galatians 2:7. 'Those who were reputed to be the main support of the church, James and Cephas and John. . . .' This order of names seemed so unnatural to the fathers that it was rewritten as 'Peter and James and John' by Marcion, Irenaeus, Tertullian, Origen, Gregory of Nyssa, Jerome, Ambrose, Ephraim and Augustine. The same rearrangement is to be found in several of the oldest manuscripts of the Epistle.

These few indications from the Epistles are of no great significance, although they have been used with considerable ingenuity from the patristic age up to the present time. The gospels are the primary source of information about St. Peter and his authority over the church, the first half of the Acts is a secondary source, and the rest of the New Testament is of little value, since it does not treat directly of the matter in question. The indications which can be gleaned from these other books tend to confirm the gospel picture of St. Peter but it is possible to over-emphasize their importance.

[1]Chapman, J., *Bishop Gore and the Catholic Claims*, London, 1905, p. 195.
[2]I Cor. 1:12 and 3:21.
[3]Chrysostom, *Homilies on I Cor.*, No. 3, M.P.G., Vol. 61, col. 24.
[4]Chrysostom, op. cit., No. 21, M.P.G., Vol. 61, col. 172.

3

ST. PETER IN PATRISTIC THOUGHT

ALTHOUGH the gospels are the primary source of information about St. Peter, a complete examination of his position must take into account the attitude of the early church, since the Christians of those days were so well qualified to understand the intentions of Christ. The attitude of the first generation is to be found in the Acts of the Apostles, but for the succeeding ages search must be made in the writings of the fathers. It is true that they are yet one stage farther removed from Christ, but their value lies in the fact that they witness to the living teaching of the church at a time when the oral tradition was still current.

Although the fathers did not write systematic studies on the theology of the church, they did compose exhaustive commentaries on the Scriptures. In this way St. Peter was forced upon their attention, and their exegetical writings, especially on Matthew's sixteenth chapter, provide an approach to this question, which owing to their theological climate might otherwise have been overlooked.

It is a regrettable fact that there is no altogether satisfactory study of the position of St. Peter in patristic thought. Both in the past and in the present day he has tended to be eclipsed by St. Paul, whose theology has occupied the attention of ancient and modern scholars. Dom J. Chapman's books (one of which has already been referred to) have a fair amount of relevant information, but the only complete examination of even one aspect of the matter is the recent study by J. Ludwig, *Die Primatworte Mt. 16:18, 19, in der Altkirchlichen Exegese*.[1]

The powers bestowed on St. Peter were very wide in their scope, and extended to several different spheres. The scriptural passages which treat of them, notably Matthew's famous text, include the idea of Peter's superiority over the other Apostles, the power to forgive sins, the first appearance of episcopal authority, and a close connexion between the whole bestowal of the powers and with Peter's acknowledgement of the true nature of Christ. Such a wealth of information about the person of Peter was bound to be appreciated only gradually, and the various

[1]Munster, 1952. Followed extensively in this chapter.

aspects of his powers and status were excogitated one by one, according to the provocation of circumstances. A modern Catholic, influenced by the defence against Protestantism, would consider that the Apostle's seniority was the most obvious meaning of the various Petrine texts. This was not the case in the early church. The aspect which most occupied their attention was the connexion with Peter's faith, so that the actual promises were overshadowed in their minds by Peter's acknowledgement of the divinity of Christ.[1]

This orientation of their thought was the direct result of the early heresies, nearly all of which were connected with the person of Christ. The first of these heresies to cause serious anxiety to the church was Gnosticism, and it is in the anti-Gnostic writings that Matthew's Petrine text is first alluded to. The writer in question is St. Justin, who was martyred most probably in the year 165. He was at pains to clarify the position of Christ, whose uniqueness had been obscured by the Gnostic theory that there were many intermediaries bridging the gap between the Father and the world. Peter is then spoken of precisely because the Father had revealed to him the true nature of Christ. 'One of the disciples, hitherto called Simon, learnt, through a revelation from the Father, that Jesus Christ is the Son of God. For that reason he acquired the name Peter.'[2] It is evident from the wording that St. Justin had in mind Matthew 16. His understanding of it is by no means exhaustive, nor exclusive of other deductions, but its principal merit in Justin's eyes is its connexion with the divinity of Christ.

The same background of Gnosticism must be borne in mind when examining the next writer, St. Irenaeus. His treatment of the matter is more developed, and he had to face the allegation that St. Paul alone had received the full revelation from Christ. In his famous treatise *Adversus Hæreses* (written in the last decades of the second century) he makes several references to St. Peter's knowledge of Christianity and it is clear that he, like St. Justin, is relying on Matthew 16. How could Peter be accused of ignorance, asks Irenaeus, when the Lord himself had declared that it was not from flesh and blood but from the Father that he had derived his knowledge.[3] Although, as will be seen later, St.

---

[1] Modern scholarship has become increasingly critical of the extent to which M. 16 teaches the divinity of Christ. A full examination of the problem lies outside the scope of the present study. The ancient writers were almost unanimous in seeing in the text a reference to the divine filiation of Christ.

[2] *Dialogue with Trypho*, 100:4, M.P.G., Vol. 6, col. 709.

[3] *Adv. Hær.*, III, 13, 2, M.P.G., Vol. 7, col. 912.

Irenaeus was aware of the Roman primacy, he himself does not say precisely how he connected it with the Apostle Peter. His account of the foundation of the Roman church, and the list of the bishops of Rome, mentions both Peter and Paul as the founders. Possibly this might appear to be prejudicial to the position of St. Peter, but since it was only the intention of Irenaeus to establish Apostolic connexion for his churches it would be outside his aim to differentiate between the Apostles.[1]

The last of the anti-Gnostic apologists to be considered is the African Tertullian, who wrote at the beginning of the third century. Tertullian's treatment of St. Peter has the special interest that he does not confine himself to the Christological sphere. Other implications in the position of Peter are becoming explicit and the text of Matthew 16 is no longer confined to the question of Peter's faith. In the treatise *De Præscriptione Hæreticorum*, which dates from the orthodox period of Tertullian's life, he speaks of Peter's knowledge of Christ in a manner which is reminiscent of the earlier apologists. Yet there is a subtle difference in his starting-point which reveals his wider conception of St. Peter's role in the church. He defends Peter's knowledge of the full revelation by the words 'Was anything hidden from Peter, who was called the rock on which the church was built, and who possessed the keys of the kingdom of heaven, together with the power of binding and loosing in heaven and on earth ?'[2] Three distinct powers are alluded to, the roles of being the foundation, and the keybearer, together with the competence to bind and loose. It is important to remember that from this early date the church understood the rock as being Peter as a person, not his faith, and still less anything other than Peter. In his other writings, *De Monogamia* and *Scorpiacae* the idea, of the foundation is spoken of, but the power most fully appreciated was that of binding and loosing. In the current African theology the import of this text was understood as applying to the power of forgiving sins, not indeed as the exclusive prerogative of Peter, but received by him for the sake of the church.[3]

When Tertullian became a Montanist, some time after the year 207, it was precisely the power of forgiving sins which he challenged in the treatise *De Pudicitia*. The events which stimulated him to write are not altogether clear. It is reasonably certain that Pope Callixtus had relaxed the penitential discipline to the extent that he would allow adulterers and

[1]Ludwig, op. cit., p. 9.
[2]*De Præscriptione Hæreticorum*, ch. 22, C.S.E.L., Vol. 70, p. 20.
[3]Ludwig, op. cit., pp. 11, 12.

fornicators to avail themselves of sacramental forgiveness. The only sources which record the innovation are the *Philosophumena* of Hippolytus and *De Pudicitia* of Tertullian.[1] Both these writers were bitterly opposed to the relaxation and their condemnations of it are so exaggerated as to be reliable only for the main outlines of the affair. The twenty-first chapter of *De Pudicitia* has, however, the distinction of being the first recorded quotation of the actual text of Matthew 16. After addressing his adversary as the supreme pontiff (*Pontifex Maximus*), bishop of bishops and the author of an edict, he proceeds to question his competence in the matter of forgiving sins with the words: 'If, because the Lord has said to Peter, "Upon this rock I will build my church", or "Whatsoever thou shalt have bound or loosed on earth, shall be bound or loosed in the heavens", you therefore presume that the power of binding and loosing has derived to you, that is, to every church allied to Peter's, what sort of man are you, subverting and wholly changing the manifest intention of the Lord, conferring, as that intention did, this gift personally upon Peter? "On thee", he says "will I build my church; and I will give to thee the keys", not to the church; and "whatever thou shalt have loosed or bound", not what they shall have loosed or bound . . . Hence the power of loosing and binding committed to Peter had nothing to do with the capital sins (i.e. adultery and fornication) of believers . . . For in accordance with the person of Peter, it is to spiritual men that this power will correspondingly appertain, either to an apostle or to a prophet.' Two questions arise out of this passage which are relevant to the present study. Did Callixtus inaugurate his penitential reform by an edict which appealed to Matthew 16? And for what precise reason did Tertullian object to the power then claimed by his adversary?

The first question has provoked a considerable divergence of opinion. De Rossi was the first scholar to interpret *De Pudicitia* as referring to an edict of Callixtus and the opinion received widespread support after Harnack had championed it. More recently it has been accepted by many eminent theologians including Batiffol, Caspar, and van den Eynde. At first sight the theory has much to support it. Callixtus did indeed reform the penitential discipline in this fashion and Tertullian must have had some highly placed bishop in mind. However, this interpretation has been denied by G. Esser, K. Adam, G. Bardy, and

---

[1]*Philosophumena*, 9:12, M.P.G., Vol. 16 (iii), cols. 3386, 3387; *de Pudicitia*, passim, M.P.L., Vol. 2, cols. 1029 ff.

most energetically by P. Galtier.[1] The arguments brought forward have
considerable weight. It has been pointed out that the titles which Tertullian employs mean very little. *Pontifex Maximus* was a pagan title,
and the expression was only used of the Popes at a much later date.
Bishop of bishops is quite obviously irony. Furthermore Hippolytus
appears to know nothing of the alleged edict. He has much to say against
the relaxations of Callixtus but makes no mention of any edict. In the
circumstances the omission is surprising and constitutes a fairly strong
argument against its existence. Finally the expression 'every church
allied to Peter's' (*omnem ecclesiam Petri propinquam*) is such an awkward
way of saying 'Rome' that one is tempted to infer that he meant anything
but Rome. In view of these arguments it seems more probable that
Tertullian had in mind Agrippinus the bishop of Carthage rather than
Callixtus.

On the strength of this conclusion it is possible to attempt a recon-
struction of the probable course of events which provoked the writing
of *De Pudicitia*, and thereby to answer the second question to which it
gave rise, namely, for what precise reason did Tertullian object to the
penitential procedure of his adversaries. In Rome Pope Callixtus relaxed the penitential discipline in favour of the 'capital sins'. The
liaison between Rome and Carthage was such that the change would
almost certainly be adopted in Africa. At what point did the text of
Matthew 16 enter upon the scene? Rome can be counted out, not only
for the reasons cited above which indicate that Tertullian was writing
against Agrippinus, but also because at that time Rome no longer used
the text in connexion with penance.[2] However, in Africa it was still
employed for the remission of sins, and could well have been invoked
by Agrippinus, or even by Tertullian himself if Agrippinus had not
done so.[3] Tertullian, now a Montanist, had restricted the signification of
the text. Peter's church is for him the non-localized ideal unity of the
church. In contrast to this is the local church 'every church' (*omnis
ecclesia*). When the local church is in communion with the world-wide
united church it is 'allied' (*propinqua*) to Peter's church. It would seem
therefore that the local church would be in a position to receive the
powers given to Peter, but that is precisely what Tertullian disputes.
From his Montanistic standpoint, he declares that the power to forgive

---

[1] Arts. in the *Revue d'Histoire Ecclésiastique*, 'Le Véritable Édit de Calliste',
1927, pp. 465–88, and 1928, pp. 41–51.
[2] Ludwig, op. cit., p. 17.
[3] Ludwig, op. cit., p. 14.

sins was given to Peter personally and not for the church. Henceforth the forgiveness of sins would be the prerogative of 'spiritual men'; that is to say Montanists like Tertullian.

Tertullian's understanding of St. Peter's role in the church, particularly during his orthodox period, shows a decided advance on that of his predecessors. Peter is shown to have some kind of primacy in the church and it is clear that the power to forgive sins is included in it: and moreover this power is to be passed on to the church. As with the previous writers, this is not an exhaustive understanding of the position of St. Peter, but it shows a steady progress in the orthodox development of the appreciation of his role in the church.

Rome at this time, as is reasonable, had a clearer notion of the prerogatives of St. Peter than most other churches. By the middle of the third century the text of Matthew 16 was understood there as the basis of the universal authority of the popes, yet this conception was probably being formed even at the beginning of the century. The defence of the church against the second-century heretics had clarified the notion of apostolic succession, and when it appears from the evidence of Hippolytus that in his time Matthew 16 was no longer used of penance, it is only reasonable to assume that it was because Rome used it even then of the primacy.[1]

Confining the inquiry for the moment to the Western fathers, the next writer to be examined is St. Cyprian, whose personality dominated the African church during the short period that he was a Christian, from 249 until 258. His attitude to St. Peter, the church, and the episcopate, can be judged from his constant references to the subjects in his letters. Letter 33 to the lapsed is typical of his ecclesiology. 'Our Lord, whose commands we must reverence and obey, when arranging the dignity of the episcopate and the external form of the church, speaks in the gospel to Peter and says, I say to thee that thou art Peter and on this rock I will build my church. . . . Thence through the passage of time, and the episcopal succession, the election of bishops and the external form of the church persevere, so that the church is built upon the bishops, and every item of its government is regulated by those same rulers.'[2] The same theory is to be seen in many of his other letters[3] and it represents his definitive judgement on the matter.

---

[1]Ludwig, op. cit., p. 17.
[2]Letter 33:1, ed. Hartel in C.S.E.L., Vol. 3, ii, p. 566.
[3]Letters 43:5, 66:8, 71:3, 73:7.

The 'external form of the church' (*ratio ecclesiae*) which he mentions so often is the result of the incarnation of the church, if it may thus be described. In Cyprian's thought, the church is primarily a heavenly institution and hence invisible. At a certain time, this heavenly church commenced an earthly and visible life, becoming perceptible in virtue of its structure of episcopal government. The occasion when the church acquired this visible framework and commenced its earthly existence was the incident at Caesarea Philippi. Hence for Cyprian, the significance of Matthew 16 is that it marks the origin of episcopal government.

Cyprian applied these general principles to the problem of schism when he wrote his celebrated treatise *De Ecclesiae Catholicae Unitate* (On the Unity of the Catholic Church). The fourth chapter of this work has provoked endless discussion since it has been preserved in two versions. One version appears to be more pro-Roman and contains the word 'primacy' (*primatus*); for the sake of convenience it may be called the 'primacy' text. The other version is not so obviously pro-Roman, it omits the word 'primacy' and may be called, the 'non-primacy' text. A third type of text is formed by various combinations of these two.[1] The passage in question has caused so much dispute that the two versions must be compared.[2]

The Primacy Text

'*Ego tibi dico (inquit) quia tu es Petrus, et super hanc petram aedificabo ecclesiam meam, et portae inferorum non vincent eam. Et dabo tibi claves regni coelorum : et quae ligaveris super terram, erunt ligata et in coelis; et quaecumque solveris super terram erunt soluta et in coelis*' (M. 16:18, 19).
Et eidem post resurrectionem suam dicit: 'Pasce oves meas' (J. 21:17). *Super illum aedificat ecclesiam et illi pascendas oves mandat.*
Et quamvis apostolis omnibus parem tribuat potestatem, unam tamen

'I say to thee (he says) that thou art Peter and upon this rock I will build my church, and the gates of hell shall not overcome it. I will give to thee the keys of the kingdom of heaven. And what thou shalt bind upon earth shall be bound also in heaven, and whatsoever thou shalt loose on earth shall be loosed also in heaven' (M. 16:18, 19).
And he says to him again after the resurrection: 'Feed my sheep' (J. 21:17). It is on him that he builds the church, and to him that

[1] For a detailed study of the textual problems of *De Unitate*, cf. Bévenot, M., *St. Cyprian's De Unitate*, London, 1939.
[2] Text in Ludwig, op. cit., p. 23, based on C.S.E.L., Vol. 3, i, pp. 212–14. Trans., Bévenot in *St. Cyprian, The Lapsed and the Unity of the Catholic Church*, pp. 46–47 (Vol. 25 in the series, Ancient Christian Writers, London, 1957).

*cathedram constituit et unitatis origi-
nem adque rationem sua auctoritate
disposuit. Hoc erant utique ceteri
quod fuit Petrus,*

*Sed primatus Petro datur et una
ecclesia et cathedra una monstratur.
Et pastores sunt omnes, sed grex unus
ostenditur, qui ab apostolis omnibus
unanimi consensione pascatur.*

*Hanc ecclesiae unitatem qui non
tenet, tenere se fidem credit? Qui
catherdam Petri, super quem fundata
ecclesia est, deserit, in ecclesia se esse
confidit?*

he entrusts the sheep to feed. And
although he assigns a like power to
all the Apostles, yet he founded a
single chair, thus establishing by his
own authority the source and hallmark of the (church's) oneness.
No doubt the others were all that
Peter was, but a primacy is given
to Peter and it is (thus) made clear
that there is but one church and
one chair. So, too, even if they are
all shepherds, we are shown but
one flock which is to be fed by all
the Apostles in common accord. If
a man does not hold fast to this
oneness of Peter, does he imagine
that he still holds the faith? If he
deserts the chair of Peter upon
whom the church was built, has he
still confidence that he is in the
church?

The Non-Primacy Text

*'Ego tibi dico (inquit) quia tu es
Petrus, et super hanc petram aedificabo ecclesiam meam, et portae
inferorum non vincent eam. Et dabo
tibi claves regni coelorum : et quae
ligaveris super terram, erunt ligata
et in coelis; et quaecumque solveris
super terram erunt soluta et in
coelis'* (M. 16:18, 19.)

*Super unum aedificat ecclesiam Et
quamvis apostolis omnibus post resurrectionem suam parem potestatem
tribuat et dicat: 'Sicut misit me
Pater, et ego mitto vos: accipite
Spiritum Sanctum: si cujus remiseri-
tis peccata remittentur illi, si cujus
tenueritis, tenebuntur'* (J. 20:21),
*tamen ut unitatem manifestaret,
unitatis eiusdem originem ab uno
incipientem sua auctoritate disposuit.
Hoc erant utique et ceteri apostoli
quod fuit Petrus pari consortio
praediti et honoris et potestatis sed*

'I say to thee (he says) that thou art
Peter and upon this rock I will
build my church, and the gates of
hell shall not overcome it. I will
give to thee the keys of the kingdom
of heaven. And what thou shalt
bind upon earth shall be bound
also in heaven, and whatsoever thou
shalt loose on earth shall be loosed
in heaven' (M. 16:21, 19).

It is on one man that he builds the
church and although he assigns a
like power to all the Apostles after
his resurrection, saying: 'As the
Father hath sent me, I also send
you. Receive ye the Holy Spirit: if
you forgive any man his sins, they
shall be forgiven him; if you retain
any man's sins, they shall be
retained' (J. 20:21), yet in order
that the oneness might be unmis-
takable, he established by his own
authority a source for that oneness

exordium ab unitate proficiscitur, ut ecclesia Christi una monstretur, quam unam ecclesiam etiam in cantico canticorum Spiritus sanctus ex persona Domini designat et dicit: 'Una est columba mea, perfecta mea, una est matri suae, electa genitrici suae' (Cant. 6:8). *Hanc ecclesiae unitatem qui non tenet, tenere se fidem credit?*

Qui ecclesiae renititur et resistit in ecclesia se esse confidit, quando et beatus apostolus Paulus hoc idem doceat et sacramentum unitatis ostendat dicens: 'Unum corpus, et unus spiritus, una spes vocationis vestrae, unus Dominus, una fides, unum baptisma, unus Deus' (Eph. 4:4)?

having its origin in one man alone. No doubt the other Apostles were all that Peter was, endowed with equal dignity and power, but the start comes from him alone, in order to show that the church of Christ is unique. Indeed, this oneness of the church is figured in the canticle of Canticles when the Holy Spirit, speaking in Our Lord's name says: 'One is my dove, my perfect one : to her mother she is the only one, the darling of her womb' (Cant. 6:8). If a man does not hold fast to this oneness of the church, does he imagine that he still holds the faith? If he resists and withstands the church, has he still confidence that he is in the church, when the blessed Apostle Paul gives us this very teaching and points to the mystery of oneness saying: 'One body and one spirit, one hope in your calling, one Lord, one Faith, one Baptism, one God' (Eph. 4:4)?

When Hartel edited *De Unitate* in the Vienna series, he assumed that the primacy text was a forgery interpolated for the sake of defending the Roman primacy. This view was widely accepted until Dom John Chapman demonstrated, in a now famous series of articles, that both the versions are of Cyprianic origin.[1] Chapman considered that the non-primacy text was written first, in the year 251, and that a few months later Cyprian altered it to the primacy text before sending it to Rome for use in the campaign against the anti-Pope Novatian. Chapman's first conclusion is almost universally accepted, but more recent scholarship has reversed the chronology. D. van den Eynde[2] and O. Perler[3]

[1] Arts. in the *Revue Bénédictine*, 'Les Interpolations dans le Traité de S. Cyprien sur l'Unité de l'Église, 1902, pp. 246–54; 357–73; 1903, pp. 26–51; 1910, pp. 447–64.

[2] Art. in *Revue d'Histoire Ecclésiastique*, 'La double édition du De Unitate de S. Cyprien', 1933, pp. 5–24.

[3] Arts. in *Römische Quartalschrift*, 'Zur Datierung der beiden Fassungen des vierten Kapitels De Unitate Ecclesiae', 1936, pp. 1–44, 49–57; 'De Catholicae Ecclesiae Unitate cap 4–5, Die ursprünglichen Texte, ihre Überlieferung, ihre Datierung', 1936, pp. 151–68.

have shown that the primacy text was written first in 251, having in mind the schism of Novatian rather than that of Felicissimus in Carthage; later, at the time of the dispute about heretical baptism Cyprian modified it, since his adversaries were using it in a pro-Roman sense which he had never intended. Hence the deletion of the word 'primacy'. In addition to giving a most reasonable explanation of why the text should have been changed, the evidence in support of this theory is very convincing. An analysis of the structure of the primacy text shows that it is planned with remarkable precision and executed with a corresponding polish and balance. The chapter begins with two Petrine texts to indicate that unity is to be preserved in the church, since its hierarchy began with one man. Then follow three pairs of phrases in which the first is a declaration of the subsequent equality of the apostles, and the second is an assertion that unity is nevertheless preserved. Finally two perfectly balanced rhetorical questions emphasize the obvious conclusion. By contrast, the non-primacy text, though not devoid of style, is no more than a fragmentary survival of the precise structure of the primacy text, from which it must have taken its origin. The content, too, reveals the date of the non-primacy text. Three of its scriptural quotations, John 20:21, Canticles 6:8, and Ephesians 4:4, occur only in those of Cyprian's writings which date from the period of the baptismal dispute; that is to say, after the year 255.

The debates over the text have been matched by similar disagreements about the meaning. Cyprian used the Petrine text of Matthew to defend episcopal authority, but many later theologians, influenced by the papal connexions of the text, have interpreted Cyprian in a pro-papal sense which was alien to his thought. It is in a sense unfortunate that the schism should have started in Rome. Cyprian would have used Matthew 16 to defend the authority of any bishop, but since he happened to employ it for the sake of the Bishop of Rome, it created the impression that he understood it as referring to papal authority. In Cyprian's ecclesiology the unity of the church is secured by two means, the authority of the bishops, and the role of Peter at the beginning. With scriptural passages, among which is Matthew 16, he defends the oneness of government in the local church. Since the local church is the microcosm of the universal church, the safeguarding of unity in the one will ensure it for the other.

The precise role which Peter played in securing the unity of the church is even now disputed. Catholics as well as Protestants are now generally agreed that Cyprian did not attribute a superior authority to Peter. However, there is an almost equal division of opinion as to whether he saw Peter merely as the model of unity, or also as some kind of source of the unity which he exemplified.

The 'exemplar' theory was defended consistently by H. Koch[1] and has been followed by many eminent scholars, including the Catholics Batiffol[2] and Bardy.[3] Advocates of this opinion point out that Cyprian himself on more than one occasion says explicitly that the unity of the church is modelled on Peter. In the fourth chapter of *De Unitate* he enunciates the principle clearly 'a primacy is given to Peter, and it is [thus] made clear (*monstratur*) that there is but one church and one chair'. Moreover it is alleged that for Cyprian a foundation is merely the first in a chronological series. Examples of this are seen in his other writings. Abraham is said to be the foundation of faith,[4] that is to say, he was the first believer. In much the same sense Cyprian speaks of the fear of God as the origin of religion,[5] allegedly because it is the initial attitude of the soul to God.

This interpretation of Cyprian was challenged by Chapman, particularly on account of the reduction of a 'foundation' to the role of chronological priority.[6] Indeed, it seems that there is much to commend Poschmann's theory of Peter as the causal source of unity as well as the exemplar.[7] Its principal merit is that it gives an adequate meaning to a series of expressions in Cyprian's writings which describe Peter as being the model of unity, and something more. For example, in Letter 33 quoted above Cyprian cites Matthew 16 as the origin of episcopal authority, and then adds: 'Thence through the passage of time, and the episcopal succession, the election of bishops and the external form of the church persevere. . . .' (*'Inde per temporum et successionum vices, episcoporum ordinatio et ecclesiae ratio decurrit.'*) The most satisfactory understanding of this sentence seems to be that the episcopal succession and with it the external form of the church both

---

[1]His definitive work on the subject was *Cathedra Petri*, Geissen, 1930, cf. esp. pp. 40–46.

[2]Batiffol, *Cathedra Petri*, pp. 112–13, 135–40.

[3]Bardy, *La Théologie de L'Eglise de S. Irénée au Concile de Nicée*, Paris, 1947, p.233.

[4]*De Bono Patientiae*, ed. Hartel in C.S.E.L., Vol. 3, i, p. 414.

[5]*De Habitu Virginum*, C.S.E.L., Vol. 3, i, p. 188. Discussed, together with preceding reference by Koch, op. cit., pp. 40–42.

[6]Chapman, J., *Studies in the Early Papacy*, London, 1928, pp. 29–34.

[7]Poschmann, B., *Die Sichtbarkeit der Kirche nach der Lehre des hl. Cyprians*, Paderborn, 1908, pp. 17–21. Also *Ecclesia Principalis*, Breslau, 1933, pp. 15–18.

take their origin from Peter's reception of authority at Caesarea Philippi. The same idea is expressed with perhaps even more clarity in Letter 59, written when the Carthaginian schismatics had attempted to gain recognition in Rome: 'They have the audacity to travel to Peter's chair and to the original church from which the episcopal unity has arisen.' ('*Navigare audent et ad Petri cathedram atque ad ecclesiam principalem, unde unitas sacerdotalis exorta est. . .*')[1] The original church (*ecclesia principalis*) is the episcopal authority at Rome, understood as having begun at Caesarea Philippi. From this starting-point the unity of the church received not merely the exemplar on which it would be modelled, but the source from which it took its veritable origin. Admittedly the interpretation of this letter is by no means unanimous, yet it must be remembered that if Cyprian had wished to describe Peter merely as the model of unity there are any number of clearer ways in which he could have done it. Other writings of Cyprian go even farther and name the two aspects of Peter's function, namely that of being model and source of unity. In Letter 73 the following sentence occurs: ('It is to Peter, on whom he built the church and in whom he has established and demonstrated the origin of unity [*unde unitatis originem instituit et ostendit*] that the Lord has conferred the power of . . .')[2] Similar clear expressions are to be found in *De Unitate*. In the fourth chapter Christ is said to have established in Peter the 'source and hallmark of the church's oneness' (*unitatis originem adque rationem*). The *ratio* is the external form of unity and the *origo* is naturally its causal source.[3] In chapter five the theory of Peter's being a causal source as well as a model of unity is confirmed by the examples which Cyprian furnishes. The unity of the church is likened to the sun and its rays, the tree trunk and its branches, the spring and the streams, and finally the mother and her children: in other words, causal sources of the unity in their related members. Thus it would appear that a fair estimate of Cyprian's understanding of St. Peter must go beyond the notion of a mere model of church unity and include the idea of his being the causal source from whom the bonds of unity take their origin.

An adequate judgement on the value of Cyprian's thought must wait until its sequel is studied; namely the role which Peter's successor plays in the church. Cyprian's theory of the episcopate and the papacy is the

[1] Letter 59:14.
[2] Letter 73:7.
[3] Bévenot, M., op. cit., p. 103; Camelot, P-Th., Art. 'S. Cyprien et la primauté', *Istina*, 1957, p. 430.

natural complement of his opinion on St. Peter, but for the sake of clarity it will be examined in Chapter 7. For the present it can be seen that Cyprian attributes some kind of primacy to Peter in the grant of power which he received at Caesarea Philippi. In this grant of authority he became, moreover, the foundation of the church and received episcopal power which appeared for the first time in the church. In all these matters Cyprian is in accord with the general ecclesiastical tradition. In one matter only is he at variance with the authentic tradition, in his refusal to accord seniority to St. Peter, whose unique position was being clarified at this time.

Cyprian's refusal to recognize the superior authority of St. Peter had the effect of provoking a firm clarification of the matter by Pope St. Stephen. As has been stated above, there is reason to believe that the Roman church applied the text of Matthew 16:16 to the primacy of St. Peter as early as the beginning of the third century. There can be little doubt that Pope Stephen used the text, in the middle of the century, specifically to defend his authority against the consequences of Cyprian's theory regarding St. Peter. In the course of the dispute about the validity of heretical baptism Stephen sent a letter to Cyprian of which only fragments have survived. Cyprian's Letter 74 to Pompeius contains the Pope's instructions in the matter of the reconciliation of baptized heretics. The next letter in the collection (75) indicates what Stephen said about St. Peter. Apparently Cyprian sent the whole of the correspondence to his ally Firmilian of Cappadocia, whose reply is of unusual value, since his sarcastic remarks about the Pope have preserved a reliable indication of what Stephen actually said. It is this letter of Firmilian, translated and probably re-edited, which has come to be included in the correspondence of St. Cyprian.[1] The key sentence is as follows: 'I am justifiably angry at this obvious and manifest stupidity of Stephen, who boasts about his particular bishopric, contending that he holds from St. Peter that succession upon which the foundations of the church were established, thereby producing many other rocks (*petras*) and constituting the structures of many new churches.' This illuminating sentence shows how far the Roman theology of St. Peter had developed by this time. It can be seen that the text of Matthew was understood as referring to the foundation of the church, and that it indicated the superiority of St. Peter. It is, moreover, clear that Pope Stephen was claiming to have inherited the powers which St. Peter had been granted in this text.

[1]Letter 75.

It is not surprising that the community at Rome should have been the first to give definitive form to the theology of St. Peter's position in the church. The action and correspondence of the subsequent popes reveals a consistent and deepening appreciation of this theory. However, it must be borne in mind that the detailed exposition of, for instance, St. Leo does not go beyond the scope of the principles already understood by St. Stephen. In other words the development was uniformly consistent.

*   *   *   *   *

During the third century the Eastern church had not as a whole achieved the intellectual brilliance which was to distinguish it later on. However, the school of Alexandria had already established its tradition of learning and its most distinguished representative, Origen, was a contemporary of Cyprian. In seeking his opinion of St. Peter one is able to use not mere controversial works as with Cyprian but systematic studies of theology and apologetical treatises of a more comprehensive scope than those of the second century. In view of this it is most natural to seek his study on St. Peter in the commentary which he wrote on the Gospel of St. Matthew, bearing in mind, of course, that in these biblical commentaries he was concerned with the mystical rather than the literal sense. The Petrine text of Matthew 16 interests him chiefly on account of its seventeenth verse: 'It is not flesh and blood, it is my Father in heaven that has revealed this to thee.' Thence his whole interest is focused on the heavenly enlightenment which Peter has received.[1] The notion of enlightenment which is here alluded to could be called Christian Gnosticism. Origen drew a distinction between the faith of the ordinary Christian and the enlightenment of the perfect soul. Progress towards this enlightenment was brought about by the twofold method of prayer and asceticism until the knowledge of God and things divine became the contemplation of the enlightened or perfect souls.

It is in the context of this enlightenment that Origen refers to St. Peter in his famous apologetical treatise 'Against Celsus'. The relevant passage is as follows:—'However, to those who by following him, have received power to go after him even as he is ascending the high mountain, he has a more divine form. Anyone who is a Peter (Πέτρος) sees this; for Peter was capable of having the church built on him by the *Logos* (Λόγος) and attained such ability that no gate of Hell could prevail

[1] *Comm. on Matt.*, G.C.S., Origen, Vol. 10, p. 84.

against him.[1] The distinction between the believers and the perfect
is maintained, and without equivocation they are called 'rocks' on whom
the church is built. This is an extension of an idea which is based on his
consideration of the union of the soul with Christ. Since the name Christian was already given to the followers of Christ, on account of the
intimacy of the union between them, Origen saw no difficulty in extending to them the other title which is attributed to Christ in I Cor. 10:4;
namely 'the rock that was Christ'.[2] On such a view the bestowal of the
title of 'rock' in Matthew 16 had little that was out of the ordinary. Peter
was then merely the first Christian Gnostic.[3] As a result the church is
not built on Peter alone, but on all those who receive similar heavenly
enlightenment.[4]

This latter statement is pursued to all its logical conclusions. The
text of Matthew which is normally applied only to St. Peter and the
church is applied in all its aspects to the other 'rocks'. The gates of hell
will not prevail against them, they all possess the power of the keys, and
the power of binding and loosing (i.e. judging) is likewise enjoyed by
the perfect.[5]

Such, is the rather startling view of Origen on St. Peter, and in
particular the relevance of the classical text of Matthew 16. It is true
that these commentaries are mystical in their treatment rather than
literal, but it must be admitted that Origen has sacrificed the literal
sense with remarkable freedom.[6] Needless to say, the passages in question have often been invoked in an anti-Petrine and anti-papal sense.
Batiffol has cast doubts on the correctness of such an interpretation.[7]
The whole problem is complicated by such factors as Origen's *penchant*
for departing from the literal sense, as well as by the more down-to-earth
factor of the loss of so many of his exegetical works.[8] Undeniably
his theory on St. Peter is perplexing and it is significant that it
did not command any notable following in the subsequent patristic
tradition.[9]

---

[1]*Contra Celsus VI*, 77, G.C.S., Origen, Vol. 2, p. 147.
[2]*Comm. on Matt.*, G.C.S., Origen, Vol. 10, p. 88. cf. p. 84.
[3]Ludwig, op. cit., p. 40.
[4]*Comm. on Matt.*, G.C.S., Origen, Vol. cit., p. 86.
[5]*Comm. on Matt.*, G.C.S., Origen, Vol. cit., pp. 96, 98.
[6]cf. Batiffol, *L'Église Naissante*, p. 393.
[7]Batiffol, op. cit., p. 392.
[8]Of the *Scholia* none has survived in its entirety. Less than half the *Homilies*
have been transmitted even including translations and fragments. Finally of his
Commentaries even less is extant than of the *Homilies*,
[9]Ludwig, op. cit., p. 45.

The next Eastern writer to be considered is Eusebius, the Bishop of Caesarea in Palestine. As a thinker he was not original, but compensated for this defect by the diligence of his researches into the studies of his predecessors. At the time when Diocletian was systematically destroying the Christian writings Eusebius was making every effort to collect them for the already famous library at Caesarea. In his own books, too, he has preserved quotations from many early Christian authors whose writings would otherwise be unknown today. He became Bishop of Caesarea on the eve of Constantine's edict of religious toleration, played a prominent part in the council of Nicea, and died in 339 or 340.

His definitive judgement on the position of St. Peter is difficult to ascertain (if indeed he did arrive at such a decision), since his writings record three different views. In the *Ecclesiastical History* he says without any explanation or qualification: 'Peter upon whom the church of Christ is built, against which the gates of hell shall not prevail . . .'[1] Elsewhere he speaks of Christ as the foundation of the church in such a way as to exclude St. Peter. For instance in his commentary on the Psalms the reference to the foundations of the earth in Psalm 17 leads him to consider the foundation of the church.[2] Using Matthew 16, he declares that this foundation is a rock, which is then identified as Christ on the authority of I Cor. 10:4. This interpretation of the text of Matthew which seems so strange to the modern reader indicates a problem which perplexed quite a number of the early fathers. Their theology of the church was, thanks to St. Paul, so thoroughly Christocentric that it was difficult for them to envisage a foundation other than Christ. To this predisposition must be added the realization that the Greek fathers, not to mention the Latins, had lost sight of the play upon words, being ignorant of the Aramaic original of the Petrine text of Matthew. The reconciliation of the respective roles of Christ and Peter as elaborated by writers such as St. Jerome was not appreciated by all the fathers, so that many of them, while estimating correctly the position of St. Peter, would yet misinterpret the text of Matthew 16.

The third opinion which Eusebius put forward was an interpretation of Matthew 16 which envisaged the rock of the church neither as Christ nor precisely Peter himself, but as the faith which he manifested in his

[1]H. E., VI, 25. cf. also II, 14.
[2]M.P.G., Vol. 23, col. 173.

acknowledgement of Christ.[1] This latter view of Eusebius, together with his other innovation, namely that the rock of Matthew 16 was Christ, had considerable influence on the later exegesis of the text in question, both in the Eastern and the Western church.[2]

The Egyptian Serapion seems to have held an estimate at least of the Petrine text which closely resembles that of Eusebius. He became Bishop of Thmuis, near Alexandria, in 339 and was a friend of the great Athanasius. His most important surviving work is a treatise against the Manicheans, in the twenty-second chapter of which he deals with St. Peter.[3] Although he applies the text of Matthew 16 to the Apostle in person, he omits all reference to the rock which is the foundation of the church. The omission has the appearance of being deliberate and is hard to account for, unless he, too, like Eusebius, considered that the rock in question was not to be understood as St. Peter.[4]

The same anxiety not to prejudice the position of Christ seems to have been the inspiration of St. Cyril of Jerusalem. He, too, omits to call St. Peter 'the rock' in circumstances which would seem to make the identification perfectly natural. He describes the rejection of the synagogue and its replacement by the church, adding that the change over took place when Christ said 'Upon this rock . . .'[5] His failure to mention Peter's role in the church can best be appreciated as a desire to safeguard his neophytes from misunderstanding Christ's unique place. This does not mean that he failed to attribute to Peter his rightful place among the human rulers of the church. Elsewhere in his famous *Catechism* he speaks of Peter as the 'First Apostle', or as the 'Prince of the Apostles, and the keybearer of the Kingdom of heaven',[6] or in slightly different words: 'Peter who bears with him the keys of heaven.'[7] In this respect Cyril is particularly valuable. Despite his unwillingness to apply Matthew 16 to St. Peter in the way which seems most obvious to the modern exegete, his Petrine doctrine is perfectly orthodox. Protestant polemical writers have frequently drawn attention to the divergencies of patristic interpretation of Matthew 16 and inferred thereby that the fathers were uncertain about St. Peter's position in the church. The

---

[1]*Theopany*, IV, 11; G.C.S., Eusebius, Vol. 3, ii, p. 181.
[2]Ludwig, op. cit., p. 47.
[3]M.P.G., Vol. 40, col. 920.
[4]Ludwig, op. cit., p. 47.
[5]St. Cyril, *Catech.*, 18:25, M.P.G., Vol. 33, col. 1045.
[6]St. Cyril, *Catech.*, 11, 3, M.P.G., Vol. 33, col. 693; and 17:17; M.P.G., Vol. 33, col. 997.
[7]St. Cyril, *Catech.*, 6, 15, M.P.G., Vol. 33, col. 564.

case of St. Cyril indicates how this problem should be approached, since for several of the fathers the exegesis of Matthew 16 did not necessarily indicate their definitive thought on the role of St. Peter.

★ ★ ★ ★ ★

From the fourth century onwards the quantity of patristic writing is so great as to require systematic division if it is to be studied. It is perhaps clearer to follow logical divisions rather than attempt to pursue a purely chronological sequence. The consideration of St. Cyril of Jerusalem leads on quite naturally to that group of fathers whose lives were dedicated to the defence of orthodoxy against the Arians. Their opinion of St. Peter is constant and determined: without any hesitation he is identified as the rock and foundation of the church. Their certainty shows such a marked contrast with the hesitations of some of their predecessors that it would seem that something out of the ordinary had prompted it. Ludwig has suggested that they were helped by the urge to disassociate Christ from any suggestion of 'creature status' and thereby to consider Peter rather than Christ as the rock foundation of the church.[1] Another characteristic which illuminates the whole question of the patristic opinion of St. Peter is the fact that they sometimes speak of the rock as being Peter's faith as well as his person. Although it is possible to maintain that Eusebius could hold inconsistent opinions on a given subject, the same cannot be said of the great rivals of the Arians, among whom are some of the most distinguished of the fathers of the church. Since they cannot be accused of inconsistency, one is forced to admit that the difference between interpreting the promises as referring to Peter or Peter's faith was, in their opinion, negligible. The examples which follow will show how the two notions harmonize in their thought.

St. Basil the Great, who died in 379, makes the formal identification between St. Peter and the foundation of the church, in terms which indicate that he must have had in mind the text of Matthew 16: 'Peter upon which rock the Lord promised that he would build his church.'[2] The role which his faith played is indicated quite naturally in his treatise *Against Eunomius*, where he says that it was Peter 'who, on account of the pre-eminence of his faith, received on himself the building of the church.[3] His contemporaries the two Gregories say much the

---

[1]Ludwig, op. cit., p. 49.
[2]Basil, *In Isaias*, II, 66, M.P.G., Vol. 30, col. 233.
[3]Basil, *Adversus Eunomius*, II, 4, M.P.G., Vol. 29, col. 577.

same thing. Gregory of Nazianzen wrote in his *Theological Discourses*: 'Seest thou that of the disciples of Christ, all of whom were exalted and deserving of the choice, one is called a rock, and is entrusted with the foundations of the church.[1] Gregory, too, harmonizes this perfectly with the role played by Peter's faith, since he declares that it was in virtue of that faith that he merited such a distinction.[2] The third of these famous Cappadocians, Gregory of Nyssa, accords fully with the preceding two, and a single representative quotation will suffice to indicate his thought: 'The memory of Peter, the head of the Apostles, is celebrated; and glorified indeed with him are the other members of the church; but the church of God is firmly established upon him. For he is, in accordance with the gift conferred on him by the Lord, the unbroken and most firm rock upon which the Lord built his church.'[3]

Among the champions of the church in the Arian crisis it is usual to include one Western father, St. Hilary of Poitiers. The four years of exile which he spent in the East (356–360) were employed most profitably in the study of the Eastern theology, and as a result his thought has much in common with the Greek fathers who were his contemporaries. He is in no doubt about the senior position of St. Peter and interprets the text of Matthew 16 in this sense. In his commentary on the passage in question he speaks thus of St. Peter: 'O Blessed keeper of the gate of heaven, to whose disposal are delivered the keys of the entrance into eternity; whose judgement on earth is an authority already decided in heaven . . . O, in thy designation by a new name, happy foundation of the church, and the rock worthy of the building of that which was to scatter the infernal laws, and the gates of the Underworld, and all the barriers of death.'[4] Precisely the same estimate of Peter is to be found in other parts of his writings. In his commentary on the psalms he described him thus: 'The door keeper of the heavenly kingdom', or 'Peter, upon whom he was about to build the church'.[5] The same theme is to be found elsewhere in Hilary with one exception. A passage in his *De Trinitate* is not so clear and could be interpreted as indicating that the rock of Matthew 16 is Peter's faith. The words are (after a series of examples of faith) '. . . and after his acknowledgement of the heavenly mystery (*sacramentum*), the blessed Simon, supporting the edifice of the

---

[1]Gregory Nazianzen, *Discourse*, 32:18, M.P.G., Vol. 36, col. 193.
[2]cf. Gregory Nazianzen, *Discourse*, 28, M.P.G., Vol. 36, col. 52.
[3]Gregory of Nyssa, *Panegyric on St. Stephen*, M.P.G., Vol. 46, col. 733.
[4]Hilary, *Comm. on Matthew*, M.P.L., Vol. 9, col. 1010.
[5]*Comm. on the Psalms*, 141:8, 131:4, C.S.E.L., Vol. 22, pp. 804 and 663.

church, and receiving the keys. . . .'[1] Sometimes this passage is isolated and alleged as evidence that Hilary did not view St. Peter as the foundation of the church. The clear testimony of his other writings cannot be made to yield to one doubtful quotation. It is reasonable, as Ludwig suggests,[2] to understand this as a rhetorical embellishment, which would be a legitimate application of the scriptural text once its literal meaning had been established.

Slightly later than St. Hilary is another anti-Arian champion, Didymus the Blind, who died in 398. His theory of St. Peter adds nothing new to the general opinion of his day. In his treatise on the Trinity he identifies Peter as the rock spoken of in Matthew 16, and extends the notion to his controlling thereby the entry into the church.[3]

The preoccupation with the purity of the orthodox faith can be seen in the thought of Epiphanius of Salamis. Although he was of the Eastern church he may well have been influenced by Western attitudes, since he was present at the synod of Rome in 382 at which the position of St. Peter was clarified in reaction to the pretensions of Constantinople. The various influences blended harmoniously and his writings about St. Peter show how smoothly the notions of 'faith' and 'primacy' complement each other in the minds of these fathers. In his *Ancoratus* he describes St. Peter thus: 'The first of the Apostles, that firm rock upon which the church of God is built, so that the gates of hell, that is to say the heresies and heresiarchs, will not prevail against it. For in every way was the faith confirmed in him who received the key of heaven, in him who looses on earth and binds in heaven. For in him are found all the subtle questions of faith.'[4] The same ideas are to be found elsewhere in the *Ancoratus* and also in his apologetical work the *Panarion*, better known as *Adversus Hæreses*, which contains the passage: 'Peter, who was the very chief (κορυφαιοτατος) of the Apostles, who became for us truly a firm rock, founding the faith of the Lord, upon which the church was in every way built . . .'[5]

The last of this group of anti-Arian fathers is Asterius of Amasea, who died in 410, and is of particular interest because he harmonizes the two passages of the New Testament which speak of Christ and Peter as the 'rock'. In his homily on Saints Peter and Paul he has this important

[1]Hilary, *De Trin.*, VI, 20, M.P.L., Vol. 10, col. 172.
[2]Ludwig, op. cit., p. 60.
[3]Didymus, *De Trin.*, I, 30, M.P.G., Vol. 39, col. 416.
[4]*Ancoratus*, 9:6, G.C.S., Epiphanius, Vol. 1, p. 16.
[5]*Adversus Hæreses*, 59:7, M.P.G., Vol. 41, col. 1029.

passage: 'The only begotten calls Peter the foundation of the church
. . . no man can lay a foundation other than that which is laid which is
Jesus Christ. But with a similar appellation did He adorn also that first
disciple of His, describing him as a rock of the faith. Through Peter
therefore . . . the stability of the church is preserved incapable of fall
and unswerving. . . . Peter is called the rock of faith, the foundation
and substructure of the church of God.'[1] Further on in the same homily
he applies to Peter the text of John 21:15: 'He entrusts to this man the
catholic and universal church, after having asked him three times
"Lovest thou me"? . . . Peter received the world in charge; as it were
for one fold, one shepherd, having heard "Feed my lambs"; and the Lord
gave wellnigh in his own stead, that most faithful disciple to the pro-
selytes as a father, and pastor and instructor.'[2]

The opinion of the anti-Arian fathers is therefore quite clear. Peter
is regarded as the senior Apostle, and the foundation of the church. In
their minds this honour is in no way incompatible with the position
which Christ occupies, nor does the excellence of Peter's faith blind
them to the fact that something more is indicated in the texts of
Matthew and John.

★   ★   ★   ★   ★

Before moving westwards to study the Italian and African opinions
it will be convenient to consider the smaller group of Syrian fathers
who flourished in the fourth century. Their situation is somewhat
unique, since they were far removed from the centres of the Arian controversy, and can be relied upon to give a primitive unbiased testimony
to the ancient tradition of the church. For the present inquiry they have
the particular advantage that their Syriac versions of the Scriptures preserved the play upon words which was present in the Aramaic form of
the promise of Matthew 16, thereby preserving them from one of the
difficulties which beset the Latin and Greek fathers.

The earliest of the Syrian fathers of importance is Aphraates, who
died about the year 360. In his homily 7, *De Paenitentibus*, he urges his
listeners to imitate Simon, '. . . the chief of the disciples . . . the Lord
accepted him, set him up as the foundation, called him the rock and
structure of the church'.[3] The same opinion is voiced in his other

---

[1] Asterius, Homily 8, M.P.G., Vol. 40, col. 268.
[2] Asterius, Homily 8, M.P.G., Vol. 40, col. 281.
[3] Aphraates, Homily 7:15, *De Paenitentibus*, ed. Parisot in *Patrologia Syriaca*,
Vol. 1, col. 335.

'Demonstrations', where he declares that the church was established on Peter, who is called the 'prince of pastors', and who is the foundation of the church, while James and John are the columns.[1]

The greatest name in this school is undeniably that of St. Ephraim, who died in 373. His commentary on Matthew 16 has already been discussed in connexion with the authenticity of the Petrine promise,[2] and it is only necessary here to recall the relevant details. On account of his writing 'The gates of hell shall not overcome thee', Harnack alleged that the *Diatesseron* which lay before Ephraim made no mention of Peter's being the rock. The ancient versions of the Diatesseron show that this was not the case. The text of Tatian's compilation contained the usual form of the promise. This is, moreover, confirmed by other phrases from Ephraim's commentary, such as his calling Peter the rock, and declaring that the church would not be destroyed because it was the work of Christ.[3] These remarks of Ephraim show not only that his text was as it is today, but also that he understood that Peter was the rock.[4] Elsewhere he upholds the senior position of Peter in so far as the church is built on him, he is responsible for all of it, and he is the source of truth and sanctification for the disciples.[5]

The lesser writers of the later period testify to the persistence of this view of St. Peter in the Syrian church. For example, Isaac of Antioch, who died at the end of the fourth century, declared that the church was built on Simon as the Ark of the Covenant was built on Moses.[6]

The tradition in this remote region of the church was so strong that it remained unshaken despite the Monophysite crisis. The poems of the Monophysite Bishop Jacob of Bathnae, who died in 521, bear witness to the preservation of the traditional estimate of St. Peter. The Apostle is described as the one on whom the church was built, and who was given as a gift the power to resist both death and satan.[7]

[1]Aphraates, *Demonstrationes*, 10:4; 23:12; *Patrologia Syriaca*, Vol. I, col. 454; Vol. II, col. 35.
[2]cf. p. 8.
[3]The original has perished; fragments of an Armenian version have survived. Latin version by J. B. Aucher and G. Mösinger, *Evangelii Concordantis Expositio*, Venice, 1876, pp. 153, 154.
[4]Ludwig, op. cit., p. 52.
[5]Ed. Lamy in *Hymni et Sermones*, Malines, 1882–1902, Vol. I, cols 373, 411, 435, 533; Vol. III, col. 783; Vol. IV, cols. 533, 621, 681–7, 737–45.
[6]Quoted in Landersdorfer, P. S., *Ausgewhälte Schriften der syrischen Dichter*, Munich, 1911, p. 161.
[7]Quoted in Landersdorfer, op. cit., p. 328.

The Nestorian and Monophysite crises were followed eventually by the Mohammedan invasions which strangled the intellectual life of this region. However, in its time of prosperity it bequeathed to the church a unanimous consensus of opinion on St. Peter. There can be no doubt as to the constancy with which the Syrian church subscribed to his primacy.

★   ★   ★   ★   ★

Another convenient grouping of patristic opinions is the series of Italian bishops and theologians of the period after the Arian crisis. It is hardly necessary to mention that the bishops of Rome are unwavering in proclaiming the primacy of St. Peter. It would be superfluous to quote from all of them, particularly as only two have merited the title of 'father of the church' on account of their constructive contributions to the science of theology.

The first important writer of this period was Ambrose of Milan, one of the greatest bishops of all time, who died in 397. It has been suggested that he was somewhat anti-Petrine, since in the exegesis of Matthew 16, he identifies consistently the 'rock' with Peter's faith.[1] For example, in his treatise on the incarnation he says as follows: 'He is called the foundation, because he was able to sustain not just his own faith, but that of all. . . . (Peter's) faith therefore is the foundation of the church, for not of the flesh of Peter but of his faith was it said that the "gates of hell shall not prevail against it".'[2] By extension this title is applied, in a manner reminiscent of Origen, to all believers, who will likewise resist the gates of hell.[3] Despite these rather rhetorical uses of the scriptures, Ambrose is clear in testifying to the primacy of St. Peter, which is, of course, perfectly compatible with his view that the 'rock' was Peter's faith. The title which he usually applies to Peter is that of *firmamentum ecclesiae* (support of the church), as, for instance, in his commentary on St. Luke, where he is speaking of the ship of Peter as the image of the church: 'That ship in which prudence is present, from which unbelief is absent, is not tossed about . . . for how could it be disturbed, since it was presided over by him, in whom is the support of

---

[1]For instance, F. Homes Dudden, while maintaining that Ambrose assigned to Peter a special place in the church, endeavours to minimize it because he doesn't identify the 'rock' with Peter in person. *St. Ambrose, His Life and Times,* Oxford, 1935, Vol. II, pp. 640–1.

[2]Ambrose, *De Incarnationis Dominicae Sacramento,* 5:34, M.P.L., Vol. 16, col. 827.

[3]Ambrose, *In Luc. Expos.,* VI, 98, C.S.E.L., Vol. 32 (iv), p. 275.

the church.[1] The underlying thought in Ambrose's estimate of St. Peter is that he merited the primacy because of the quality of his faith.[2] This consideration provides the key to the understanding of a sentence in the treatise on the Incarnation, where St. Peter's primacy is described as a 'primacy of confession and not honour, a primacy of faith not order'.[3] When it is understood that Ambrose wished to emphasize the role of Peter's faith in his meriting the primacy, it is evident that this passage is not incompatible with the rest of his thought, still less does it demote St. Peter.

The emphasis which Ambrose placed on the faith of St. Peter commanded some following. His influence can be seen in Cassian and Maximus of Turin. The former interprets the 'rock' of Matthew 16 quite simply as the faith of the church.[4] This does not entail any failure to appreciate St. Peter's senior position in the Apostolic college. In his treatise against Nestorius he asks his readers to pardon him for devoting so much time to St. Paul's theology of the Incarnation. He continues thus: 'If then the authority of a greater person would please you . . . let us interrogate not an inexperienced youth . . . nor a woman . . . but that great man, the disciple of disciples, that master among masters [*sed summum illum et inter discipulos discipulum, et inter magistros magistrum*], who wielding the government of the Roman church possessed the authority [*principatum*] in faith and priesthood. Tell us therefore, tell us we beg of you, Peter, prince of the Apostles, tell us how the churches must believe in God.'[5]

Maximus lived during the middle of the fifth century and was therefore able to draw upon the writings of Leo the Great and Augustine, in addition to St. Ambrose. Most probably it was from the latter that he derived the notion that the 'keys' of Matthew 16:19 referred to Peter's faith,[6] but that consideration did not entail for him a diminution of Peter's primacy. He applies to Peter the title of 'rock', and seems to have had in mind St. Augustine's contention that Peter is the rock only by derivation from Christ: 'This is Peter on whom Christ freely bestowed a sharing in his name. For just as Christ is the rock, as the Apostle Paul taught, so through Christ Peter is made a rock, when the

[1] *In Luc. Expos.*, IV, 70, C.S.E.L., Vol. 32 (iv), p. 175. Also *De Virginitate*, XVI, 105, M.P.L., Vol. 16, col. 292.
[2] *De Fide*, IV, 5, M.P.L., Vol. 16, col. 653.
[3] *De Incarnationis Dominicae Sacramento*, IV, 32, M.P.L., Vol. 16, col. 826.
[4] Cassian, *Contra Nestorium*, III, 14, C.S.E.L., Vol. 17, p. 279.
[5] Cassian, *Contra Nestorium*, III, 12, C.S.E.L., Vol. 17, p. 276.
[6] Maximus, Sermon 27, M.P.L., Vol. 57, col. 587.

Lord says to him: "Thou art Peter and upon this rock I will build my church . . ." [1] His judgement on the Apostle's seniority is clear from other homilies; for instance: 'Hence from heaven Christ summoned him (Peter) to be the comfort of the church and the support [*firmamentum*] of all believers'; or again: 'Peter therefore had such merit in the sight of God that after the steering of a small boat, the governing of the whole church was entrusted to him.' [2]

Dating from the time of St. Ambrose is a set of commentaries on the epistles of St. Paul, by an unknown author to whom the Renaissance scholars gave the name *Ambrosiaster*. It is, moreover, generally agreed that the book known as the *Hundred-and-twenty-seven Questions on the Old and New Testaments* was also of his authorship. To a certain extent his views tend to weaken the position of St. Peter. In the first place he bestows the title of 'primacy' (*primatum*) on St. Paul in a sense which would seem somewhat prejudicial to Peter. [3] Moreover, the 'rock' in the Petrine promise is for him simply faith: 'The Lord said to Peter: On this rock I will build my church; that is: in this confession of catholic faith I will consolidate the faithful for [eternal] life.' [4] In spite of these opinions it is not to be thought that he really minimized Peter's authority. Paul's first visit to Peter is appraised thus: 'It was right indeed that he should be anxious to see Peter; for he was the first among the apostles, and was entrusted by the Saviour with the care of the churches. [5] The import of the title 'first' is made clear in his commentary on II Cor. 12:12: 'Andrew followed the Saviour before Peter; and yet it was not Andrew but Peter who obtained the primacy.' [6] In other words, it cannot be thought that it derived from a possible 'firstness' in the chronological order.

Of all the fathers it would appear that St. Jerome presents the clearest and most carefully thought out theory of St. Peter. In this matter he was helped by his thorough knowledge of the Biblical languages as well as a solicitude to establish the literal meaning of the text rather than any rhetorical or homiletic elaborations. His testimonies to St. Peter are so numerous and so unequivocal that it is necessary only to select a few passages to give a just estimate of his thought. [7] In the first place the

[1] Homily 63, *In nativitate Petri et Pauli*, M.P.L., Vol. 57, col. 394.
[2] Homilies 69 and 70, M.P.L., Vol. 57, cols 393, 399.
[3] *Comm. on Galatians*, M.P.L., Vol. 17, col. 349.
[4] *Comm. on Ephesians*, M.P.L., Vol. 17, col. 380.
[5] *Comm. on Galatians*, M.P.L., Vol. 17, col. 344.
[6] *Comm. on II Cor. 12:12*, M.P.L., Vol. 17, col. 332.
[7] A detailed examination of his views on St. Peter and the see of Rome is to be found in J. Chapman, *Studies in the Early Papacy*, London, 1928, pp. 99–132.

identification of Peter as the 'rock' is abundantly clear. For instance, in his commentary on Matthew he describes the giving of the new name thus: 'As Christ himself gave light to the apostles, that they might be called the light of the world, and as they obtained other names also from the Lord, so to Simon also, who believed in the rock Christ, He bestowed the name Peter; and according to the metaphor of a rock, it is rightly said of him "I will build my church upon thee." . . .'[1] Secondly, he is not confused by the passage in I Cor. 10:4 which refers to Christ as a rock. In Jerome's theory Peter derives his privilege from Christ in such a way that the titles of both harmonize without difficulty, as is expressed in his commentary on Jeremias: 'Christ is not alone in being the rock, for He granted to the apostle Peter that he should be called "Rock".'[2] Jerome also clarified the meaning of the 'gates of hell' and declared without hesitation that it referred to the church's security from heresy, rather than a promised immortality.[3] His championing of the position of St. Peter even led him to the extreme of interpreting the quarrel between the Apostles at Antioch as a fabrication staged for the benefit of the gentile converts. This theory, which did not impress St. Augustine, is of course quite fantastic, yet it serves as a confirmation of Jerome's thoroughly pro-Petrine attitude.[4]

As has been mentioned above, the Popes themselves, needless to say, upheld the primacy of St. Peter. Evidence of their views is to be found principally in their letters, which reveal a uniform pattern of thought. The text of Matthew 16 is the *locus classicus* on which they base their claims for St. Peter, whose primacy is clearly appreciated, but in a way which shows little advance on the position adopted by Pope Stephen in the third century. These papal letters cannot be classified with the books and sermons of the fathers, but they did have an influence in their own fashion, on account of their official character, and the diversity of regions to which they were sent. Before proceeding to St. Leo, whose writings merit closer examination, there is one document of Roman origin which deserves to be mentioned, on account of the circumstances in which it was made known. It is the statement of the papal and Petrine claims made by the legate Philip at the council of

[1]Jerome, *Comm. on Matt. III, 16, 18*, M.P.L., Vol. 26, col. 117. Also Letters 15:2, 41:2, C.S.E.L., Vol. 54, pp. 63, 312.
[2]Jerome, *Comm. on Jeremias, III, 65*, C.S.E.L., Vol. 59, p. 202.
[3]*Comm. on Matt.*, loc. cit.
[4]Their correspondence on the matter is to be found among the letters of St. Jerome, Nos. 56, 67, 112, 116, M.P.L., Vol. 22, cols. 566, 648, 916–31, 941.

Ephesus in 431: 'There can be no doubt, indeed it has been known by all generations, that the holy and most blessed Peter, prince and head of the apostles, support of the faith, and foundation of the catholic church, received from our Lord Jesus Christ, the Saviour and Redeemer of the human race, the keys of the kingdom, and to him was also given the power of binding and loosing sins.'[1] The statement needs no comment, its meaning is perfectly clear. It is, moreover, a characteristic example of the Roman opinion in the fourth and early fifth centuries and shows their precise and clear evaluation of the role of St. Peter in the church.

In the middle of the fifth century the Roman see was occupied by Pope Leo, justly called 'the Great'. He is the first Pope whose intellectual attainments compare with those of the great Eastern theologians, and he is rightly considered as one of the fathers of the church. His theory of the papacy and St. Peter is expressed in his correspondence, and more elaborately in the sermons which he preached each year on the anniversary of his consecration as bishop of Rome.

The basis of the Petrine position, for Leo, as for the other popes, is the text of Matthew 16 (supported, too, by the Petrine texts of Luke and John), which he applies to the Apostle without any confusion between the roles of Peter and Christ. His bestowal of the titles of 'rock' to both of them is reminiscent of St. Jerome, as in the following example: '. . . as my Father has manifested to thee my divinity, so also do I make known to thee thy distinction. "For thou art Peter": that is, whereas I am the inviolable rock; I the cornerstone who made both one; I the foundation besides which no one can lay another; yet thou also art a rock, because thou art consolidated by my might, that those things which are my own in virtue of my power shall be extended to thee by participation with me.'[2] The amplitude of this power is understood as taking in the whole church, and in a sense the whole world: 'Out of the whole world the one Peter is chosen to be over both the calling of the nations, and over all the Apostles, and all the fathers of the church; that although in the people of God there be many priests and many shepherds, Peter shall rule all of them by his authority, not excluding the overall authority of Christ.'[3]

The exact role of Peter's faith in his receiving the primacy would appear to be that of a meritorious cause. In various contexts he uses the

[1] Mansi, IV, col. 1295.
[2] Leo, Sermon 4:2, M.P.L., Vol. 54, col. 149.
[3] Leo, Sermon 4:3, M.P.L., Vol. 54, col. 151.

Petrine text of Matthew when speaking of Peter's faith and his acknowledgement of Christ, as well as Christian faith in general.[1] It would be
somewhat *simpliste* to accuse St. Leo of inconsistency or contradiction
on account of these varied applications of the text of Matthew. He is
employing a procedure quite common in the sermons of the fathers,
namely that of using the text in an applied sense once the literal meaning
has been established.[2]

The persistent influence of Leo's thought can be seen in other
writers of the Italian school. His contemporary St. Peter Chrysologus,
the metropolitan of Ravenna, is a faithful echo of the master. His dealings with Eutyches and his sermons testify formally to the primacy of
St. Peter. A sentence from his Sermon No. 154 is typical: 'Let Peter
hold his long-established headship over the Apostolic choir; let him
open to those who enter the kingdom of heaven.'[3] The style is rhetorical,
but the writer's thought is perfectly clear. The same opinion can be
seen in the work of Arator, a deacon of the Roman church in the sixth
century, who wrote a poetical commentary on the Acts of the Apostles.
St. Peter is described as the unshakeable rock of faith.[4] Since he is
actually dealing with the name Peter, it is reasonable to suppose that he
had in mind the text of Matthew 16 as the source of the Apostle's
prerogative.

A fitting conclusion to the Italian school of thought is Pope St.
Gregory the Great. Although he cannot be regarded as an original
thinker, his writings are a lucid and faithful testimony to the tradition
of the early church, and they exerted a considerable influence on the
subsequent thought of the West. His exposition of the position of St.
Peter is in perfect conformity with all that his predecessors had taught.
He is in no doubt about the primacy of the Apostle. He understands it as
a responsibility for the whole church, and like St. Leo he deduces it not
only from the *locus classicus* of Matthew 16 but also from the Petrine
texts of Luke and John. One quotation from his letter No. 40 is truly
representative of his opinion: 'Who could be ignorant of the fact that
the holy church is consolidated in the solidity of the prince of the
Apostles, whose firmness of character extended to his name so that he

[1]A series of such applications has been collected by Batiffol, *Siège Apostolique*,
Paris, 1924, pp. 420–1.
[2]That the basic signification of 'the rock' is Peter's person is defended by
T. G. Jalland, *The Life and Times of St. Leo The Great*, London, 1941, p. 65.
[3]Chrysologus, Sermon 154, M.P.L., Vol. 52, col. 608. Also Sermon 107,
M.P.L., Vol. 52, col. 437.
[4]Arator, *De Actibus Apostolorum*, I, 1013, M.P.L., Vol. 68, col. 171.

should be called Peter after the "rock", when the voice of the Truth says "I will give to thee the keys of the kingdom of heaven". To him again is said "When after a little while thou hast come back to me, it is for thee to be the support of thy brethren." . . ."[1]

In general, then, the Italian school from Ambrose to Gregory the Great presents, but for minor divergences, a consistent view of the superior position of the Apostle Peter. This distinction is understood as being closely related to the quality of his faith, and it results in his being responsible for the whole church.

*   *   *   *   *

The next part of the church to be examined is Africa. After the death of Cyprian the African church went through a period of comparative mediocrity, devoid of great leaders or thinkers. At the beginning of the fourth century the church there was torn by the Donatist controversy which was the culmination of the African unwillingness to recognize the validity of sacraments administered by heretical or, in this case, sinful ministers. For the present examination the Donatists present a phenomenon of particular interest. Although they were severed from the universal church, and held divergent views of their own on certain subjects, they remained faithful in spite of it to the traditional attitude to St. Peter. Not only did they interpret Matthew 16 in the sense of giving a primacy to St. Peter, but they followed it to the logical conclusion of maintaining a Donatist bishop in Rome.[2] The only known divergence from this general opinion is that of Tyconius, who does not apply the text of Matthew to St. Peter. In his *Book of Rules* he speaks of the church founded on the rock, and which is secure against the assault of the underworld. The cause of this security might well be expected to be its protection by St. Peter, but in fact he gives as the reason 'because the firm foundation of God stands fast, as it is written. The lord knows his own'.[3] In the context his failure to mention St. Peter is most reasonably understood as a deliberate omission arising out of the conviction that Peter was not the 'rock' of the church. In all fairness, though, it must be recognized that he did not consider the rock to be either Christ or the Apostles or the faith of the church.

The only distinguished champion of the true faith who disputed with

---

[1]Gregory the Great, Letter 40 in Book VI, M.P.L., Vol. 77, col. 898.
[2]Ludwig, op. cit., p. 62.
[3]Tyconius, *Book of Rules*, ed. Burkitt in *Texts and Studies*, III, i, Cambridge, 1894, p. 63.

Donatists, before Augustine, was Optatus of Milevis, who died in 370 or thereabouts. His exposition of the role of St. Peter in the church is based on two concepts dear to the Africans which he developed in a sense which was considerably more pro-Roman than that which is to be found in Tertullian or Cyprian. They are the power of the keys, and the chair (*Cathedra*) of Peter, understood as his teaching authority. The unique position suggested by the possession of the *Cathedra* is fairly evident, and Optatus makes it quite clear that Peter has a special function as the Teacher for preserving the unity of the church. The notion of unity he derived apparently from St. Paul, since he uses the image of the head and the limbs to explain it. The notion is expressed succinctly in his apologetical treatise against Parmenian: 'You cannot fail to be aware that in Rome the episcopal Cathedra (chair) was conferred first on Peter, in the which chair has presided Peter the head of all the apostles (whence he is called "Cephas"), and in this chair unity is safeguarded for all.'[1] Although the exclusiveness of Peter's position is not so immediately apparent in the power of the keys Optatus insists that they were given to him first and that he bestowed the power on the other Apostles, as he declares in the same treatise: 'For the sake of unity the blessed Peter both merited to be preferred before all the apostles, and he alone received the keys of the kingdom of heaven to pass on to the others.'[2] The prominence given to the keys and the episcopal chair are typical of the African thought of that day, and it does not weaken his theory of Peter that he did not stress the 'rock'.

The greatest of the African thinkers, and indeed the unequalled genius of the whole of the West was St. Augustine of Hippo, who died in 430. His opinion of St. Peter is closely linked with his view of the church. On account of his inclination to neo-Platonism he was disposed to regard the church on earth as the image of the invisible church which was a more perfect entity than the visible manifestation. This notion found admirable confirmation in St. John's image of the vine and the branches, as well as in St. Paul's metaphor of the Head and members: the mystical body of Christ. The contact between the visible and invisible worlds was achieved through the sacraments and in a special sense by St. Peter. At this point it will be convenient to let St. Augustine speak for himself and the following passage from Tract 124 on St. John

[1]Optatus of Milevis, *Adversus Parmen*, II, 2, C.S.E.L., Vol. 26, p. 36. He confused the Greek *Kephale* (head) with *Cephas*.
[2]Optatus, op. cit., VII, 3, C.S.E.L., Vol. 26, p. 171.

is a clear explanation of his theory: 'Forgive us our debts as we forgive our debtors. So does the church act in blessed hope through this troublesome life; and this church, symbolized in its generality, was personified in the Apostle Peter [*gerebat figurata generalitate personam*] on account of the primacy of his apostleship. For as regards his own personality he was by nature one man, by grace one Christian, by still more abounding grace one, and yet also the first Apostle, but when it was said to him "I will give unto thee the keys of the kingdom of heaven, and whatsoever thou shalt bind upon earth shall be bound in heaven; and whatsoever thou shalt loose upon earth shall be loosed in heaven", he represented the universal church, which in this world is shaken by divers temptations, that come upon it like torrents of rain, floods and tempests and falleth not, because it is founded upon a rock from which Peter received his name. For rock [*petra*] is not derived from Peter, but Peter from *petra*; just as Christ is not called so from the Christian, but the Christian from Christ. For on this very account the Lord said "On this rock I will build my church", because Peter had said "Thou art the Christ the son of the living God". On this rock therefore, he said, which thou hast confessed, I will build my church. For the Rock [*petra*] was Christ: and on this foundation was Peter himself also built. For other foundation no man can lay than that which is laid which is Jesus Christ. The church therefore which is founded in Christ received from him the keys of the kingdom of heaven in the person of Peter, that is to say, the power of binding and loosing sins. For what the church is essentially in Christ, such representatively is Peter in the rock [*quod est enim per proprietatem in Christo Ecclesia, hoc est per significationem Petrus in petra*]. And in this representation Christ is to be understood as the Rock, Peter as the church. This church accordingly which Peter represented, so long as it lives amid evil by loving and following Christ, is delivered from evil.'[1]

It is clear in the first place that for Augustine, Christ is the foundation of the church, and it would appear that he was guided in this by I Cor. 3:11: 'The foundation which has been laid is the only one which anybody can lay; I mean Christ Jesus.' In addition to this St. Peter is closely associated with him in a way which needs careful elucidation. The very least that one can say is that Peter acted as an ambassador for the church in receiving for it the various spiritual powers. This much could hardly be denied, yet it does not seem to do full justice to the

[1]Tract 124:5 in *John*, trans. M. Dodds, Edinburgh, 1874.

thought of Augustine. There are a series of phrases in various of his writings which can best be understood if Peter is envisaged as personifying the church. In sermon 149 there is the phrase 'Peter bore the person of the church' (*'Petrus personam gerit ecclesiae'*).[1] Or again in the same sermon 'Peter bore the figure of the church' (*'Petrus figuram gestabat ecclesiae'*). The same idea is also expressed in the words 'In Peter there was the sacred image of the church' (*'In Petro esset ecclesiae sacramentum'*).[2] The full meaning of this enigmatic phrase, which he employs consistently of St. Peter, is indicated by the sentence in the passage quoted above from the 124th Tract on St. John: 'For what the church is essentially in Christ such representatively is Peter in the rock.' In other words, Augustine is saying that the relationship which the invisible church bears to the invisible Christ is reproduced at the visible level by the relationship of Peter to *'Petra'* (the visible Christ). This function is far above that of ambassador; yet surely Peter is not to be made coterminous with the whole church? Augustine seems to have foreseen the danger of this exaggeration, for when speaking of the bestowal of the power of the keys he says: 'Is it to be thought that Peter received the keys and not Paul? That Peter received them, but not James and John? . . . Since in the realm of symbolism Peter bore the person of the church, that which was given to this individual was given to the whole church.'[3]

Peter is, then, more than an ambassador for the church, but less than the whole church. He receives the spiritual powers from Christ on behalf of the church, and in his person he externalizes the invisible church. As Ludwig has expressed it, 'He focuses in himself, like a lens, the rays of the invisible church'.[4]

This judgement is confirmed by St. Augustine's attitude to the Roman see in his own day. The question will be dealt with more fully later on, but for the moment it is sufficient to draw attention to certain aspects of his papal theory which could not be sustained if he had considered Peter to be no more than an ambassador for the church. For Augustine, the basis of the papal authority is the fact that the power of St. Peter lives on in the see of Rome. This he expresses in the letter to Gloriosus, saying that Rome is the church 'in which the authority of the apostolic office [*cathedra*] has always stood fast'.[5] As a result of this he

[1] Sermon 149:7, M.P.L., Vol. 38, col. 802.
[2] Tract 50 in *John*, M.P.L., Vol. 35, col. 1762.
[3] Sermon 149:7, M.P.L., Vol. 38, col. 802.
[4] Ludwig, op. cit., p. 77.
[5] Letter 43:7, C.S.E.L., Vol. 34 (i), p. 90.

recognized the superior teaching authority of the Roman bishop which he described as an 'abundant source' of doctrine when he had recourse to Pope Innocent I in the Pelagian crisis.[1] On the juridical plane, too, he regarded communion with the Roman see as necessary for membership of the universal church.[2]

The foregoing estimate of the position of Peter must be regarded as the genuine and authentic judgement of St. Augustine. In addition to this he adopted a somewhat different attitude in the commentary on the psalms, where he identified Peter as the rock on which the church is built.[3] There is nothing in this latter view which contradicts the previous picture, though it does introduce another aspect to the consideration of St. Peter's position. Later in his life, though, St. Augustine repudiated this, not absolutely, but so as to leave his readers free to decide for themselves whether to regard Peter or Christ as the 'rock'.[4] This passage has been seized upon by controversialists who would almost infer from it that St. Augustine had no clear picture of St. Peter's role in the church. Such a view is unwarrantable. The retraction does not affect Augustine's basic theory of St. Peter and it was probably motivated by a desire to conciliate the Donatists by stressing the connexion of the church with Christ rather than the Apostles.[5]

The circle of St. Augustine's immediate followers seems to have reacted rather sharply to his decision in the *Retractationes*, which is all the more surprising since they are usually faithful echoes of the master. Paul Orosius, the Spanish priest who was a contemporary and disciple of Augustine, holds fast to the identification of Peter and the rock foundation of the church.[6] The same opinion is voiced by another of Augustine's circle, Paulinus of Nola, who adopts a more comprehensive view, since he calls Peter the rock, though he is aware that the title is primarily Christ's in accordance with I Corinthians.[7] St. Prosper of Aquitaine likewise solves the difficulty presented by the texts in I Corinthians by pointing out, as had so many others, that Peter derived

[1] Letter 177, C.S.E.L., Vol. 54, p. 688.

[2] Letter 53:2 to Generosus, C.S.E.L., Vol. 34 (ii), p. 153. *Psalm Against the Donatists*, C.S.E.L., Vol. 51, p. 12. cf. Batiffol, *Le Catholicisme de S. Augustin*, Paris, 1929, pp. 192–209.

[3] Augustine, *Enarrationes in Psalmos*, 55:15, M.P.L., Vol. 36, col. 656; *idem*, 69:4, M.P.L., Vol. 36, col. 869, etc.

[4] *Retractiones*, I, 20, 2, C.S.E.L., Vol. 36, p. 97.

[5] Ludwig, op. cit., pp. 74 and 79.

[6] Paul Orosius, *Liber Apologeticus contra Pelagianum de arbitrii libertate*, 23:5, 27:3, etc., C.S.E.L., Vol. 5, pp. 641, 647.

[7] Letter 23:43, C.S.E.L., Vol. 29, p. 198.

his quality of being the 'rock' solely by dependence on Christ. This view he expresses in the book *The Calling of All Nations*, where he describes Peter as 'the most firm rock, who from the principal Rock received a share of his virtue and his name'.[1]

The later reaction to Augustine was not so independent, and tended to follow the great doctor almost slavishly. Fulgentius, who died in 533, reproduces Augustine's notion of Peter personifying the church when he says of him: 'To Peter, that is, to his church, he gave the power of retaining and forgiving sins on earth.[2] Somewhat later in the century Cassiodorus identifies Christ with the 'rock' in his commentary on the Psalms,[3] which is all the more surprising since he must have had before him Augustine's commentary in which he declared that the 'rock' was Peter.[4] The climax of this tendency to imitate Augustine is to be seen in the writings of St. Isidore of Seville, who died in 636. In his *Allegories and Etymologies* he reproduces Augustine's theory of St. Peter in every detail.[5] Needless to say, his estimate of St. Peter shows no doubt about the primacy of the Apostle.[6]

These later Latin writers, though not all from Africa, form a fitting conclusion to the African school of thought. They are distinctive in their preoccupation with the power of the keys and the teaching authority (*Cathedra Petri*). The different emphasis which they stress does not make their testimony to St. Peter in any sense divergent, and it is apparent that this school, too, but for minor inconsistencies, upholds the primacy of St. Peter.

*   *   *   *   *

Finally it is necessary to consider the school of Antioch, which came into prominence in the fifth century. The first of the Antiochean fathers to be studied is also the greatest representative of the school, St. John Chrysostom, who died in 407. He is one of the most prolific of the Greek writers and on the subject of St. Peter Abbot Chapman discovered more than ninety passages which are relevant to the question of his authority.[7] Despite their number the thought is consistent and it is

[1]*De Vocatione Omnium Gentium*, II, 28, M.P.L., Vol. 51, col. 714.
[2]*De Remissione Peccatorum*, II, 20, M.P.L., Vol. 65, col. 571. Also *De Fide*, III, 37, M.P.L., Vol. 65, col. 690.
[3]*Complexiones in Psalmos*, 45:5, 86:1, and 103. M.P.L., Vol. 70, cols. 330, 618, 729.
[4]Ludwig, op. cit., p. 83.
[5]*Allegoriae*, 137, M.P.L., Vol. 83, col. 117. *Etymologiae*, VII, 9, 2, M.P.L., Vol. 82, col. 287.
[6]*De Eclesiasticis Officiis*, II, 5, M.P.L., Vol. 83, col. 781.
[7]Studied exhaustively in *Studies on the Early Papacy*, pp. 72–98.

possible to analyse accurately his attitude to St. Peter. Before examining
his scriptural exegesis a general indication of the trend of his thought can
be derived from the extravagance of the titles which he bestows on the
Apostle. This quotation from the sermon on almsgiving is typical of
many: 'Peter that head of the Apostles, the first in the church, the friend
of Christ, who received the revelation not from man but from the
Father . . . this Peter, and when I say Peter, I mean the unbroken
Rock, the unshaken foundation, the great apostle, the first of the disciples, the first called, the first to obey.'[1] Even making allowance for
Oriental adulation and poetical licence it is quite clear that St. Peter is
to be considered as being quite different from the other Apostles.

In his interpretation of the Petrine promise of Matthew 16, Chrysostom understands the rock as Peter's faith and sometimes as his acknowledgement of Christ, but not in such a way as to lessen his primacy.
The fifty-fourth homily on St. Matthew elucidates the whole text: 'And
I say to thee: Thou art Peter, and upon this rock I will build my church,
that is upon the faith of this confession. Hence he shows that many will
believe, and raises his thoughts higher, and makes him Shepherd.'[2]
As Chapman remarks, it is alien to the thought of Chrysostom to consider the notions of Peter as the rock or his faith as the rock as if they
were in watertight compartments.[3] The other Petrine texts of John and
Luke he also applies to Peter and indeed in a sense which indicates
Peter's superior authority. In the opinion of Chapman, the most important testimony to the primacy of St. Peter is the homily on the election
of Matthias, principally on account of the magnitude of the event which
was taking place: 'One must be ordained to be a witness (to the resurrection) that their college might not be left mutilated. Then why did it
not rest with Peter to make the election himself? What was the motive?
(i.e. for consulting the rest.) This, that he might not seem to bestow it
out of favour.'[4] There is some doubt about the authentic text in this
passage, but the safer form has been given, and on either reading it is
clearly implied that Peter could have appointed Matthias on his own
authority.

Prior to the time of Chrysostom the church of Antioch had been split
by the notorious schism in which Rome and Alexandria had supported

[1]*De Eleemos.*, III, 4, M.P.G., Vol. 49, col. 298.
[2]Homily 54, on Matt., M.P.G., Vol. 58, col. 534.
[3]Chapman, op. cit., p. 79.
[4]Homily on Acts, M.P.G., Vol. 60, col. 36. cf. remarks by Chapman, op. cit.,
p. 89.

Paulinus against Meletius, who appears to have had the better claim to the bishopric. Although Meletius was never formally excommunicated, the situation produced rather a strained relationship with Rome, since he had by far the greater following in Antioch, and the claims of his party were ultimately recognized. In addition to this, Rome had caused further resentment in Antioch by according to the church of Alexandria a rank above that of Antioch in the celebrated *Decretum Gelasianum* of 382. An echo of this resentment is probably to be detected in Chrysostom's sermon on the consecration of the church,[1] where he seems to protest against an exclusive claim to possess St. Peter, saying that whoever holds the faith of Peter possesses the Apostle himself. This is the only discordant note in his many words on St. Peter, but it does not weaken the conclusion that Chrysostom 'believed and taught, and was ever anxious and careful to teach that St. Peter was really the chief ruler of the Church.'[2]

The antipathy to Rome which finds its echo even in the works of St. John Chrysostom became more pronounced as the Eastern church came more and more under the control of the emperor and affected eventually their estimate of St. Peter. Although they were not influenced by the Eusebian idea that the 'rock' of the church was Christ, the lesser Antiocheans betray an unwillingness to admit that Peter was the rock. Theodore of Mopsuestia, who died a quarter of a century after Chrysostom, declared that the rock on which the church was built was Peter's confession of faith.[3] The same opinion is repeated by Palladius of Helenopolis in his *Dialogue on the life of St. John Chrysostom*. Without any elaboration he states that the rock in Matthew 16 is Peter's confession.[4] The complete absence of reasons or arguments in support of the contention is an indication of how widely the view was accepted at that date.[5] Such an opinion was, in fact, held also by Theodore of Ancyra, Basil of Seleucia, and Nilus of Ancyra, in the first half of the fifth century.[6]

In all fairness it must be pointed out that Nilus expresses this view in a very pro-Petrine passage. He is comparing the various apostles with parts of the body. The head represents Peter, whom he calls the leader

---

[1] M.P.G., Vol. 51, col. 86.
[2] Chapman, op. cit., p. 73.
[3] From a hitherto unpublished MS. quoted in Ludwig, op. cit., p. 54.
[4] Op. cit., ch. 19, M.P.G., Vol. 47, col. 68.
[5] Ludwig, op. cit., p. 97.
[6] Basil of Seleucia, *Oratio*, XXV, M.P.G., Vol. 85, col. 297. Nilus, quoted in the *Catena of Procopius of Gaza*, M.P.G., Vol. 87 (ii), col. 1693.

of the apostles (κορυφαιότατος τῶν ἀποστόλων), and continues 'who was called Cephas, and prepared the building of the church in the confession of faith'. Likewise for Basil, St. Peter is the leader (κορυφαῖος) of the Apostles, and the chief (προστάτης) of the disciples of Christ.[1]

More variety is to be seen in the opinions of Theodoret of Cyr, who died in 458. He seems to have been confused by the texts of I Corinthians so that he declared at one time that the rock foundation of the church was faith,[2] and at another that it was Christ.[3] Elsewhere he applies the notion to all the Apostles.[4] It is difficult therefore to say that he had a conclusive judgement on the problem, yet it is evident that he did not acknowledge the primacy of St. Peter.[5]

Before concluding the study of the school of Antioch, reference must be made to St. Cyril of Alexandria, whose theology on the question of St. Peter resembles closely that of Antiochean fathers. The life work of St. Cyril, for which he is renowned in the church, was his upholding of the orthodox faith against Nestorius, principally at the Council of Ephesus in 431. This preoccupation with Christological questions influenced his exegesis of the text of Matthew 16 in a manner which is reminiscent of the earliest fathers who were writing against Gnosticism. Although he alludes frequently to the text, it is the Christological application which interests him and the resultant picture of St. Peter is inconclusive. For instance when, commenting on the passage he writes: 'Then he also names another honour: "Upon this rock I will build my church; and to thee will I give the keys of the kingdom of heaven." Observe how he summarily manifests Himself Lord of heaven and earth for . . . He promises to found the church, assigning immovableness to it, as He is the Lord of strength, and over this he sets Peter as shepherd. Then he says, "And I will give thee the keys of the kingdom of heaven." Neither an angel nor any other spiritual being is able to speak thus.'[6] The application to Peter of the title 'shepherd' is deceptive, since he applies it elsewhere[7] to all the Apostles and it cannot therefore indicate a peculiar authority for Peter. It seems to have been his consistent opinion that the 'rock-foundation' of the church was Peter's

[1]Nilus, ref. as above, Basil, *Oratio*, XVII, M.P.G., Vol. 85, col. 217.
[2]*Comm. on the Canticle of Canticles*, II, 14, M.P.G., Vol. 81, col. 108.
[3]Letter 146, M.P.G., Vol. 81, col. 1396.
[4]*Commentary on Psalms*, 47:3, 86:1, M.P.G., Vol. 80, cols. 1212, 1561.
[5]Ludwig, op. cit., p. 102.
[6]*Comm. on Matt.*, ad. loc., M.P.G., Vol. 72, col. 424.
[7]Hitherto unpublished MS. quoted in Ludwig, op. cit., p. 99.

immovable faith.[1] Although it seems a small matter to distinguish Peter's faith from his person in the function of being the foundation of the church, it does not appear that Cyril did, in fact, isolate St. Peter himself for that role and in this respect he is at one with the later Antiocheans.

Although the opinion unfavourable to the superiority of St. Peter gained a considerable following in the East under the influence of the school of Antioch, it is important to bear in mind that it was not universal. The Eastern liturgy is an indication of the persistence of the belief in his primacy, and several writers of this period give clear testimony to it. Proclus shows implicitly, in his sermon on the Transfiguration, that Peter is the foundation of the church,[2] and his witness is all the more valuable since he was from 434 to 446 bishop of Constantinople. The same opinion is found again in the first half of the seventh century in the works of the monk John Moschus[3] and his friend Sophronius, the celebrated patriarch of Jerusalem[4] who was the first opponent of the monothelite heresy. Another famous champion of orthodoxy against the Monothelites was Maximus the Confessor, who died in 662. His attitude to St. Peter must be inferred from his opinion of the Bishop of Rome. He attributed to Rome a superior authority in matters of faith which he related to the power of the keys. It is reasonable therefore to conclude that he must have recognized some kind of superiority for St. Peter.[5]

Last of all, in this survey of the later Eastern writers, is the opinion of St. John Damascene, whose death in 749 brought to a close the patristic era. He is true to the Oriental mentality in the fact that he has left no systematic treatise on the church. Nevertheless his attitude to St. Peter can be gleaned from his extensive writings. In his homily on the Transfiguration he follows the lead of the school of Antioch by identifying the 'rock' of the church with Peter's faith.[6] In common with many of the Greek fathers, his opinion of Peter does not stop there, since he

[1]*Dialogue on the Trinity*, IV, M.P.G., Vol. 75, col. 865; *Comm. on Isaias*, IV, 2 (44, 23), M.P.G., Vol. 70, col. 940.
[2]M.P.G., Vol. 65, col. 768.
[3]*Pratum Spirituale*, M.P.G., Vol. 87 (iii), col. 3012.
[4]*Sermon on SS. Cyrus and John*, M.P.G., Vol. 87 (iii), col. 369.
[5]Maximus, *Opuscula Ad Petr. Ill.*, M.P.G., Vol. 91, col. 144. *Letters to Rome*, M.P.G., Vol. 91, cols. 137, 139. cf. remarks of Ludwig, op. cit., p. 103.
[6]M.P.G., Vol. 96, col. 556, cf. also *Liber de recta sententia*, M.P.G., Vol. 94, col. 1429. Elsewhere he says the 'rock' is Christ! M.P.G., Vol. 96, col. 548.

declared that the government of the whole church had been entrusted to him.[1]

The school of Antioch (and those who were influenced by it) presents a conflicting set of opinions. St. Chrysostom and some followers uphold the primacy of St. Peter, while St. Cyril of Alexandria and others deny it. This opposition is probably to be accounted for, in part at least, by the antipathy towards Rome bred by the Pope's favouring Paulinus in the schism. This resentment was aggravated by the precedence given to Alexandria in the Roman scale of dignities. It does not appear, however, that this is the complete explanation for appearance of the anti-Roman opinion on St. Peter, since allowance must be made for the influence of the Constantinian religious policy. The matter will be discussed in more detail at a later stage in this book, but for the present the conclusions must be anticipated in order to show its effect on the Eastern opinion of St. Peter. The subjection of the church to the state in the government of Constantine and his successors was such that it was virtually incompatible with an independent church and a papacy. The Eastern church tacitly acquiesced in this system in practice, chiefly because they had no adequate theological understanding of the nature of the visible church. The change in their attitude to St. Peter as evidenced by the later Antiochean writers shows how their theology had begun to follow the leadings of the régime to which they had been subject for more than a century.

★   ★   ★   ★   ★

Standing apart from the main body of patristic writings is the group of documents known as the Pseudo-Clementine literature. In view of their doubtful origins, these documents would not be considered in any study of St. Peter but for the fact that they have been used quite extensively by controversialists. The purpose of these writings is principally didactic and the alleged details of the life of Clement of Rome are present merely to serve as a framework for the missionary sermons of St. Peter. Of the writings which are extant there is a collection of twenty homilies, ten books of the so-called *Recognitions*, and various other fragments. The Homilies are allegedly the sermons of St. Peter which were witnessed by St. Clement. They are accompanied by letters from Peter and Clement to James the bishop of Jerusalem, and their tone is

[1]Homily on the Transfiguration, sections 2, 6, 16, M.P.G., Vol. 96, cols. 548, 553, 569.

that of the Judaist heretics, the Ebionites and Elkasaites. Christianity is depicted as no more than a purified Judaism and the theology of God is monotheistic to the extent of excluding the doctrine of the Trinity. The ten books of the *Recognitions* have survived only in the Latin version of Rufinus and the Judaist tone has been modified, conceivably by Rufinus himself. Their composition, authorship and dating have caused a great deal of controversy and even today the problems are still far from solution. In view of the biographical details which are common to all the Pseudo-Clementines, it is reasonable to conclude that they had a common source. This document was probably of Jewish-Christian heretical origin, emanating from Syria at the beginning of the third century.[1] It is probable that they remained unknown in the West until they were available in the Latin version of Rufinus at the end of the fourth century.

Their bearing on the Petrine primacy has been variously interpreted. The Anglican Puller declared that they were pro-Petrine to the extent of being the basis of the Roman claims.[2] Their support for St. Peter has also been defended by Scott,[3] and more recently by Clavier.[4] On the other hand, they have been interpreted as favouring the superiority of St. James by Jalland[5] and Cullmann.[6] Disagreement such as this, and among non-Catholic authors, is an indication that these writings are not altogether clear in their indications about the primacy either of Peter or James. In fact, passages can be found which appear to favour both. The letter addressed to James from Clement bears the inscription 'Clement to James, the Lord and bishop of bishops, who rules the holy church of Jerusalem, and the churches everywhere, excellently founded by the providence of God'.[7] On the other hand a very modern-sounding papal notion is to be heard in the words of Peter to Clement: 'I appoint for you this man Clement as bishop, to whom I entrust my chair of teaching. I give him the power to bind and loose, thereby all that he commands on earth will be valid in Heaven. Then he will bind what is to be bound, and he will loose what is to be loosed.'[8]

---

[1]Quasten, *J. Patrology*, Maryland and Utrecht, 1950, Vol. I, p. 60.
[2]Puller, F. W., *Primitive Saints and the See of Rome*, London, 1900, p. 41.
[3]Scott, S. H., *The Eastern Churches and the Papacy*, London, 1928, pp. 23, 24.
[4]Clavier, H., 'La Primautée de Pierre d'apres les Pseudo Clementines', *Revue d' Histoire et de Philosophie Religieuses*, 1956, pp. 298–307.
[5]Jalland, *The Church and the Papacy*, p. 61.
[6]Cullmann, op. cit., p. 202.
[7]M.P.G., Vol. 2., col. 32.
[8]M.P.G., Vol. 2., col. 36.

Whatever be their final judgement on the relative positions of Peter and James, the pseudo-Clementines are of little evidential value to the present study, since they do not represent the authentic patristic tradition. They are no more than the opinions of a small and obscure sect,[1] and do not bear witness to the true tradition of the church. This consideration is important principally because it shows that the notion of James's superseding Peter is not supported by the genuine patristic evidence.[2]

*   *   *   *   *

The examination of patristic opinions about St. Peter has necessarily been somewhat lengthy, yet it is possible to deduce some accurate general conclusions. First, the divergences in the opinions of the fathers are more apparent than real. Their ignorance, for the most part, of Aramaic caused them some difficulty in understanding Matthew 16:18, which was further complicated by their preference for considering Christ as the 'rock' in accordance with I Corinthians. However, this confusion did not obscure their estimate of St. Peter. St. Cyril of Jerusalem and St. Chrysostom are just two examples of fathers who misunderstood Matthew 16:18, but acknowledged the primacy of St. Peter. The word misunderstood, in the previous sentence, is perhaps too strong. Their preoccupation with Christological questions disposed them to examine this text from the standpoint of Peter's confession rather than the promises of Christ. What their judgement would have been had they been faced with the circumstances of the Reformation is not a fair question. It is, however, unwise to exaggerate the difference between the building of the church on Peter or Peter's faith. These apparent divergences have been greatly overestimated in the post-Reformation polemics, which have tended to obscure the large measure of agreement between the fathers.

The second general conclusion which emerges from this study of the fathers is their moral unanimity, in the fourth century, about St. Peter's position. This achieving of agreement is of the utmost importance. In the first three centuries the matter is not discussed greatly, and there is a tendency to hesitation. Cyprian is more typical of this period than Origen, since he attributed to Peter an imperfect primacy, whereas

[1]James, M. R., *The Apocryphal New Testament*, Oxford, ed. 1955, p. xxv.
[2]The fragments of Hegesippus and Clement of Alex. quoted by Eusebius in *Eccles. Hist.*, II, i, and II, xxii, cannot reasonably be interpreted as meaning any more than James's designation as Bishop of Jerusalem.

the latter seems to have been ignorant of any seniority in the position of the Apostle. However, in the fourth century, which is the golden age of patristic theology, moral unanimity is to be seen in all the schools of thought. The primacy of St. Peter is then upheld by the Syrians, the anti-Arians of East and West, the Italians and the Africans. In the following century this unanimity is maintained with but one exception, namely a section of the school of Antioch.

To some this measure of agreement may seem insufficient. Admittedly it is not as strong as, for instance, in the patristic testimonies to the doctrine of the Trinity. This comparison must be qualified by one very important reservation. Patristic opinions about the Trinity are more unanimous, it is true, but only in the period after the Arian crisis. Before that event they show perhaps more divergence than the early testimonies to St. Peter. It is well known in the history of theology that heresies crystallized the true doctrine and provoked a unanimity in the fathers which was lacking in the earlier period. Thus, the post-Nicene fathers are more in agreement in their Trinitarian theology than their predecessors before 325. The relevance of this principle to the question of St. Peter is obvious. In the patristic age the primacy never became a theological issue of the magnitude of the Trinitarian or Christological questions. As a result there was never the same pressure for clarification as there was for these other doctrines. The consensus of opinion about St. Peter must therefore be judged in comparison with other doctrines which were not disputed during the patristic era, such, for instance, as the theology of the sacraments. It can safely be asserted, then, that the measure of agreement on the primacy of St. Peter is as good, if not better, than that which is to be found on any other doctrine which did not become a matter of serious controversy in the period of the fathers.

★   ★   ★   ★   ★

The final witness to the mind of the early church, and thence to the mind of Christ, is the liturgy. Being the official prayer of the church, it is a testimony to the belief not of individuals but of the whole community. Needless to say, the liturgical feasts do not all date back as far as the fathers, but they compensate in official status for what they lose in antiquity. Above all the liturgy represents the mentality of the church prior to the schism between East and West, and it was too firmly established to be changed after the separation.

It would be superfluous to search for testimonies to St. Peter in the liturgy of the Western church. Even the most superficial knowledge of the matter shows that the Western liturgy is in full accord with the tradition of St. Peter's authority over the whole church. What is frequently overlooked, though, is the strength of this attitude in the Eastern liturgy. A pro-Petrine liturgy is to be found as far afield as among the Jacobites of India,[1] and the Greeks and Russians honour him as head of the Apostles even at the present day.

In the liturgy of the Greeks and Russians the feast of SS. Peter and Paul is observed on June 29th. To give solemnity to the occasion, it is preceded by a period of fasting, similar to Lent, which begins on the first Sunday after Pentecost. The hymn of the dawn office contains the following verse:

'Thou art rightly called the rock,
In whom the Lord consolidated the unshaken faith of the Church,
The Lord appointed thee as prince and shepherd of the rational sheep,
So that thou mightest admit all those who approach in faith.'[2]

The *Book of Homilies* assigns to this feast one of the sermons of St. John Chrysostom, in the course of which St. Peter is addressed as 'Leader and commander, supreme pastor of the Apostles'.

These are not random examples. The tone of the whole liturgy is consistent in this matter. Many other feasts could be referred to but the feast of the Dormition of the Virgin is the most deserving of mention. For this feast, the *Book of Homilies* contains a sermon of John of Thessalonika, who died in about the year 630. He describes the death-bed scene of the Blessed Virgin, and tells how she wished to give to St. John the palm branch which the Angel Gabriel had presented to her on the occasion of the Annunciation. St. John is unwilling and says: 'I cannot accept it without the other apostles while they are not here, in case there should be a quarrel among us, for among us there is one senior to me who has been set in charge of us.' The identity of the senior Apostle is soon disclosed. When all are assembled St. Peter is unwilling to be the first to pray, but the others persuade him with the words: 'Father Peter: thou hast been set in charge of us, do thou pray before us.' When the actual funeral ceremonies are taking place Peter turns to

[1]'Apologia of Fr. Abraham', in *Eastern Churches Quarterly*, 1957, No. 3, p. 87.
[2]Quoted in Jugie, M., *Theologia Dogmatica Christianorum Orientalium ab Ecclesia Catholica Dissidentium*, Paris, 1926, Vol. IV, p. 334 ff.

John and says: 'You are a virgin, and you must chant the hymns at the bedside, holding the palm.' To this John replies: 'You are our father and supervisor, it is for you to stand at the bedside chanting, while we give place to you.'

These brief extracts are typical of the attitude of the Eastern and Western liturgies to St. Peter and are all the more significant in the East since they represent the pre-schismatical tradition.

In conclusion then, to this examination of the mind of the early church, it must be remembered that the testimonies of the New Testament and the fathers were not in any sense trying to prove a case in favour of one or other of the Apostles. The relevant passages must be allowed to speak for themselves and not be constrained to fit any preconceived theories. The first half of the Acts shows St. Peter in the position of authority over the early Christian community, then the switching of attention to the gentile mission focuses the attention on St. Paul. Since the powers given to Peter by Christ were of a permanent nature, it is hard to subscribe to the idea of his demotion. The evidence in favour of such a theory is very fragile, and the idea was not entertained in the early church. In the age of the fathers it was taken for granted that St. Peter continued to hold the authority which he was seen to have before the New Testament diverted its attention elsewhere. This indeed is the most natural way to interpret the ancient documents, and no other judgement on St. Peter was seriously maintained until the doctrine of the papacy entered the field of polemics.

4

ST. PETER IN ROME

In his *Ecclesiastical History*, St. Bede indicates that even in Anglo-Saxon times Englishmen had begun to make pilgrimages to Rome to honour the tombs of the Apostles.[1] In the Middle Ages men and women came from all parts of Europe for the same purpose, and it is superfluous to remark that all were convinced that the bodies of Saints Peter and Paul were buried beneath their respective basilicas. Luther declared, at one time, that not even the Cardinals in Rome knew whether St. Peter's body was there or not. However, the matter does not appear to have aroused much interest among the early Reformers, and the first scientific attack against the traditional view was that of Spanheim at the end of the seventeenth century. The negative view was followed fairly widely in German rationalistic circles, and the well-known English writer Gibbon declared, in his *Decline and Fall of the Roman Empire*, that not one of the immediate disciples of Christ would have been put to death outside the confines of Palestine. The reaction came at the end of the nineteenth century, when distinguished historians such as Harnack, Duchesne, and H. Lietzmann defended the traditional view. The fact of Peter's coming to Rome is now almost universally accepted, but some scholars are still unwilling to subscribe to it, as, for example, C. Guignebert and K. Heussi.

The first source of information about St. Peter's journeys is the New Testament. The starting-point is quite clear. St. Peter was present in Jerusalem for the Council of the Apostles, which is most probably to be assigned to the year 49. The next stage of his journey is not so easy to date with the same precision. The meeting of Peter and Paul at Antioch, recorded in Gal. 2:11 almost certainly took place after the Council of Jerusalem, and probably quite soon after it.[2]

After Antioch it is more difficult to trace his movements with certitude. The First Epistle which bears his name is addressed to: 'The

[1] Bede, *Ecclesiastical History*, V, 7.
[2] Zeiller, J., in *L'Église Primitive*, Vol. I of Fliche & Martin, *Histoire de L'Église*, Paris, 1946, p. 225.

elect who dwell as foreigners up and down Pontus, Galatia, Cappadocia, Asia, and Bithynia' (I Pet. 1:1). It seems reasonable to infer from these names that St. Peter spent some time preaching the gospel in these regions. The view was held by Origen[1] and has received fairly wide support.[2] The discussions as to the authenticity of the Epistle do not affect this precise question. Catholics are unanimous in defending the Petrine authorship, and this view is to be found among authoritative non-Catholic authors, such as E. G. Selwyn,[3] although many Protestant scholars will not subscribe to it. For those who accept the Petrine authorship there is no complication in the import of this passage at the beginning of the Epistle. For those who deny it, though, the ultimate result is the same, since an anonymous writer wishing to pose as St. Peter, would not adopt any biographical indications except those which were to be found in the early Christian tradition. The evidence of the First Epistle of St. Peter on the Apostles' journey to Rome is thus independent of the problem of its authenticity.[4]

The next place of sojourn can be fixed with more certainty. Writing to the Corinthians, St. Paul reproaches them for their party strife: 'Each of you, I mean, has a cry of his own, I am for Paul, I am for Apollo, I am for Cephas, I am for Christ' (I Cor. 1:12). Since St. Paul and Apollo are known to have been at Corinth, it is reasonable to infer that Peter, too, was there at one time, making converts who subsequently formed a Petrine faction. This Epistle has been assigned to many different years, but among reputable scholars its date varies from the year 55 to 58. It appears, then, that St. Peter must have departed from Corinth before that time. Later on Dionysius, the Bishop of Corinth in the second half of the second century, declared unhesitatingly that the church there had been founded by the two Apostles Peter and Paul.[5]

The next indication from the New Testament is one of silence. St. Paul's Epistle to the Romans and the Acts of the Apostles make no mention of St. Peter's presence in Rome. Had he been there at the time of St. Paul's writing it is inconceivable that he would not have mentioned him. Similarly, the chapters of the Acts which describe St. Paul's arrival and imprisonment in the city, would almost certainly have referred to the other Apostle had he been there at the time. The Epistle

[1]Eusebius, *Ecclesiastical History*, III, 1.
[2]Zeiller, op. cit., p. 227.
[3]*The First Epistle of St. Peter*, 1946, pp. 32, 38.
[4]cf. Cullmann, op. cit., p. 75.
[5]Letter to Rome recorded in Eusebius, H. E., II, xxv, 8.

to the Romans was written perhaps in 56 or perhaps as late as 59, and St. Paul arrived in Rome in the year 60. It is reasonable, then, to deduce that St. Peter was absent from Rome at that particular period. Duchesne considered that he arrived there after St. Paul's first release; that is to say, some time after the year 62.[1] Whether he was there before is not easy to decide. The church at Rome was well established when St. Paul wrote his Epistle to the Romans, and the Christians there originated in the Jewish community which was St. Peter's special missionary field. It is unlikely that the church there could have been in such a flourishing condition, even before St. Paul's arrival, but for the work of an Apostle.[2] St. Paul did not visit the city before his arrival as a prisoner, so it is possible that St. Peter was there at an earlier date. The theory of his arriving in the city twenty-five years before the date of his martyrdom has little to commend it.

The actual presence of St. Peter in Rome is clearly indicated in his Epistle already cited, where it concludes with the words: 'The church here in Babylon, united with you by God's election, sends you her greeting' (I Pet. 5:13). The reference to Babylon would have caused no difficulty to the early Christians, since it was commonly accepted as a pseudonym for the city of Rome. It is used as such in the canonical Apocalypse (17:5), and it occurs several times in various apocryphal works of the period. It is to be found in the Sibylline Oracles[3] and in the Fourth Book of Esdras. The Apocalypse of Baruch likewise employs the term when lamenting over Rome's destruction of Jerusalem:

'Moreover I, Baruch, say this against thee, Babylon:
> If thou hadst prospered,
> And Zion had dwelt in her glory,
> It would have been a great grief to us
> That thou shouldst be equal to Zion.
>
> But now, lo! the grief is infinite,
> And the lamentation measureless,
> For lo! thou art prospered
> And Zion desolate.'[4]

[1] Duchesne, L., *Early History of the Church*, Vol. I, p. 45, being the trans. of 4th French ed. of *Histoire Ancienne de l'Église*.

[2] Besson, M., *Saint Pierre et les origines de la Primauté Romain*, Geneva, 1928, p. 66.

[3] *Sibylline Oracles*, V, 159, ed. J. Gefken, 1902 (in G.C.S.), pp. 111–12.

[4] *Apocalypse of Baruch*, XI, 1 and 2, ed. R. H. Charles, London (S.P.C.K.), 1917, p. 41.

The inference is clear. St. Peter wrote the Epistle from Rome; and once again this fact is not affected by the question of the authenticity of the Epistle.

The last indication which the New Testament gives about the subsequent career of St. Peter is the prophecy of his martyrdom which is recorded in the last chapter of St. John's Gospel: 'As a young man, thou wouldst gird thyself and walk where thou hadst the will to go, but when thou hast grown old, thou wilt stretch out thy hands, and another shall gird thee . . .' (J. 21:18).

The reference to the stretching out of the hands is a clear anticipation of his ultimate crucifixion, which other sources record as having taken place during the Neronian persecution.

Before turning from the New Testament to examine other sources of evidence it will be convenient to consider the radical theory by which K. Heussi attempts to rule out the possibility of St. Peter's voyage to Rome. In the Epistle to the Galatians, St. Paul speaks about the three Apostles, Peter, James, and John, whom he describes as the 'pillars' of the church. These men he declares approved of the doctrines which he was preaching, and in parentheses he says of them 'it matters little to me who or what they were' (ὁποῖοί ποτε ἦσαν οὐδέν μοι διαφέρει) (2:6). The most natural understanding of the passage is that St. Paul used the past tense because he was describing an incident of the past. Heussi interprets it as a reference to the fact that these apostles were dead when he wrote Galatians![1] The identity of Peter and John causes no difficulty, but the James in question needs to be clarified. Heussi considers that he is James the son of Zebedee, who was put to death by Herod Agrippa (Acts 12:2). It is clear, however, that the James in question is James the 'brother of the Lord', who was the upholder of the Jewish traditions. The weakness of Heussi's theory is that, if it were true, it would prove too much. Scholars are agreed that the Epistle to the Galatians was written between the years 54 and 58. The suggestion that John and James the 'brother of the Lord' were dead at that date is contrary to every relevant piece of evidence in the primitive history of the church. If, then, the text cannot refer to the death of James and John, it can hardly indicate the death of Peter.

The New Testament evidence, then, for the last years of St. Peter's life is fragmentary, but clear in the main outlines. His going to Antioch is firmly established; evidence for his presence in Asia Minor and

[1] *Die Römische Petrustradition in kritischer Sicht*, Tübingen, 1955, pp. 1–7.

Corinth is of a more conjectural nature, but the deductions are not forced. The indication of a Roman origin of the First Epistle of St. Peter, is eminently reasonable, although one might be reluctant to subscribe to St. Peter's presence in the city if there were no other evidence.

The writers of the early church have far more to say about St. Peter's presence in Rome than had those of the New Testament. At the end of the first century the indications are rather general, but by the end of the second century the testimonies are explicit and quite detailed. This increase in precision is to be explained by the fact that the cult of the martyrs was by then well established, and the church had been emphasizing her Apostolic connexions in face of the Gnostic and Marcionite heresies. It is not therefore surprising that much of the evidence concerns the martyrdom and burial of the Apostle in Rome. Some period of ministry can legitimately be inferred therefrom, and in fact several of these writers furnish details of St. Peter's work while he lived at Rome.

The earliest of these non-scriptural writers to treat of St. Peter and his death at Rome is St. Clement in his well-known letter to the church at Corinth, whose date of composition is generally agreed to have been the year 96. The relevant allusions to St. Peter and his death are to be found in chapters 5 and 6:

'But, to drop the examples furnished by antiquity. Let us come to the athletes nearest to us in time. Let us take the noble examples of our own generation. It was due to jealousy and envy that the greatest and most holy pillars were persecuted and fought to the death. Let us pass in review the good Apostles: Peter, who through unmerited jealousy underwent not one or two, but many hardships and, after thus giving testimony, departed for the place of glory that was his due. Through jealousy and strife Paul demonstrated how to win the prize of patient endurance: . . . . These men who had led holy lives were joined by a great multitude of the elect that suffered numerous indignities and tortures through jealousy and thus became illustrious examples among us.'[1]

The way in which St. Clement draws out the moral lessons from fragmentary biographies is an indication that the careers in question were too well known to his audience to need detailed description. As Cullman has shown,[2] the context and circumstances clarify what is not

[1]Text, Funk, F. X., *Patres Apostolici*, Tübingen, 1901, I, p. 104, Trans. Kleist, J. A., in *Ancient Christian Writers*, London, 1946, I, p. 12.
[2]Cullmann, op. cit., pp. 79–99.

explicit in the actual text. The reference to their martyrdom 'among us' indicates that the people in question underwent death in Rome, and this is confirmed by various indications in the text. The examples chosen in the preceding part of the letter are of members of the same communities, and moreover victims of jealousy within communities, both of which would indicate that St. Peter is to be connected with the other martyrs. Since St. Paul was certainly martyred in Rome, it is reasonable to say the same for St. Peter and the rest. Further precisions are lacking,[1] but the indications thus furnished justify the reasonable inference that St. Peter did suffer martyrdom in Rome.

Not long after Clement had written to the Corinthians, St. Ignatius wrote a letter to the church at Rome. The saintly Bishop of Antioch was on the way to that city, under arrest, and shortly to suffer martyrdom. The letter to the Romans was written from Smyrna during the reign of the Emperor Trajan and probably a little before the year 110. The reference to St. Peter is very short: 'Not like Peter and Paul do I issue any orders to you. They were Apostles, I am a convict; they were free, I am until this moment a slave.'[2] This association of the two Apostles with Rome is far from being a categorical assertion that either of them visited the city. However, it is known that St. Paul dwelt there, and as Duchesne remarked, 'supposing he [Peter] did come, Ignatius would not have spoken otherwise; whereas if he had not, there would have been no point in Ignatius's argument'.[3]

Towards the end of the second century this tradition is seen to be firmly established throughout the whole church and in a manner which is comparatively detailed. A survey of the principal Mediterranean churches shows that they were all well aware of the martyrdom and burial of saints Peter and Paul in Rome.

The earliest of this particular group of testimonies is that of Dionysius of Corinth, who wrote to Rome during the pontificate of Pope Soter. The letter can be dated approximately as belonging to the year 170, and although it has not survived, the relevant passage has been preserved by Eusebius, who introduces it thus: 'Denis Bishop of the Corinthians, in a letter addressed to the Romans, thus fixes the point that Peter and Paul both suffered martyrdom at the same time. "You

---

[1]Unfortunately the sentence in 5:3 is ambiguous. Λάβωμεν πρὸ ὀφθαλμῶν ἡμῶν τους ἀγαθοὺς ἀποστόλους. It could mean 'our eyes' or 'our Apostles'.
[2]Ignatius, *Epistle to the Romans*, 4:3. Text, Funk, F. X., op. cit., I, p. 256. Trans. Kleist, op. cit., p. 82.
[3]Duchesne, op. cit., I, p. 46.

have also, by such an admonishment, united Rome and Corinth the two trees which we owe to Peter and to Paul. For just as both the one and the other planted at Corinth and taught us, so after teaching together in Italy, at the same time they suffered martyrdom".'[1]

Eusebius is the only source for the next witnesses who are from the church of Alexandria. He quotes from Clement of Alexandria, who, at the turn of the century, wrote concerning the origin of St. Mark's gospel, 'Peter preached the word of God publicly at Rome, and under the inspiration of the Holy Spirit made the Gospel known. Those who assisted at his sermons, and they were numerous, exhorted Mark, who for a long time had been Peter's companion, and whose memory held many of his sayings, to put these things in writing.'[2] Some thirty years later Origen, the brilliant pupil of Clement, spoke of St. Peter in his commentary on Genesis (50:3): 'Peter appears to have preached in Pontus, in Galatia, in Bithynia, in Cappadocia, and in Asia to the Jews of the Diaspora. Finally he, too, came to Rome, and there he was crucified, head downwards, having asked to suffer in this fashion.'[3]

In Africa it is Tertullian who reveals the local tradition on the career of St. Peter in Rome, and in various of his writings he alludes to the work and martyrdom of the Apostle. The writings in question can be ascribed with a fair degree of accuracy to the first decade of the third century. In his most famous treatise, *De Præscriptione Hæreticorum* (36), he extols the church of Rome with a reference to the Apostles. 'O happy church! The Apostles lavished upon it their teaching and their blood. Peter there suffered a death like to that of the Lord.' In a later work, *De Baptismo* (4), he says that St. Peter baptized in the Tiber, and later still, in the *Scorpiace*, (15) he adds more details: 'Nero was the first to persecute the nascent faith at Rome with punishments. Then it was, that Peter was girt by another, when he was fixed to the cross.'[4]

The testimony of St. Irenaeus is particularly valuable. He was Bishop of Lyons in Gaul in the last decades of the second century, but having come there from Smyrna, he was acquainted with the traditions of the East as well as the West. His allusions to St. Peter's being in Rome are brief but clear, as in the *Adversus Hæreses*, where he records that the

---

[1]Eusebius, H. E., II, 25. Most of these testimonies are set out with admirable clarity in Hughes, P., *History of the Church*, London, 1952, Vol. I, pp. 59–66.

[2]Eusebius, H. E., VI, 14.

[3]Eusebius, H. E., III, 1.

[4]Tertullian, C.S.E.L., Vol. 20, p. 204; M.P.L., Vol. 2, col. 59; C.S.E.L., Vol. 20, p. 178.

gospel of St. Matthew was written 'while Peter and Paul were preaching the gospel at Rome and founding the church there'.[1]

Finally in Rome itself, as is natural, the memory of the two Apostles was very vivid. During the pontificate of Zephyrinus (199–217), Caius the priest wrote a treatise against Proclus of Asia Minor. Proclus had claimed that Asia possessed the tombs of the four prophetesses who were the daughters of Philip. Caius replied with the claim: 'I can show you the *tropaia* of the Apostles. Go to the Vatican, or along the Ostian way, there you will find the *tropaia* of the founders of this church.'[2] The word τρόπαιον has occasioned a certain amount of controversy, since it can mean a tomb or a commemorative monument such as might have been used to designate the place of death. Despite this uncertainty in the word, the context leaves little doubt about its signification in the present instance. Proclus had boasted the possession of the tombs of the prophetesses and it would be natural to reply by referring to distinguished tombs in Rome. This was how it was understood by Eusebius (who had the complete text of Caius in front of him), since he prefixed the quotation with the words, 'speaking of the places where the sacred remains of the Apostles were laid he says . . .'

Many other testimonies are extant, but being of a later date they are of less value evidentially; one could not exclude the possibility that they were re-echoing the earlier tradition without deriving their knowledge from independent sources. However, there is one witness of the later period who merits attention, since it is clear that his information is derived from an independent source. The writer in question is Macarius Magnes, who wrote no earlier than the end of the third century.[3] Concerning St. Peter he wrote: 'He was crucified after having fed the sheep for only a few months.'[4] The interest of this text lies in the fact that the writer derived his information probably from the anti-Christian Porphyry and, despite his own manifest antagonism, the tradition of Peter's crucifixion was too strong to be denied. Admittedly there is no reference in the text to Rome, but the tradition of Rome as the site of Peter's death was then too strong to be impugned, and he had to make his derogatory remark about the length of his ministry there.

There was a time when it was alleged that the belief that St. Peter

---

[1]Irenaeus, *Adv. Hæreses*, III, 1, i; M.P.G., VII, 844.
[2]Quoted by Eusebius, H. E., II, 25.
[3]Cullmann, op. cit., p. 109.
[4]Macarius Magnes, *Unigenitus*, III, 22; ed. Harnack, *Texte und Untersuchungen*, 1911, Vol. 37 (iv), p. 56.

came to Rome rested solely on the apocryphal accounts which circulated in the second and third centuries. Such a theory is now generally abandoned in view of the fact that the orthodox tradition is equally emphatic about the matter, and indeed some of the reliable sources are older than the apocrypha.[1] If the apocrypha alone recorded the matter, as is the case for some of the extravagant stories of the childhood of Christ, then it would be dangerous to credit them. However, when they recount what is also to be found in the accredited witnesses of the early church, then they testify to the strength of the prevalent tradition.

The historical evidence is enhanced by one more factor, namely the complete absence of any rival tradition. Even when the authority of the bishops of Rome was in dispute in the third and fourth centuries, and when they made explicit claim to inherit the powers of St. Peter, no one attempted to deny that the Apostle had indeed been martyred and buried in Rome.

In view of the unanimity of this tradition, throughout the world and at an early date, the fact of St. Peter's death in Rome must be regarded as established. In fact, Dr. Salmon, the author of the standard Protestant work against Papal infallibility, remarked that if the evidence for this fact is not accepted, then there is little else in the early history of the church which can be credited.[2]

As a result of these testimonies, it can be affirmed that St. Peter came to Rome and worked there for some appreciable time; later he was martyred in the persecution of Nero, and was probably buried in the city. The date of his arrival cannot be established, but his death is better known. Eusebius assigned it to the year 67, being under the impression that the persecution of Nero took place then. However, it would appear that this date is too late. In fact, the Neronian persecution began in the year 64 and modern authors generally consider this to have been the year of St. Peter's death.[3]

Before passing to the examination of other relevant indications about St. Peter's coming to Rome, it is important to recall the validity of the writers already cited. It has been suggested that they were dependent upon the Epistle of Clement, which was well known in the early church.[4] It cannot be ruled out that the text of Clement was indeed in the posses-

[1]Zeiller, J., op. cit., p. 228.
[2]Quoted in Butler, B. C., *The Church and Infallibility*, London, 1954, p. 120.
[3]Duchesne, op. cit., p. 47; Zeiller, op. cit., p. 233; Tricot, D.T.C., art. cit., col. 1753.
[4]Lowe, op. cit., p. 30.

sion of the authors quoted, yet it must be remembered that they were not exclusively dependent upon it. The additional details which they supply, different in nearly every case, are a sufficient guarantee of the fact that other sources of information were available, freeing them from an absolute dependence on Clement. Another argument brought against the reliability of the historical tradition defended above is the silence on the matter among all writers of the mid second century. This is the frailest of all arguments. In the particular case it should be remembered that the literary activity of the Christians at that epoch was not considerable, and of the books then composed little has survived. Of the Roman writers of that period, St. Justin is the only one whose writings have been preserved in a reasonable quantity. He mentions Simon Magus on several occasions, but makes no reference to St. Peter's journey to Rome.[1] The omission may seem unusual in the present day, but in his time there were many reasons which can explain why he would not have done so. He was writing before there was a general interest in the cult of the martyrs, he was at Rome where the tradition was too strong to need retelling, and above all he was writing against the Jews and pagans, for whom the matter would have had little interest or relevance.

The details, too, of these early ecclesiastical writers are worthy of acceptance, even the matter of the burial. Caius claimed that he knew of the *tropaia* at the Vatican and on the Ostian Way. This part of the early tradition has been considered as unreliable. Cullmann suggests that an interest in their tombs must have come later in the evolution of the tradition.[2] It would be natural, he contends, that the place of burial should be associated with what was known to be the place of death, and once it was appreciated that there were well-established cemeteries in those two places the tendency to consider the Apostles as being buried there is quite easy to understand. In fact, though, the matter is not quite so simple. St. Paul was put to death at the Tre Fontane some considerable distance from the place spoken of by Caius, and as Lowe has shown,[3] the improbabilities of this place for the burial of St. Paul are so great that Caius could hardly have invented it. If the memory of their burial places had really been lost, then it would have been natural for the Christians to assign them imaginary graves in a Christian burial

[1]Cullmann, op. cit., p. 103.
[2]Cullmann, op. cit., p. 136.
[3]Lowe, op. cit., p. 34.

place, and probably together, in view of the joint cult which they received. The *a priori* unlikelihood of the burial of St. Paul on the Ostian way, and to a lesser degree of St. Peter at the Vatican, is, in fact, a strong argument in favour of the reliability of the testimony of Caius.

The historical conclusion that St. Peter was martyred in Rome gives rise to three related but distinct questions. In the first place was it possible for the early Christians to obtain the body of St. Peter after his execution? Secondly, did they in fact secure it and bury it? Finally, what was the subsequent fate of the relics? Have they been preserved under the basilica of St. Peter? Even if a negative answer were given to each of these questions, it would not invalidate the conclusion of the historical evidence, namely that St. Peter had come to the city and suffered martyrdom there. However, positive answers would afford confirmation for the findings of history and for that reason, and for the sake of completeness these three questions must be examined briefly.

Despite its straightforward appearance, the first question is wrapped in considerable obscurity, both from the point of view of the Roman law and the particular fate of the corpses of the martyrs in the Neronian persecution. According to Tacitus,[1] Nero had the victims executed and burned in his gardens on the Vatican hill. The earliest testimony to the crucifixion of St. Peter is Tertullian,[2] but this detail accords well with the general indications of Tacitus. These facts have given rise to various doubts. Would it be possible to recognize the remains of St. Peter and distinguish his body from that of the other martyrs? Would not the corpses of all the victims be cast into the Tiber or some kind of common grave? Did the Roman law at that time permit the burial of the body of a criminal by his relatives?[3]

These difficulties are indeed formidable, but not incapable of a certain elucidation. The methods available then for the burning of the bodies were not as thorough as have been devised subsequently, and since they were burned in order to illuminate Nero's festivities they would not have suffered the more complete combustion effected in an enclosed furnace. It is reasonable to suppose that at least the skeletons would have survived for burial, nor is it by any means certain that every victim of this persecution was actually burned. As for the subsequent recovery, identification and burial of the bodies, little can be said of the

[1] Tacitus, *Annales*, XV, 44.
[2] Tertullian, *De Præscriptione Hæreticorum*, 36, M.P.L., Vol. 12, col. 49; *Scorpiace*, 15, C.S.E.L., Vol. 20, p. 178.
[3] Cullmann, op. cit., p. 135; Lowe, op. cit., p. 44.

Neronian persecution, but in the later persecutions the bodies of the martyrs were recovered in the face of difficulties which were just as great.

The theory of a common grave even for criminals is not entirely in keeping with the contemporary mentality with regard to the dead. Both the Jews and the Romans took care to provide for the decent burial of corpses, and Roman law was very strict in safeguarding the subsequent inviolability of the tomb. It was as a result of this attitude that the early Christians took care to give honourable burial to the bodies of the martyrs even before the religious cult of their relics became established. A case in point is the burial of the first martyr, St. Stephen.

The law on this matter in the first century is by no means certain. One might hope that the circumstances of the burial of Christ would furnish some evidence for a solution. The Jewish law demanded that the bodies of criminals should be buried on the day of execution,[1] and it does not appear that there was any difficulty in obtaining the necessary permission from Pilate for the friends of Christ to effect it. It is possible that this incident reveals the state of Roman Law at that time; namely, that the relatives of an executed criminal could obtain the body for burial. However, one cannot exclude the possibility that it was no more than the Roman practice of adaptation. As a rule, the Romans used to respect the religious susceptibilities of their subjects, so that it is possible that the burial of Christ shows no more than the Roman toleration of the Jewish religious law in Palestine.

Literary testimonies to the situation are very rare, but there is a phrase from Petronius which appears at first sight to rule out the chances of honourable burial for the body of a criminal. The passage is of interest, particularly because it dates from about the end of the first century: *Miles qui cruces asservabat, ne quis ad sepulturam corpus detraheret* (The soldier who was on guard at the crosses, in case anyone should take down the body for burial. . . .).[2] Although this seems to settle the matter in favour of a negative solution to the problem under consideration, a closer inspection yields another result. One of the peculiar cruelties of death by crucifixion was the length of time taken for death to be accomplished. A strong man would survive for several days, and even after he was dead the body was left for a time to enable the birds and dogs to dishonour it as it decayed. This ultimate indignity was part of the punishment, and it is highly probable that the soldier

[1] Deuteronomy 21:23.
[2] Petronius, *Satyricon*, 111, ed. Loeb, p. 230.

spoken of by Petronius was stationed there to ensure that the full
penalty should be exacted before burial might be allowed. The exposure
of the dead body of Cleomenes[1] is likewise inconclusive, since he had
not been the victim of a judicial sentence. The manner of his death was
an act of brutality which cannot be taken for an indication of the legal
execution of that period.

From the time of Justinian there is explicit evidence that the bodies
of criminals were given up for burial: *Corpora animadversorum quibusli-
bet petentibus ad sepulturam danda sunt* (The bodies of criminals are to
be handed over for burial to whomsoever shall apply).[2] It is unfortunate
that this testimony is so late. Although it is perfectly clear in itself, there
is no absolute guarantee that the law was the same in the reign of Nero.
The only other relevant consideration is the fact that throughout the
persecutions the Christians did, in fact, obtain the bodies of the
martyrs for burial. Whether this was done in defiance of the law or with
its approval or connivance is hard to say, but the fact of their being
obtained is undeniable. In conclusion, then, to the question of the
recovery of the body of St. Peter, it is reasonable to admit, in the present
state of knowledge on the subject, that such a recovery was indeed
possible.

What now of the fact? Did the Roman Christians actually recover
the remains of St. Peter and give them burial? To solve this question
it is reasonable to search in the fields of archaeology and liturgy, whence
information could be obtained which would be of value not only in
answering the immediate question of St. Peter's burial, but in confirming or weakening the fact of his being in the city at all.

In this field of inquiry the liturgy is of value, since originally the cult
of the martyrs was strictly local. That is to say, they were accorded public worship in the cities in which they were executed and buried. At a
later date it became customary to honour martyrs in churches far
distant from the scenes of their deaths, but the presence of a truly
primitive liturgy is a strong indication that the martyr in question had
been present at the place where later he was honoured.

The earliest written testimony to the cult of the Apostles in Rome is

[1]Plutarch, *Cleomenes*, 39, ed. Loeb, *Lives*, Vol. 10, pp. 140, 141.
[2]*Digest*, XLVI, 24, 3, ed. Momsen, Berlin, 1872, p. 821. 24, 1, has an interesting reference to Augustus: *Corpora eorum qui capite damnantur cognatis ipsorum
neganda non sunt: et id se observasse etiam divus Augustus liber decimo de vita sua
scribit . . . eorum quoque corpora qui exurendi damnantur peti possunt, scilicet ut
ossa et cineres collecta sepulturae tradi possunt.*

an entry in the *Calendar of Filocalus*, a document which was drawn up in 354: *III Kal. Jul. Petri in catacumbas et Pauli Ostense Tusco et Basso cons* [The third of the calends of July (i.e. June 29th) Peter at the catacombs and Paul at the Ostian (Way) in the consulate of Tuscus and Bassus].[1] The consulate of Tuscus and Bassus was in 258 and it can only refer to the origin of the feast. That is to say in that year either one or both of the feasts mentioned was instituted.

Documents dating from the end of the fourth century indicate that the cult was then established at three places: St. Peter at the Vatican, St. Paul in the basilica at the Ostian Way and both of them at the catacombs on the Appian Way. Why there should be three places which were associated with the cult of the Apostles is a problem which has exercised the minds of scholars for half a century. Perhaps the most interesting feature of its complexities is that archaeology reveals the same threefold cult.

At the beginning of the present century the catacombs on the Appian Way, under the basilica of St. Sebastian, were examined by A. de Waal and P. Styger. The most spectacular discovery was that of several hundred *graffiti* (inscriptions) invoking the names of Peter and Paul. It was possible to date the beginning of this activity and the business of writing the names of the Apostles must have commenced between the years 260 and 280 or thereabouts. This date accords reasonably well with the year 258 in the calendar of Filocalus and seems to show fairly conclusively that the two Apostles were honoured there from the year 258.

The more recent excavations under the Vatican have not revealed as much as might have been hoped. One discovery of paramount importance is that of the *tropaion* mentioned by Caius. Under the high altar of the present church the remains of a funereal monument have been revealed which can be assigned to the period A.D. 160 to 170. All scholars are agreed that this is the monument of which Caius boasted. Underneath it there is a simple grave which could be assigned to the latter part of the first century. Is there any reason for thinking that this is the grave of St. Peter? The archaeological evidence is not conclusive for or against such an identification. The identification is possible, and would seem to be suggested by one singular factor. The grave appears to have been discovered when the monument had already been partially completed. The rest of the monument was then redesigned to make it correspond to the position of the grave below, and in doing so destroyed

[1] Text in *Liber Pontificalis*, ed. Duchesne, Paris, 1886–94, Vol. I, p. 11.

the symmetry of the memorial as originally planned. Although it is not an apodictic proof, this fact can readily be explained by the hypothesis that the workmen who were constructing the monument discovered what they considered to be the grave of St. Peter.

At a later date the monument over this grave became the focal point of the basilica of Constantine, which became the principal place for the cult of St. Peter from the middle of the fourth century. It seems almost certain that Constantine's architects considered that the monument marked the site of the grave, and this would account for the church's becoming the centre of the cult of St. Peter.

To explain the threefold character of the Apostolic cult, L. Duchesne suggested that the relics of the Apostles had been moved from their original graves in the persecution of Valerian (258) to the catacombs, and thence moved back when the Constantinian basilicas had been completed. This would certainly explain the origin of the cult at the Appian Way, but it is a hypothesis which entails considerable difficulties. It is, in fact, only an attempt to rationalize the threefold cult, and since the Vatican excavations have yielded nothing to confirm it, the majority of modern writers reject it. Of the other explanations which have been offered, that of J. Ruysschaert seems to be the most satisfactory.[1] It is suggested that the relics were never moved from the original tombs at the Vatican and Ostian Way, but that the worship of the Apostles was conducted at the Appian Way at a period when the tombs did not offer the same facilities for liturgy. After the completion of the Constantinian basilicas, it was natural that the cult centres should focus on the tombs, embellished as they then were with the magnificent churches.

The result of these various excavations and researches is that archaeology confirms the literary evidences of a very early cult of the Apostles in the city. In its own right archaeology cannot prove that St. Peter was buried there, but it suggests that such was the case. The problem of deciding upon the exact relationship between the three shrines does not interfere with the general inference, namely that this primitive liturgy confirms the historical conclusion that St. Peter was martyred in Rome.

A suitable conclusion to the examination of St. Peter's coming to Rome is a brief allusion to the episcopal lists.[2] These afford evidence

---

[1] Art. 'Les Documents litteraires de la double Tradition romaine des Tombes apostoliques' in the *Revue d' Histoire Écclésiastique*, 1957, pp. 791–831.

[2] A detailed study of this intricate question lies outside the scope of this book. The standard work on the subject is still E. Caspar's *Die älteste römische Bischofsliste*, Berlin, 1926.

relative to the immediate inquiry, and provide an introduction to the next question, which is the problem of succession. These lists of bishops were drawn up in the second century as part of the church's defence against the Gnostics and Marcionites. The general character of the anti-heretical measures was a 'closing of the ranks'. Liturgical freedoms were curtailed considerably, the canon of Scripture was clarified, and the teaching authority of the bishops was emphasized. This last measure was achieved by stressing the Apostolic character of the tradition of the church and the continuity of authority from the time of the Apostles to their successors the bishops. This attitude accounts for the episcopal lists which appear to have been drawn up in all the churches of Apostolic foundation, giving the names of the bishops back to the Apostle who first established the church. The oldest undisputed witness to the list of the Roman church is Irenaeus, whose testimony is as follows: 'When therefore the blessed Apostles (i.e. Peter and Paul) had laid the foundations and erected the church (i.e. Rome) they entrusted the liturgical office of the episcopate to Linus. And Anacletus succeeds him, after whom Clement is ordained to the episcopate in the third place from the Apostles.'[1]

The subsequent records of the list are substantially the same, and with one exception, they all begin with the name of Peter.[2] Therefore the first and obvious inference from these lists is that St. Peter came to Rome. Furthermore, they indicate the attitude of the early church to the question of succession. This principle of the transmission of powers to the later office-holders was well known to the primitive church. The earliest enunciation of it is to be found in the letter of St. Clement to the church of Corinth: 'Our Apostles, too, were given to understand by our Lord Jesus Christ that the office of the bishop would give rise to intrigues. For this reason, equipped as they were with perfect foreknowledge, they appointed the men mentioned before, and afterwards laid down a rule once for all to this effect: when these men die, other approved men shall succeed to their sacred ministry.'[3] It is possible to conceive of a variety of methods by which the authority could be transmitted. Of them all the most obvious and natural is to consider that the powers should pass to the person who assumes control in the place where the Apostle, or other ruler, died. Such a method as this is implicit

[1]Irenaeus, *Adv. Hæreses*, III, 3, iii, M.P.G., Vol. 7, col. 849.
[2]The exception is the Index Catalogue of Corby (ii), in the *Liber Pontificalis*, ed. Duchesne, Vol. I, p. 31.
[3]Clement of Rome, *Letter to Corinth*, ch. 44, ed. Funk, op. cit. Vol. I, p. 154.

in the episcopal lists, and years later the bishops of Rome, and nowhere else, claimed formally that they had inherited the authority of St. Peter, who died in their city.

In conclusion, then, to this study of the latter period of St. Peter's life, it can be established beyond reasonable doubt that he came to Rome and suffered martyrdom there. Evidence for the subsequent history of his relics is not so conclusive, yet it appears probable that his remains were buried at the Vatican and never moved from there.

Excursus

ARCHAEOLOGICAL AND LITURGICAL
EVIDENCE RELATIVE TO ST. PETER'S PRESENCE
IN ROME

OF the three places which are associated with the memory of the Apostles, the first to be examined by archaeologists was the basilica of St. Sebastian on the Appian Way. The excavations took place between the years 1915 and 1925 under the direction of A. de Waal and P. Styger, and the results, published by H. Chéramy, have been made readily accessible for the English reader in the study of J. Toynbee and J. Ward Perkins.[1]

The excavations under the present church revealed a group of buildings some of which were used for the cult of the Apostles. Access to this region was provided by a stairway leading from a side road which joined the Appian Way. The stairway led into a *triclia*, or drinking-room, to the west of which is a courtyard. Both the courtyard and the *triclia* are bounded to the north by a monument known as a columbarium in which are constructed niches to contain funereal urns. Below the level at which these buildings was constructed, and elsewhere around the site, there are numerous graves and burial structures.

Prior to its use as a cemetry, the place was a quarry and was in use for this purpose in the first century or earlier. Quarrying ceased about the end of the first century and the changeover from a pagan to a Christian cemetery took place about the year 200 in circumstances which cannot be ascertained.[2]

Nothing in the region has been found which could be described as the grave of an Apostle, but the walls of the *triclia* and the courtyard are covered with inscriptions to Peter and Paul. Thirty-three of these *graffiti* are preserved on the walls and a further 179 have been found scattered in the soil. They are far from elegant in style and spelling, but they reveal a devout and popular cult of the Apostles. The usual theme

---

[1]Chéramy, H., *Saint Sebastien hors les Murs*, Paris, 1925; Toynbee, J., and Ward Perkins, J., *The Shrine of St. Peter and the Vatican Excavations*, London, 1956.
[2]Toynbee and Ward Perkins, op. cit., p. 172.

is a simple invocation such as: *Petrus et Paulus in mente abeatis Antonius Bassus* (Peter and Paul be mindful of Antonius Bassus). Some, however, make explicit reference to the *refrigerium*, as, for instance: *Petro et Paulo, Tomius Coelius refrigerium feci.* (I Tomius Coelius, have performed a refrigerium in honour of Peter and Paul).[1] The *refrigerium* was a pagan practice of holding a commemorative meal at the tomb of a dead relative or friend. The celebration of these meals in honour of the saints was not wholeheartedly approved by the church, and its occurrence is an indication of the rather popular character of the cult here.

The period of this cult at the Appian Way can be dated with a fair amount of accuracy. There is no trace of the Constantinian monograph among the *graffiti* and this factor, taken together with the fact that the church above was built by Constantine, indicates that the cult was established before the end of the third century. The commencement is limited by the date of the last of the graves below the courtyard. The occupants of these tombs, the *Innocentii*, assumed for their burial the names of the Emperors Popenius and Gordianus, who reigned between the years 238 and 244. It seems probable, then, that the cult originated in the period between 260 and 280 with a certain margin each side of these two limits.[2] This dating accords quite well with a certain datum of the liturgy as will be examined later on.

As far as the present study is concerned, these excavations are of interest in so far as they throw light on the problem of the fate of the bodies of the Apostles. The inference is quite simple. The numerous *graffiti* and the celebration of the *refrigerium* cannot readily be explained unless the relics of the saints were present in this very place by the Appian Way, or at least somewhere in the city. The former view would appear to receive support from the famous inscription which Pope Damasus wrote for this shrine: *Hic habitasse prius sanctos cognoscere debes nomina quisque Petri pariter Paulique requiris* (Here you should know that the saints once dwelt, you who are seeking the names of both Peter and Paul).[3] It has been suggested that this inscription of Pope Damasus and the other evidence in this same place indicate that the shrine marked the actual house where the Apostles dwelt while they lived in the city.[4] Such a view, however, gives rise to difficulties which

[1]Quoted in Chéramy, op. cit., p. 58, also in D.A.C.L., Vol. 14, art. 'Pierre' by H. Leclerq, cols. 888–93.
[2]Toynbee and Ward Perkins, op. cit., p. 178.
[3]Diehle, E., *Inscriptiones Latinae Christianae Veteres*, 1952, No. 951.
[4]Cullmann, op. cit., p. 120.

are almost insurmountable. The inscriptions of Pope Damasus were never placed on dwellings, and other traditional residences of the Apostles, such as the Mamertine prison and the church of St. Pudentiana, have never had a similar cult. It is, moreover, unlikely that the two Apostles would have shared the same house[1] on a site which was then a quarry. Although the theory that the Appian Way was the resting-place of the bodies of the Apostles will have to be abandoned, it is by no means devoid of probability, and many eminent scholars have subscribed to it, although, as has been noted above, the excavations did not reveal any direct indication of an apostolic grave.

Although the basilica of St. Peter had always been regarded as occupying the site of the tomb of the Apostle, excavations were not undertaken until 1939. Pope Pius XI had expressed the wish to be buried in the crypt, and the work of preparing a tomb revealed that the pavement of Constantine's church was only a few inches below the floor of the present crypt. Pope Pius XII thereupon ordered a complete examination. The difficulties of excavating without endangering the present church, together with many other complications, have combined to make the undertaking one of the most difficult in the history of archaeology. The official report was published in 1951[2] and the results are accessible to the English reader in the study of J. Toynbee and J. Ward Perkins.

The key to the study of St. Peter's is the church of Constantine. Contemporary records are strangely silent about the construction, yet it is known to have been built in the first half of the fourth century. The recent excavations have revealed two remarkable facts about the site. The position chosen for the church was in the middle of a cemetery which was still in use. The building operations therefore necessitated the destruction of many of the graves, and the closure of the cemetery for the future. Such a procedure was seriously at variance with Roman law and sentiment, and its implementation would probably have been impossible but for the fact that Constantine still retained the authority of Pontifex Maximus. In addition to this, the site itself was far from convenient, since the place chosen was on sloping ground. It is reasonable to infer from these indications, that Constantine was very anxious to focus his church on an exact place.

[1]Chéramy, op. cit., p. 57.
[2]The official report is: *Esplorazioni sotto la Confessione de San Pietro in Vaticano, eseguite negli anni 1947–49*, by B. M. Appoloni Ghetti, A. Ferrua, E. José, E. Kirschbaum, C. Serafini, Rome, 1951.

The examination of the pre-Constantinian remains has been complicated by the subsequent history of the church. The sanctuary was modified considerably by the building operations of Gregory the Great about the year 600, and again by those of Callixtus II in the twelfth century. Although the church escaped damage when the city was sacked in 410 and 451, it is probable that the ornaments of the shrine itself were pillaged by the Saracens in 846[1]. Pope Nicholas V decided to demolish the Constantinian basilica, and the second half of the fifteenth century saw the commencement of the work which ultimately destroyed nearly every vestige of the old church. However, great care was taken once again to arrange for the positioning of the Renaissance church, and the High Altar of the present building is once again exactly above the previous shrine.

The question which immediately presents itself to the mind is to ask what was located at this site which so strongly influenced Constantine and the Renaissance architects? The recent excavations have disclosed an ancient monument beneath the shrine of Constantine. This monument consisted of a recess in the wall which is known as the Red Wall. Sufficient of the original masonry has survived to enable the main outlines of the edifice to be ascertained. The monument thus conjectured consisted of a semicircular niche flanked by columns and surmounted by an arch. In addition there seems to have been a stone slab placed horizontally, dividing the niche into almost equal parts, and supported at its outside edge by two columns. At the base of the monument, level with the floor and in front of the niche there was some kind of emplacement to hold perhaps a stone slab which covered the earliest 'structure.'[2] This monument was constructed as the Red Wall was being built, and as a result it can be dated with a considerable degree of accuracy, since the wall was constructed between the years A.D. 160 and 170. There is little doubt that this monument is the *tropaion* which was spoken of by the priest Caius at the beginning of the third century. The identification is accepted by nearly all scholars and it receives additional confirmation from a passage in the *Liber Pontificalis*. It is recorded that Pope Anacletus built a *memoria* (shrine) to St. Peter, and was himself buried near it.[3] A critical analysis of the passage will entail certain corrections, and if the name Anicetus is read instead of Anacletus the passage makes

---

[1] Toynbee and Ward Perkins, op. cit., p. 228.
[2] Toynbee and Ward Perkins, op. cit., pp. 140–4.
[3] *Liber Pontificalis*, ed. Duchesne, L., Paris, 1886–94, Vol. I, p. 125.

very good sense. The excavations reveal no trace of a shrine built before the end of the first century, but Anicetus was Bishop of Rome about the year 160, and this accords well with the dating of the Red Wall and the monument.[1]

The positioning of this monument is not without its significance. The Red Wall is not perfectly straight. There is a slight bend in it, and it was at this very point that the monument was constructed. From the nature of the case, this was the most difficult place to choose, and it indicates that in the building of the monument, as with the church of Constantine, the position had to be exact. The foundations and base of the monument confirm this in a striking manner. Below the monument the foundations of the Red Wall have been arched up to avoid disturbing the space below. A niche has been cut into the part of the wall which was below ground, corresponding to the niche above ground level, but carved out later. Finally at the ground level itself the emplacement which provided the seating for the slab, or whatever it was that covered the region below the monument, is out of alignment with the main structure. The variation from the line of the rest of the memorial is in the region of ten degrees and could not possibly have been accidental.

These last facts are so unusual that they demand a special explanation, which is attempted in the following hypothesis. The difficult placing of the monument in the first instance, is an indication that its erection at this very point was decided upon to commemorate the exact spot which may have been the traditional grave of St. Peter. The monument was planned accordingly and the foundations were dug. In the course of this operation it was discovered that there was a grave not far below the surface, in the position associated with that of St. Peter. Believing that they had found his grave, the builders modified the original plan for the foundations at that point to avoid disturbing the grave. The design for the Red Wall and the memorial could not be changed, but in order to do justice to the grave which had been discovered, the niche was continued down below the surface, and the slab which covered this grave was aligned, not with the monument, but with the grave itself. Is it possible that this grave could have been St. Peter's? In the first place the date would admit of such a possibility. Of the four graves close to the one in question two may well be as old as the second half of the first century. In default of any more precise indication for the one under discussion, it also could be assigned to the same period.

[1]Toynbee and Ward Perkins, op. cit., p. 262–5.

Secondly it is to be noted that the burials are inhumations and not just the conservation of cremated remains. Although it is not a decisive indication, it favours the theory of Christian rather than pagan burial.

The final discovery in this particular region was of a number of reburied bones. They do not appear to have been examined by every possible means, but it is said that they are of a person of advanced age and powerful physique; the skull is missing.[1]

That in outline is the situation revealed by the recent excavations. In assessing the significance of these findings and their bearing on the problem of locating the actual tomb considerable prudence is demanded. The possibility that the monument marked the site of execution is now difficult to sustain. The locality was a cemetery even in the first century, which tells against its having been the site of the atrocities. In addition to this, the commemoration of the place of execution would hardly have entailed such exactitude in the placing of the memorial.

The most straightforward and natural explanation of the facts revealed by the excavations is that the builders who were working on the monument about the year 160 considered that they had discovered the burial place of St. Peter. Conceivably they were misled in their assumption, but it must be admitted that the observers of the second century were in a better position to judge than those of the twentieth. As far as the present state of the archaeological evidence is concerned, the sober judgement of Toynbee and Ward Perkins deserves to be quoted in full: 'Although it is not certain that the monument marks the site of an earlier grave, the hypothesis that it did so explains much that is otherwise obscure; and although there is nothing to prove that this grave was that of St. Peter, nothing in the archaeological evidence is inconsistent with such an identification.'[2]

A further field of inquiry concerning St. Peter's career in Rome is the liturgy. The question of the feasts of Rome has been studied in detail by Duchesne, but it was first examined in connexion with St. Peter's presence in the city by H. Lietzmann, whose book *Petrus und Paulus in Rom*[3] still remains a standard work on the subject. The interest and the problems connected with the liturgy of the Apostles in Rome are immense, but for the present study the scope is somewhat simplified, since the facts have to be examined to see whether they confirm or weaken the

[1]Toynbee and Ward Perkins, op. cit., p. 154.
[2]Toynbee and Ward Perkins, op. cit., p. 161.
[3]Second Edition, Berlin, 1929.

historical conclusion that St. Peter came to Rome and suffered martyr-dom there.

The principle involved is quite simple. The early liturgical worship of the saints and particularly the martyrs was strictly local, since their feasts were celebrated in the cities where they had been executed and buried. Originally the celebrations were connected with the very tombs themselves and only at a later date were their feasts extended to other cities. Therefore if there is reliable evidence of an early cult of St. Peter at Rome, it will be an indication of the conviction of the Roman community that the Apostle had suffered there, and in all probability that he had been buried there, too. Thus the liturgy can give indirect evidence of his having been present in the city during his life and indeed for that part of it which immediately preceded his death.

The earliest liturgical evidence is that of the famous Roman calendar of Furius Dionysius Filocalus, papal secretary under Pope Liberius. In the year 354 he drew up this calendar, based on a source which must have dated from 336, giving among other things a list of the feast days observed in Rome.[1] The first entry concerning St. Peter is as follows: *VIII Kal. Martias natale Petri de cathedra* [The eighth of the calends of March (i.e. February 22nd) the feast of the chair of Peter]. At a later date the *cathedra* or chair was clearly understood as the symbol of the teaching authority, but it is highly probable that no such idea was entertained when this feast was instituted. On that very date the pagans used to honour the memory of the dead by ceremonial feasts known as *cara cognitio* or *carista* or even *cathedra*, the Greek name for the celebra-tions. Accordingly Duchesne advanced the theory that this feast of St. Peter was the simple adaptation of the pagan festival.[2] This opinion was regarded as possible by Batiffol,[3] but it was accepted as correct by Lietzmann,[4] and in this he has been followed by the majority of modern authors. In view of the peculiar origin of this festival it would be unwise to contradict Leitzmann's judgement, that as far as St. Peter's presence in Rome is concerned, this feast cannot be advanced as evidence in favour of a truly ancient tradition.[5]

The next entry in the calendar concerning St. Peter is of greater value: *III Kal. Jul. Petri in Catacumbas et Pauli Ostense Tusco et*

---

[1]Text in *Liber Pontificalis*, ed. Duchesne, Vol. I, p. 11.
[2]Duchesne, L., *Christian Worship*, 5th ed., London, 1949, p. 278.
[3]Batiffol, *Cathedra Petri*, Paris, 1938, p. 124.
[4]Lietzmann, H., op. cit., p. 19.
[5]Lietzmann, op, cit., p. 21.

Basso cons [Third of the calends of July (i.e. June 29th), Peter at the catacombs and Paul on the Ostian (Way) in the consulate of Tuscus and Bassus]. This entry has affinities with an entry in another ancient document, the eighth-century manuscript in Berne known as the Hieronyman martyrology, the original of which was composed about the year 420: *III Kal. Jul. Romae Via Aurelia natale Apostolorum Petri et Pauli Petri in Vaticano Pauli vero in Via Ostiensi utrumque in catacumbas passi sub Nerone Tusco et Basso consulibus* [Third of the calends of July (i.e. June 29), Rome, Via Aurelia, the feast of the Apostles Peter and Paul, Peter at the Vatican, Paul on the Ostian Way and both of them at the catacombs, suffered under Nero, in the consulate of Tuscus and Bassus].[1]

The difficulties of interpreting these passages will be discussed later, but the first observation which can be made is that the liturgy confirms the discoveries of archaeology in associating three places with the cult of the Apostles. That is to say, the shrines at the Vatican, the Ostian Way and at the catacombs on the Appian Way. The threefold cult is confirmed also by the inscription of Pope Damasus, referred to already, and the hymn attributed (justifiably) to St. Ambrose: *trinis celebratur viis festum sacrorum martyrum* (The feast of the sacred martyrs is celebrated on the three roads).[2] Many later testimonies confirm these early pieces of evidence, namely that the cult of the Apostles was celebrated in three places in Rome. Many theories have been advanced to unravel the difficulties of this multiple cult and to explain how it was related to the possession of the relics of saints.

It has been suggested by Dom L. K. Mohlberg that the cult centre on the Appian Way was in the hands of a schismatical group, the Novationists.[3] Although such an occurrence would have been possible, the evidence in favour of its having happened is slight. The wall paintings in this shrine, it is true, are somewhat different from the general trend of Christian art, the celebration of the *refrigerium* is almost unique, and the list of Filocalus omits the name of Pope Cornelius, the great enemy of Novatian. These indications are far from conclusive, and the state suppression of Novationism at the end of the fourth century can hardly explain how the place was in the possession of Pope Damasus for him to bestow upon it the famous inscription. In general it is hard

[1] Text in *Acta Sanctorum*, November II (i), p. 84.
[2] M.P.L., Vol. 77, col. 703.
[3] In *Festshrift Alban Dold*, 1952, p. 52 ff. Discussed by J. Toynbee in *Journal of Roman Studies*, 1953, pp. 14, 15.

to see how the shrine could have become so famous among the orthodox if in its origin it was nothing more than a schismatical centre set up in opposition to the traditional shrines.

Much greater support has been given to the theory of the translation of the Apostolic relics during the persecution of Valerian. This hypothesis was proposed, in modern times, by Duchesne, as a means of reconciling the threefold cult.[1] The key to the theory is the date of the consulate of Tuscus and Bassus, 258. This accords remarkably well with the dating of the shrine by archaeological evidence.[2] It is generally agreed that the cemetery passed into Christian hands about the year 200 and that the cult of the Apostles began in the middle of the third century.[3] There is therefore little doubt that the year 258 marks the beginning of the cult of the Apostles at the Appian Way. Duchesne suggested that, for the sake of safeguarding the remains of the Apostles, the original tombs were opened in the persecution of Valerian (258) and the relics of both were transferred to the site on the Via Appia. There they remained until the completion of the basilicas of Constantine at the sites of the original burial, whence they were retranslated, thus ensuring that their cult at the Appian Way would ultimately be superseded by that of St. Sebastian. The theory remained no more than a hypothesis, but it received widespread support, particularly after its acceptance by Lietzmann. One difficulty which seemed to trouble Duchesne towards the end of his life was that it entailed emending the calendar of Filocalus, which was often said to be unintelligible, to bring it into agreement with the Hieronyman martyrology in the following way: *III Kal. Jul. Petri in Vaticano Pauli vero in Via Ostiense utriusque in Catacumbas Tusco et Basso consulibus* (Third of the Calends of July, Peter at the Vatican and Paul at the Ostian Way, and both at the Catacombs, in the consulate of Tuscus and Bassus). Thus emended, the entry in the calendar of Filocalus corresponded very well with the indications of the hymn of St. Ambrose and portrayed a situation which could well be explained by the translation of the relics.

However, since the time of the Vatican excavations, support for Duchesne's theory has been on the wane. A number of difficulties had

---

[1]Published originally in *Pontificia Academia Romana di Archaeologia Memoriae*, I (i), p. 7 ff. (1923). Reproduced in considerable detail by H. Leclerq in D.A.C.L., Vol. 14, art. 'Pierre', cols. 822–979.

[2]See above, p. 100.

[3]cf. H. Chadwick, *St. Peter and St. Paul in Rome, the Problem of the Memoria Apostolorum ad Catacumbas*, in J.T.S., 1957, pp. 45, 46. Also Toynbee and Ward Perkins, op. cit., p. 172.

always been apparent, for instance the improbability of violating a tomb contrary to the Roman law, aggravated by the fact that the catacombs on the Appian Way were close to an imperial police post. It is, moreover, somewhat of an exaggeration to say that the relics were in danger at their well-known resting-places. There were occasions in the persecutions when the bodies of the martyrs were dishonoured after their execution, but there is no record of the authorities' exhuming the remains after a lapse of centuries. These difficulties were not regarded as conclusive by the supporters of the translation theory, but the Vatican excavations proved sadly disappointing to them. The search under St. Peter's has not revealed one scrap of evidence which could be advanced as positive confirmation of the theory. All that can be said is that the space below the monument of Caius has been so disturbed that it is impossible to decide whether or not anything was taken out or replaced there.[1] As a result there has been an increasing trend among modern writers to explain the threefold cult without having recourse to the hypothesis of translation.

One of the most valuable of these recent contributions is an article of J. Ruysschaert which deserves greater attention than has so far been accorded to it.[2] Ruysschaert observes in the first place that the calendar of Filocalus contains, in addition to Christmas and the feast of the Cathedra Petri, three feasts of non-Roman martyrs. In other words, the Roman church was already celebrating the cult of martyrs whose relics were not in the city. It is therefore possible to admit that the cult at the Appian Way did not necessarily demand the presence of the relics of the Apostles. A serious weakness of the translation hypothesis was the necessity of altering the calendar of Filocalus. If all bias in favour of translation is put aside, the entry is by no means unintelligible. It means simply that in the year 354 the official cult of St. Peter took place at the Appian Way, while that of St. Paul was observed at the Ostian, and that one or other of these had originated in the year 258. Why St. Paul's cult should have moved and not that of the other Apostle has been explained very satisfactorily by E. Kirschbaum, who suggested that on account of its more elaborated construction the basilica of St. Peter was not completed until several years after St. Paul's.[3] By the time that the Ambrosian hymn and the Hieronyman martyrology came to be written both the

[1]Toynbee and Ward Perkins, op. cit., p. 165.
[2]Ruysschaert, J., 'Les Documents, litteraires de la double Tradition romaine des Tombes Apostoliques', in *Revue d'Histoire Écclésiastique*, 1957, pp. 791–831.
[3]Kirschbaum, E., art. in *Ephemerides Liturgicae*, 1948, pp. 221, 229.

basilicas were completed and used for the separate worship of the Apostles, leaving a joint cult at the Appian Way. The complete silence of all other witnesses means that the calendar of Filocalus is the only contemporary source which throws light on the date at which St. Peter's was completed. Admittedly the calendar is silent about the continuing joint cult after that of St. Paul had moved to the Ostian Way, but this is not a serious difficulty and the theory of Kirschbaum and Ruysschaert has great intrinsic probability.

The possibility that the relics were not translated has been mentioned above. Ruysschaert takes the matter one stage farther and maintains that the evidence shows that they were never moved from their original resting-places at the Vatican and the Ostian Way.[1] In his *Ecclesiastical History* and *Theophany*[2] Eusebius speaks of the tombs of the two Apostles. He reproduces the statement of Caius describing the 'trophies' at the Vatican and Ostian Way, and indicates that these were their tombs even in his own day. In certain matters it is true to say that Eusebius accepted his sources uncritically, but in this case there is every reason to assume that he knew of the situation in Rome from visitors who had been to the very tombs of which he speaks. His own description, too, gives more information than that of Caius, which frees him from the accusation of being dependent solely on that source. The importance of Eusebius is considerable. If the *History* and the *Theophany* are to be ascribed to the years 312 and 333 respectively (with a certain margin in each case), his witness for the presence of the relics at the original tombs dates from the period when the 'translationists' would have them at the Appian Way. This interpretation of Eusebius is confirmed by the continuity of the *graffiti* at the Vatican which has been revealed by the recent excavations.[3] For those who hold that cult follows relics, it is a difficulty which tells against the theory of total translation of the remains of St. Peter.

A similar conclusion was reached by T. Klauser on account of the difficulties entailed in the alleged return of the relics at the time of the consecration of the Constantinian basilicas. He argues that if the relics had been brought back to their original resting places when the new basilicas were opened they would undoubtedly have been placed in precious reliquaries. No reliquary of any kind has been found under St. Peter's, and if it be alleged that its absence is to be explained by the

[1]Ruysschaert, art. cit., p. 812.
[2]H.E., II, 25; *Theophany*, IV, 7. The latter is to be found in H. Gressmann's German translation of the Syriac version, in G.C.S., Eusebius III, (ii), p.175.
[3]Toynbee and Ward Perkins, op. cit., p. 165.

plundering of the Saracens, then it is difficult to see why the chroniclers have remained completely silent about a crime of such enormity. Since there is no record or rumour of such a theft, nor any trace of a reliquary, it is reasonable to infer that the hypothetical reliquary never existed, nor was there a retranslation.[1] Although the contemporary records are silent about the opening of the Vatican basilica, it seems certain that Pope Damasus would have given more specific information about the Apostolic relics at the Appian Way if there had been a retranslation in the middle of the fourth century.

These considerations would seem to demand the abandonment of the translation theory and its replacement by the hypothesis that the relics never left their original tombs, and that the cult at the Appian Way began in 258 without their being present. The evidence which is available gives strong support to this hypothesis, but it is necessary to explain how and why the Apostolic cult began at the Appian Way in 258.

It must be admitted frankly that the immediate reason for the choice of the site at the Appian Way as the cult centre for the Apostles is not known. It is better to acknowledge this ignorance than to postulate an explanation in the legendary world of pious delusions or well-intentioned frauds. Although the immediate motive of the choice remains obscure, the general reasons which prompted such a move are fairly clear. The building of the *tropaia* in the time of Pope Anicetus was prompted by the interest in Apostolic connexions.[2] In that century the older churches were at pains to emphasize, against the Gnostics, their Apostolic foundation. It was definitely a search for the tombs which prompted the two *tropaia*, and as has been stated above, there can be little doubt that these marked the original graves.[3] In the third century the intention was different. Since the time of Callixtus the cult of the martyrs and Popes had developed considerably, and it was becoming customary to honour them with an elaborate liturgy in a Christian cemetery. For this purpose the original graves at the Vatican and Ostian Way were clearly unsuitable, and a Christian cemetery would be the most natural place to choose.[4] In this way the Christian cemetery on the Appian Way was selected for the celebration of the cult of the Apostles, though without their relics being present. Precisely why this cemetery should have been

[1] Klauser, Th., *Die römische Petrustradition im Lichte der neuen Ausgrabungen unter der Peterskirche*, Cologne and Opladen, 1956, pp. 73, 76.
[2] Klauser, op. cit., p. 74.
[3] cf. above pp. 89, 103.
[4] Ruysschaert, art. cit., p. 815.

chosen in preference to any other cannot yet be established, but it is a detail of little significance compared with the appreciation of the basic motive, of finding a place where an elaborate liturgical worship could be carried out.

The subsequent history of the various shrines can be conjectured quite easily with the help of the known facts. Constantine chose for his Apostolic basilicas the sites of the tombs at the Vatican and the Ostian Way. When these churches were opened their magnificence, together with the fact that they possessed the relics, combined to make them the principal centres of the cult of the Apostles. At the Appian Way their memory was still honoured, but little by little it gave way to the worship of St. Sebastian, whose relics were preserved there.

One item only remains to be accounted for in this very convincing hypothesis, namely the inscription of Damasus. Before analysing its text it should be remembered that if a translation had taken place, then a retranslation to the Constantinian basilicas must have occurred in the middle of the fourth century; in other words, at a time when Damasus was almost certainly in the ranks of the Roman clergy. If such were the case it is difficult to see why he did not state any accurate information about those relics in his inscription. In marked contrast to his other inscriptions he makes no mention of tombs, relics or burial. One is therefore inclined to deduce that he knew nothing definite about the Apostles' relics having been at the Appian Way, but merely wished to pay some tribute to the memory of the saints who had been worshipped there for more than a century. Whether this conjecture is true or not, Damasus's inscription is a very unsatisfactory witness to take as the first written testimony of the translation which is alleged to have taken place in 258.

The 'non-translationist' interpretation of Damasus is favoured by an important textual consideration. Ruysschaert has shown,[1] on the principles of textual criticism, that the inscription should be read not as *hic habitasse* but as *hic habitare*. The word *prius* should, moreover, refer not to *habitare* but to *requiris*. These corrections provide a reading of the text in favour of the idea of their present memory living on, thus: 'Before you seek the fame [*nomina*] of Peter and Paul, you should know that the saints live on here' (i.e. in the memory of the people and in the continuance of their liturgical cult).

Although this interpretation of Damasus is not devoid of obscurities,

[1]Ruysschaert, art. cit., p. 823.

it has greater probability than the attempt to understand it as a witness to the translation of the relics.

In conclusion, then, it would appear that the theory of a total translation of the relics in 258 must be ruled out. All the relevant evidence can be accounted for much more satisfactorily by the theory that the liturgy, and not the relics, was transferred to the Appian Way in 258. The possibility of a partial translation, for instance the skulls of the Apostles, is not ruled out, but it remains no more than a hypothesis.[1]

[1] Ruysschaert, art. cit., p. 830.

5

THE BISHOPS OF ROME IN THE FIRST TWO CENTURIES

By the end of the nineteenth century the history of the primitive church was being studied with a new critical precision. It was inevitable that this interest in history would have repercussions on the study of the Roman primacy. The facts which are displayed in the history of the early bishops of Rome need careful evaluation in their historical context. In the first place it appears, from the records which have survived, that of the thirteen bishops who ruled in Rome from the death of St. Peter until the end of the second century, only two of them exerted their authority outside the city in a manner which could be called papal. This situation contrasts sharply with the conduct of the later Popes such as Celestine and Leo, in whose pontificates scarcely a year passed without some indication of the exercise of their supreme power over the whole church. Nevertheless, it must be borne in mind that when those early bishops of Rome did exert their authority the extent of their power is seen to be truly remarkable.

This situation has received a variety of explanations. Some of the more extreme, such as the accusation of an ecclesiastical *coup d'état*, have now been abandoned. The most prevalent view that is held outside Catholic circles is that the early history of the papacy shows the process of evolution to have been at work, in much the same way as in the evolution of political systems. Other influences are said to have been operative as contributory factors to this main cause. Among these it is usual to cite the prestige of the city as the capital of the Empire, the wealth of the Roman church, the reputation of the martyrs and so on. This has been the theme of most Anglican studies on the papacy for the last half-century and their progress shows an increasing sympathy towards the Catholic point of view, even to the extent of attributing some measure of influence to the intentions of Christ.[1]

[1]For instance, Gore, C., *Roman Catholic Claims*, London, 1905, 6th ed., pp. 106–9; Scott, S. H., *The Eastern Churches and the Papacy*, London, 1928, pp. 350–5; Kidd, B. J., *The Roman Primacy to* A.D. *461*, London, 1936, p. 18; Jalland, T. G., *The Church and the Papacy*, London, 1944, pp. 542 ff.; Lowe, J., *Saint Peter*, Oxford, 1955, p. 64.

The most famous exponent of the theory of the historical evolution of the papal power was the German scholar Harnack. The idea of evolution is a dominant characteristic of Harnack's history of the church, and it is to be seen in his attitude to the papacy on two planes: the general evolutionary tendency of the church and, in particular, the evolution of the papacy within the wider framework of the church as a whole. Harnack divided the history of the early church into four stages of progress.[1] The first period which lasted until the middle of the second century was the period of pristine purity and brotherhood. This was succeeded by an era of organization which came to an end roughly at the close of the third century with the definitive establishment of episcopal government. The third period which he described was that which opened with the Constantinian toleration, and from then onwards the church tended to assimilate many of the institutions of the imperial government. This period was never supplanted in the East, but for the Western church Harnack postulated a fourth stage of progress which was the papal epoch, when the Bishop of Rome was able to increase his power owing to the collapse of the Empire in the West.

Against this general background Harnack put forward various other reasons to explain the predominance of the Roman church in the period even before the Constantinian toleration.[2] Basically this predominance was due to the ability of Rome to give the lead in the progress of organization which would ultimately set the tone for the whole of Christendom. The reasons which he cited are the fact that Rome was the first church to define the baptismal creed and the New Testament Canon, it was the first church to have an adequate notion of the Apostolic succession and thence dated events by the pontificates in which they occurred. In addition he declared that other churches followed the lead of Rome in the modification of such matters as the administration of the sacraments, and finally the various churches maintained their communion through Rome. To use his own words: 'All these causes, combined to convert the Christian communities into a real confederation under the primacy of the Roman Church (and subsequently under the leadership of her bishops).'[3] It is worth noting in passing that this explanation by Harnack, as Scott pointed out, is a reversal of the natural inference. Far from giving Rome a primacy, the church there was able

[1]Harnack, A., *History of Dogma* (trans. from 3rd German ed. by Neil Buchanan, Edinburgh, 1896), Vol. II, pp. 31–32.
[2]Harnack, op. cit., *Excursus: Catholic and Roman*, Vol. II, pp. 151 ff.
[3]Harnack, op. cit., Vol. II, p. 159.

to do these things precisely because it possessed the necessary authority.[1] In a more general way, the theory lies open to three serious criticisms: the apparent regression from the doctrine of the New Testament, the fact that the speed of the development is too rapid to be explained by the laws of historical circumstance, and a third reason which concerns the nature of the activity of the bishops of Rome, which will be discussed more fully further on. From the historian's point of view, the second of these criticisms is perhaps the most obvious, and in the succeeding chapters the events of the early papacy will be examined to see whether they are capable of explanation simply by reference to historical circumstances. If historical evolution fails one must ask whether the speed at which the papacy is seen to develop demands that one admit that a revolution has taken place, or that an extrinsic cause is at work, such as a previous arrangement by Christ.

A century ago Cardinal Newman realized the full import of this problem, not only for the doctrine of the papacy, but indeed for all the Christian dogmas. His famous treatise on *The Development of Christian Doctrine* is now regarded as the classical explanation of the way in which the teaching of Christian revelation undergoes apparent changes.[2] It is presented in a fairly complete manner in the New Testament, is seen to be in a state of apparent regression in the documents of the infant church, and is thence exposed in the writings of the fourth and fifth centuries with an elaboration which surpasses in its precision and clarity even the New Testament. If it were a question of uniform and gradual progress it might be possible to explain the phenomenon of the change by the laws governing the progress of human history and the onward march of ideas. In the case of the truths of Christianity both the rate of progress and the apparent regression in the primitive church demand another explanation.

The basic principle which influences the whole of Newman's treatment of the matter is the fact that the revealed doctrine is of such profundity and richness that it could not be assimilated fully by the first generation. The adequate expression of the church's doctrines could only be expected when the minds of Christians had pondered on the truths of faith to comprehend all that was implied and entailed in them. The subsequent development of the doctrines can be likened to the growth

---

[1]Scott, op. cit., p. 385.

[2]H. Burn Murdoch is not correct when he casts doubts upon the extent to which Newman's theory of the development of the papacy is consistent with Catholic teaching, cf. *The Development of the Papacy*, London, 1955, pp. 40–4.

of a child, there is undeniable progress without any loss of (self) identity, still less are there any contradictions between earlier and later stages. This progress was brought about by influences such as the interplay of revelation and philosophy, the inability of human thought to remain stagnant, and the constantly recurring problems and new situations which the church had to face.[1] Under such influences, and guided by God, this development is differentiated from the merely human development of ideas by the speed and surety of its advance and the homogeneous character of its progress.

Newman applied these principles to the doctrine of the papacy in order to show that the history of the bishops of Rome in the first two centuries was fully consistent with their possession of the primacy.[2] The papacy has this complication which is not shared by other doctrines, that it is an institution of government as well as a truth of the Christian revelation. As a result it is subject to influences in the practical sphere of events as well as in the realm of the progress of ideas.

A superficial view might expect to see the early bishops of Rome making frequent use of their world-wide power. The antecedent probability in favour of such activity is not lacking. It was indeed the habit of later popes, and they claimed that the power had been there from the start. Furthermore it is natural to suppose that the church would have one sovereign ruler. History has shown that there is no satisfactory way of preserving unity in an organization apart from the presence of a supreme power. Conceivably this could be a standing committee; but the Scriptures give no warrant for such a thing. The New Testament is quite clear about the human source of unity, the authority is vested in St. Peter, and possessed of this authority he occupied the superior position in the infant church. If the apostolic church needed one supreme ruler it is unlikely that the need for it would diminish as the church expanded and assumed a more complicated form of organization.

In the face of this strong probability of a popedom, the events of the first two centuries present an unexpected enigma. It must be admitted that the activities of the early bishops of Rome do not harmonize with this expectation. It is necessary to explain this retardation of the papal power, and Newman has done so according to the principles of the development of doctrine.

The emergence of the fully matured power of the popes in the later

[1]Newman, op. cit., edition of 1878 (London), pp. 29 and 33–55.
[2]Newman, op. cit., pp. 148–69.

centuries was the result of a tension between the factors of advancement mentioned just above and two groups of retarding influences. Retardation was at work in the sphere of practical exercise and in the sphere of theological elaboration and expression. The more obvious of these is the series of forces at work which tended to oppose the power of the Bishop of Rome. While the Christians were still few in numbers and widely scattered it was to be expected that their disputes would be of a limited and local character. In settling these minor disturbances it was natural that the authority of the local ruler should emerge first into prominence, and only later, at a more advanced state of the church's progress, would the universal power of the Pope be called upon.[1] During this early period, too, the effect of the persecutions should not be overlooked. Under the circumstances of the penal laws the church could not put into effect all the activities and institutions which could be expected to flourish in times of peace. At first the Christians could not even contemplate the building of churches, and general councils were out of the question until after the religious toleration of Constantine. Under such circumstances it is not surprising that the popes found it harder to exercise an international activity than was the case after the persecutions.[2] In addition to these factors there was also the question of opposition which had to be overcome within the church itself. The authority of the popes did not establish itself without overcoming reluctance and even rebellion in certain quarters. Yet even here it would be unwise to accuse the popes of ambition. The Epistles of St. Paul are ample testimony to the struggles which he endured in order to vindicate his authority; yet no one would accuse him of ambition.

From the purely theological point of view there were also influences in operation which retarded the appreciation and expression of the doctrine. A clear exposition of the doctrine of the papacy, or any other doctrine for that matter, could not reasonably be expected until the early church had had the time and opportunity to ponder upon it, and think out all its implications. When the primitive state of the church is borne in mind, it becomes apparent that St. Ignatius's failure to mention the primacy of Rome is no harder to explain than the silence of Seneca or Plutarch about Christianity itself.[3] The pattern of the early church's theology was against an early clarification of the primacy of Rome, or an

---

[1]Newman, op. cit., pp. 151–3.
[2]Newman, op. cit., p. 151.
[3]Newman, op. cit., p. 149.

elaboration of its scriptural foundation. The earliest theological treatises were polemical works against the pagans and Jews. Generally speaking they had to defend the religion against gross accusations such as atheism. In the middle of the second century these writings gave way to the defence of Christianity against the semi-philosophical speculations of Gnosticism. Since the Gnostics claimed to have received special teaching from the Apostles which had been denied to the rank and file, the defence against it took the form of emphasizing the Apostolic succession of the bishops and the authority of the church's tradition. There was as yet no place or opportunity for a study of the Roman primacy, nor was it then of much avail to probe the Scriptures, even for the vindication of the Trinity.[1] Only in the third century, when the disputes were between thorough-going Christians, is there evidence of the extensive use of scripture, and this was the period when the famous text of St. Matthew was first invoked by the popes. The third century also witnessed the first considerable disputes which affected the Pope's authority and after that the matter was enunciated with increasing clarity. The history of all the Christian dogmas is similar to this and Newman's judgement was as follows: 'It is a less difficulty that the papal supremacy was not formally acknowledged in the second century, than that there was no formal acknowledgement on the part of the church of the doctrine of the Holy Trinity till the fourth. No doctrine is defined till it is violated.'[2]

Chronologically the development began with the notion of the Apostolic succession. This was the means of ensuring the faithful transmission of the Apostolic tradition. As a result of the heresies of the second century, the church crystallized its consciousness of the role of the universal episcopate. The bishops were seen to be the guardians of the true faith handed on from the Apostles. This is the common burden of anti-heretical writers such as Irenaeus and Tertullian.

Thence the pattern of development was the progressive isolation of the Roman see, at times giving rise to a certain tension with the norm of the 'universal episcopate'. Although this latter norm of church government was the first to be excogitated formally, some idea of a papacy is already present in the second century. The testimony of Irenaeus (to be discussed later) shows how the church was beginning to disengage the notion of an imparity of authority among the Apostolic churches. In the third century the process can be seen to have progressed one stage

[1]Jalland, op. cit., p. 210.
[2]Newman, op. cit., p. 151.

farther. Although the notion of the authority of the universal episcopate is uppermost in the minds of Cyprian and his contemporaries, it is known that at that time the church of Rome was already receiving juridical appeals against the decisions of local councils of bishops.

When these considerations are borne in mind, it will be seen that the history of the popes in the first two centuries is in harmony with an institution of primacy by Christ and the retarding factors in the life of the primitive church. The subsequent maturing of the papal authority in the later centuries can be understood, then, not as the creation of a novelty, but the emergence of Christ's original plan, once the obstacles had been overcome. In the pages which follow, the history of the early papacy will be examined to see whether its progress demands explanation by the evolutionary principles of Harnack and others or by the theory of development as expounded by Newman.

The earliest surviving record of the authority of the Roman Church is the letter of St. Clement to the church of Corinth. The text does not actually bear his name, but all the ancient writers who refer to it, attribute it to Clement of Rome, the third successor of St. Peter. The event which had provoked this letter was a revolt in the church at Corinth in which some of the clergy had been expelled from office. It appears that the Corinthian church was still governed by the committee system of equal ranking *episcopoi-presbuteroi*,[1] and Clement wrote to vindicate the authority of the deposed party. It is anachronistic to imagine that there had been a juridical appeal to Rome;[2] Clement decided to intervene on his own initiative, having heard of the matter perhaps from travellers. The letter is a dignified and carefully constructed treatise on the evils of jealousy and the virtue of obedience to legitimate authority. Scholars are almost unanimous in assigning it to the year 96 on account of the reference to the persecution of Domitian.

At first sight it does not appear that the letter is of much value as evidence in favour of the Roman primacy. There is no explicit mention of the possession of a superior authority nor does the writer make any specific commands. In spite of this, the tone is decidedly authoritarian and indicates the consciousness of a superior talking to a subordinate. He tells the rebellious party: 'You, therefore, the prime movers of the schism, submit to the presbyters, and, bending the knees of your hearts,

[1]cf. Duchesne, *The Early History of the Church*, I, p. 161. The terms ἐπίσκοπος and πρεσβύτερος are employed equivalently, e.g. 21:6, 44:4 and 5, 47:6, and 54:2.

[2]Duchesne, op. cit., I, p. 161; Quasten, op. cit., I, p. 43.

accept correction and change your minds' (57:1). The consciousness of having a mandate from Christ is apparent in the following words: 'But should any disobey what has been said by him through us, let them understand that they will entangle themselves in transgression and no small danger' (59:1). This awareness of the divine authority is also to be seen in a later passage: 'You certainly will give us the keenest pleasure if you prove obedient to what we have written through the Holy Spirit . . . ' (63:2).[1]

Over and above the tone of authority which is manifested in these extracts, the circumstances under which the letter was written are important in revealing the superior position of the writer.

A few years later St. Ignatius, Bishop of Antioch, had occasion to write to some of the churches in Asia Minor. In these letters it is clear that he has no authority over the churches which he addresses. As he is not their own bishop, he tells them explicitly that he does not command them.[2] In such circumstances it would be natural for Clement to apologize for presuming to intervene in the affairs of another church. In fact, he does nothing of the kind. The first chapter of the letter begins with an apology that he has delayed so long before attending to the matter of their dispute.

If Clement had no right to interfere with the affairs of another church, it would be natural to suppose that Corinth would have resented his letter, particularly in view of the turbulent character of the Corinthian church apparent in St. Paul's time. The immediate reaction to the letter is not known, yet years later it was held in such high regard that it was read together with the Scriptures in the liturgical assembly on Sunday.[3] It is therefore reasonable to assume that it had been well received in the first instance.

Further light is cast upon the situation by examining the explanations advanced by those who do not admit that Clement had any superiority. Bishop Gore suggested that Rome had intervened because it had a bishop to govern it, whereas Corinth had not yet advanced beyond the stage of government by a committee.[4] Gore's argument does not go far enough. If Corinth needed outside assistance on account of the primitive state of its own hierarchy, would it not have been more suitable to expect assistance from Ephesus? The fact that the Apostle John was

---

[1] Text, Funk, F. X., op. cit., I, pp. 99 ff. Trans. Kleist, op. cit., pp. 9–49.
[2] Ignatius to the Magnesians, 11:1.
[3] Letter of Dionysius of Corinth, in Eusebius, H.E., IV, 23.
[4] Gore, op. cit., p. 94.

alive at Ephesus after the persecution of Domitian is attested by Irenaeus and Clement of Alexandria, and it is accepted by the majority of modern authors.[1] This intervention by Clement, during the lifetime of one of the Apostles, who was then considerably nearer to Corinth, is perhaps the strongest indication of the special position of the Bishop of Rome even at that early date.

A more recent theory to explain the intervention of Clement is that put forward by van Caulewaert.[2] It is suggested that Rome felt inclined to intervene because Corinth was a Roman *colonia*, and the social and cultural ties between them would be considerable. The presence of a Roman *colonia* at Corinth is perfectly true, yet it is hard to see why this should account for the intervention in an ecclesiastical affair. The type of liaison between church and state which it presupposes did not emerge until a much later date. In addition to this, it would seem more natural for some nearer Roman *colonia* to intervene; they were not rare in the Eastern Mediterranean. Philippi is the most obvious one, since it was also an Apostolic church. There is no other record in the history of the early church of ecclesiastical intervention arising out of political kinship.

The circumstances of Clement's action, combined with failure to find a satisfactory alternative, favour the acceptance of the most natural explanation of the incident; namely, that Rome was already acknowledged to possess some kind of superiority in relation to the other churches. It is perhaps most accurately summed up by Batiffol who described the incident as the 'epiphany of the Roman Primacy'.[3] The evidence in this case is too slight to give very much idea of the scope of the power thus exercised. It is one of the enigmatic facts of the early papacy which Newman described as telling so much about the papal authority but no more;[4] yet the mere existence of the letter is a testimony of great moment to the authority of the Roman bishop.[5]

Further evidence of this type, to some extent implicit, is to be found in the letter which was addressed to the Roman church by St. Ignatius.

[1] Irenaeus, *Adv. Hæreses*, II, quoted in Eusebius, H. E., III, 23; and Clement of Alexandria, *Quis Dives Salvetur*, 42:2; M.P.G., IX, 648. Modern authors, e.g. Batiffol, P., *L'Église Naissante et Le Catholicisme*, Paris, 1922, 5th ed., p. 155; Lebreton, J., *L'Église Primitive*, Vol. I of Fliche & Martin: *Histoire de L'Église*, Paris, 1946, p. 325; Kidd, op. cit., p. 11.

[2] van Caulewaert, R., 'L'Intervention de L'Église de Rome à Corinth vers l'an 96', in *Revue d'Hist. Eccl.*, April, 1935. Followed by Jalland, op. cit., pp. 102–3.

[3] Batiffol, op. cit., p. 146. A conclusion which is generally followed by Catholic authors and by some Anglicans, e.g. Scott, op. cit., pp. 17–22.

[4] Newman, op. cit., p. 154.

[5] Quasten, op. cit., I, p. 46.

The popularity of this writer was such that in the Middle Ages no less than thirteen letters were attributed to him. As a result, there was a time when all the letters were suspect. However, the critical examination of scholars amongst whom were Zahn, Harnack, Lightfoot, and Funk, has established the authenticity of the original seven, in which group is to be found the epistle to the Romans. The letter was written from Smyrna with a view to dissuading the Roman church from trying to procure his release. The writer's intention was not disappointed, and at the end of his journey, in the year 110, he suffered martyrdom in the Colosseum.

The noteworthy passage occurs in the title of the Epistle. The rest of the letters bear simple titles such as 'Ignatius, also called Theophorus, to the Church at Magnesia . . .' or 'Ignatius, also called Theophorus, to the holy Church at Tralles, in Asia . . .' However, when addressing the Roman church, he uses an entire paragraph expressing the highest praise. The tone is so deliberately deferential that it will not be out of place to quote a part of it: 'Ignatius, also called Theophorus, to the church that has found mercy in the transcendent Majesty of the Most High Father and of Jesus Christ, His only Son; the church by the will of Him who willed all things that exist, beloved and illuminated through the faith and love of Jesus Christ our God; which also presides in the chief place of the Roman territory; a church worthy of God, worthy of honour, worthy of felicitation, worthy of praise, worthy of success, worthy of sanctification, and presiding in love, maintaining the law of Christ, and bearer of the Father's name . . .'[1]

There is more in this passage than mere Oriental obsequiousness. The two phrases which have occasioned the most comment are 'which also presides in the chief place of the Roman territory'. (ἥτις καὶ προκάθηται ἐν τόπῳ Χωρίου Ῥωμαίων), and 'presiding in love' (προκαθημένη τῆς ἀγάπης). Both of these phrases contain the key word προκάθημαι, meaning literally, to preside, in the sense of supervising. It is reasonable to understand the same sense in the two uses of the word, since they are in the same passage. The strict sense of supervision is seen elsewhere in Ignatius's letters where he uses it of the bishop's presiding over the local church.[2] The first phrase then gives rise to the question: Over whom or what is the Roman church presiding? Con-

[1] Text, Funk, op. cit., I, p. 253. Translation, Kleist, op. cit., I, p. 80. The wording is critically established and there is little justification for Phillimore's emendation to προκαθημένη ἐν τόπῳ Χριστοῦ. (J.T.S. 1918, pp. 272 ff.)
[2] Letter to the Magnesians 6:1.

ceivably it could be a reference to the authority exercised over the local church, but in that case the phrase is a meaningless tautology. All the local churches govern themselves and Ignatius addressed them with the words 'to the holy church at Tralles in Asia', etc. Clearly the preface to the letter to Rome indicates that the church at Rome rules over something other than itself. Some kind of rule over the Roman territory or city is theoretically conceivable, but it is historically unrealistic and would have been expressed by a simple genitive.[1] The first phrase, then, shows that the Roman church presides over something other than itself, which is not specified as yet.

The answer to the question thus raised is supplied just below by the second phrase, 'presiding in love'. The *agape* with the definite article is indicated as being that over which the Roman church presides. The problem is not, however, entirely elucidated. Several theories have been advanced to explain the precise meaning of 'the love'.

Harnack considered that it was a reference to the practical charity of the Roman church, which was famous for the financial assistance which it gave to the needy. In that way the Roman community gave the lead and set the example for the other churches in the practice of the virtue of charity. This opinion is offset by a formidable difficulty; the word *prokathemai* is precise in meaning, and refers to governance over individuals or collectivities, never to virtues.[2] In view of this, Harnack's suggestion must be rejected, since it is anachronistic to imagine that the charitable relief of the Roman church was organized on the lines of, say, the International Red Cross.[3]

Another suggestion was that advanced by Funk and Chapman, namely that *agape* is equivalent to the universal church. There are passages in the letters of Ignatius where the word is used to denote the local churches and it is argued that it means the universal church in the present instance.[4] This theory has a fair degree of probability to commend it, yet it seems to be forcing the text. If St. Ignatius had wished to denote the universal hierarchical church, there are many ways in which he could have made his meaning much clearer.

The most satisfactory solution so far advanced seems to be that of J. Thiele,[5] in which he adopts a wider meaning for *agape*, so that it

---

[1]e.g. τόπου χωρίου . . . or simply Ῥώμης.
[2]Batiffol, op. cit., p. 168.
[3]cf. Quasten, op. cit., I, p. 69.
[4]Trallians, 13:1; Romans 9:3; Philadelphians 11:2; Smyrnians 12:1.
[5]Thiele, J., art. 'Vorrang in der Liebe' in *Theologie und Glaube*, 1927, pp. 701–9.

denotes the totality of the supernatural life given by Christ to man. The Roman church is thereby revealed as having the guiding role in the very essence of Christianity. This pre-eminence of Rome accords well with other indications in the letter. The church there is said to have 'taught others' (3:1), which is all the more remarkable since it received the gospel from the East. In addition, Ignatius does not address to Rome the exhortations to unity and obedience which are the common theme of the other epistles.

This letter resembles the epistle of Clement in so far as there is no categorical assertion of the Roman primacy. Nevertheless certain passages are intelligible only on the assumption that Ignatius was aware that Rome possessed some kind of superiority over the other churches.

A chronological examination of the early papacy must take cognizance next of an unusual series of events in the second century. Throughout this period there appears to have been a constant succession of visitors to Rome. What is of particular relevance to the present inquiry is the fact that they were all theologians, either orthodox or heretical. Their varied origins are described graphically by Kidd: 'To Rome then journeyed Polycarp from Smyrna; Valentinus from Egypt; Cerdo from Syria; Marcion from Sinope; Justin from Samaria; Tatian from Assyria; Hegesippus from Jerusalem; Justin's pupils Eulepstus from Cappadocia and Hierax from Phrygia; Rhodon, Irenaeus, and Florinus from Asia; Proclus and other Montanists from Phrygia; and Praxeas, their adversary, from the same region.'[1] Apart from its authority, it is difficult to see what Rome had to offer these scholars of the early church. For theology and philosophy the Eastern cities were superior, and moreover their religious life was more developed. Rome never became an intellectual centre in the church, and thus it would seem that these various teachers came to Rome to seek the official approval of their doctrines.

The case of Hegesippus gives certain indications of this quest for authority. Hegesippus himself was perfectly orthodox, but amid the troubles of the Gnostic heresies, he left his own church in Palestine to assure himself of the true doctrine. Eusebius describes how he visited various apostolic churches,[2] but his principal objective was Rome. Why? Presumably because its authority was greatest.

The last of the teachers mentioned above, Praxeas, is the most en-

[1]Kidd, B. J., *History of the Church*, I, p. 118.
[2]Eusebius, H. E., IV, 22.

lightening on the matter, owing to the account which Tertullian gives of his activities.[1] The incident concerns the heresy of the Montanists which had originated in Asia Minor in the latter half of the second century. Whether their teaching had been condemned locally is hard to say, but Tertullian declares that they had been approved by the Bishop of Rome and were therefore at peace with the churches of Asia and Phrygia. Praxeas, however, came to Rome and acquainted the 'Pope with the true doctrine of the Montanists. Thereupon the Pope repealed the former approval and excommunicated Montanus and his followers. Tertullian has no more to say explicitly, yet it is clear from his anger (Tertullian himself was by that time a Montanist) that the Roman decision was irreversible.

Thanks to the information given by Tertullian, the action of Praxeas is reasonably clear, and it supplies an explanation which can account for the Romeward journeys of the other teachers. It is evident, then, that the Bishop of Rome was already exercising a special role in matters of doctrine during the second century, and at this period can be seen the first recorded examples of what was later to become the most powerful prerogative of the Popes.

So much for the fact. What of its theoretical basis? This, too, is supplied by one of the travellers in question, the famous Irenaeus. This man was born in Asia Minor in the first half of the second century, perhaps towards the year 140. As a youth he had been taught by St. Polycarp and thus acquired knowledge of the most ancient traditions of the church. At a later date it is probable that he went to Rome, and he first appears in history in the year 177, when he had come to the city on behalf of the church of Lyons, in which church he was a priest. On his return to Lyons he was elected bishop of the city and from then on-wards he was occupied in the preservation of true doctrine in the church in face of the heretical infiltrations. One item of this work was the famous book *Adversus Hæreses* (Against the Heretics), which contains the celebrated passage relevant to the Roman church.

Irenaeus declares that the standard of orthodoxy is the teaching which is to be found in the churches of Apostolic foundation. He admits, though, that it would be a lengthy process to trace the teaching of all the Apostolic churches, so he presents his readers with a simple method of finding what they teach. The Roman church is necessarily in agreement

[1]Tertullian, Adv. Praxeas, Ch. I, C.S.E.L., Vol. 47, p. 228. Discussed by Batiffol, *Cathedra Petri*, pp. 33–34.

with all the Apostolic churches; therefore a man has only to find out what is being taught at Rome, and he can be sure of possessing the truth, since the apostolic churches could not be out of accord with Rome. Precisely why Rome should be so reliable is explained in the following famous passage from the third book of *Adversus Hæreses:*

Sed quoniam valde longum est in hoc tali volumine omnium ecclesiarum ennumerare successiones, maximae et antiquissimae et omnibus cognitae, a gloriosissimis duobus apostolis Petro et Paulo Romae fundatae et constitutae ecclesiae, eam quam habet ab apostolis traditionem et adnuntiatam hominibus fidem per successiones episcoporum pervenientem usque ad nos indicantes, confundimus omnes eos qui quoquo modo, vel per sibi placentiam vel vanam gloriam vel per caecitatetem et sententiam malam praeterquam oportet colligunt. Ad hanc enim ecclesiam, propter potentiorem principalitatem, necesse est omnem convenire ecclesiam, hoc est eos qui sunt undique fideles, in qua semper, ab his qui sunt undique, conservata est ea quae est ab apostolis traditio.[1]

But it would be very long in a book of this kind, to enumerate the episcopal lists in all the churches, but by pointing out the Apostolic tradition and creed which has been brought down to us by a succession of bishops in the greatest, most ancient and well-known church, founded by the two most glorious Apostles Peter and Paul at Rome, we can confute all those who in any other way, either for self-pleasing or for vainglory or blindness or badness, hold unauthorized meetings. For with this church, because of its stronger origin, all churches must agree, that is to say, the faithful of all places, because in it the Apostolic tradition has always been preserved by the (faithful) of all places.

It is regrettable that the Greek text of Irenaeus is no longer extant for this passage; nevertheless the Latin translation dates from the beginning of the third century, and despite its difficulties it is critically sound.

It is clear from the whole sense of the passage that St. Irenaeus intended to draw attention to the church of Rome. This time-honoured interpretation was challenged in 1957 by an interesting theory of P. Nautin,[2] who maintains that the norm of agreement is not Rome, but the universal church. The theory, though not lacking in probability, entails some serious difficulties.[3] If the *potentiorem principalitatem*

---

[1]*Adv. Haereses*, III, 3, 2. Text, ed. F. Sagnard, O. P., *Sources Chrétiennes*, Paris, 1952, Vol. 34, p. 102.

[2]Art. 'Irénée—Adv. Haer.—III, 3, 2, église de Rome ou église universelle?' in *Revue de l'Histoire des Religions*, 1957, pp. 37–78.

[3]Botte, B., art. 'À propos de l'Adversus Haereses, III, 3, 2, de Saint Irénée', *Irenikon*, 1957 (2), p. 159.

(stronger origin), is applied to the universal church in contrast to the heretics, it thereby follows that the heretics possess some kind of *principalitas*. Hardly a characteristic idea of Irenaeus! A further difficulty is derived from the phrase *omnem convenire ecclesiam*. Dom Botte has shown that the better translation of it is 'all the church'. If, then, the church with which this latter must agree (the church designated by *hanc*) is the universal church, the phrase is reduced to a simple tautology. Following in the wake of this dispute, J. Lebourlier[1] has shown that the key phrase must refer to Rome. The context and general sense of the passage indicate this so strongly that one would not be justified in referring it to some other church without a positive indication in the text that Rome, hitherto the theme of the passage, was to be excluded.

The general tenor of Irenaeus's thought is first indicated by the epithet *antiquissimae* (most ancient). The same word was used by Origen to designate the Roman church.[2] The epithet is unusual in view of the fact that Rome was a later foundation than the principal churches of the East, and Origen could hardly have been ignorant of the fact. From many points of view Jerusalem merited the title of mother church of the world, being the earliest by many years. Viewed thus, it is hard to understand the expression 'most ancient', unless it be taken as a reference to the office of St. Peter which was embodied in that church. This notion was well known to the early church, since they saw the origin of the episcopate in the promise of the keys of the kingdom.

The crucial passage which has occasioned so much discussion is the sentence beginning '*Ad hanc enim ecclesiam*' (For with this church). The reason why all the churches of the world must be in agreement with Rome is because it has a stronger *principalitas*. Various Greek words have been suggested as the original which was translated as *principalitas*. Van den Eynde and Bardy have suggested that it was ἀρχή or its cognates ἀρχαῖον or ἀρχαιότης (origin, with the implication of antiquity).[3] Philologically there is much to commend the view, and it accords well with the theory implied in the previous epithet 'most ancient'. Yet it is the former adjective which weakens the case for ἀρχή in the present instance. If the Greek original had contained ἀρχή it would seem natural

[1] Art. 'Le Problème de L'Adversus Haereses, III, 3, 2, de S. Irénée', in *Revue des Sciences Philosophiques et Théologiques*, 1959 (2), pp. 263–4.

[2] Quoted by Eusebius, H. E., VI, 14: εὐξάμενος τὴν ἀρχαιοτάτην Ῥωμαίων ἐκκλησίαν ἰδεῖν.

[3] D. van den Eynde, *Les Normes de L'Énseigement Chrétien*, Paris, 1933, p. 177, followed by Bardy, G., *La Théologie de L'Église de Saint Clement de Rome à Saint Irénée*, Paris, 1945, p. 207.

for the Latin translator to render it by 'antiquitas'. Greater probability seems to attach to the suggestion that *principalitas* stands for πρωτεία. This was maintained by Funk, Chapman, and Batiffol, who favoured it in his final judgement on the matter.[1] *Principalitas* is the quality possessed by that which is first in a series. Irenaeus uses it of Adam as father of the human race, and of God as the origin of all creation.[2] For this latter passage the Greek original has survived, and it contains the word πρωτύει. An adequate English equivalent for the idea is 'origin'; the Roman church thus has a stronger origin.

One further precision needs to be made. It is necessary to establish what Irenaeus meant when he drew attention to the origin of a church. The answer here is suggested in another passage of the *Adversus Hæreses*,[3] where Irenaeus warns the faithful to shun the heretical teachers. The true doctrine, he declares, is taught by the priests and bishops who can trace their ordination back to the Apostles. The heretics who stand apart from this original succession (*principali successione*) are to be shunned. Clearly, then, the original succession, as opposed to the heretical organization, is the succession of bishops which traces its origin back to the Apostles. The extension of this idea to the problem under consideration indicates that Rome had some kind of stronger Apostolic origin. This could hardly be a reference to the fact that it was founded by two apostles. The same could be said of Corinth, Ephesus, and especially Jerusalem. The only satisfactory explanation is to infer that the Apostle who founded the Roman church had greater authority.

The rest of the passage, though not devoid of complexity, is more straightforward. The phrase *necesse est omnem convenire ecclesiam* (all churches must agree) is generally taken to be a necessity of fact, rather than a moral obligation. Irenaeus is not dealing with the question of the supreme arbitration in disputes about belief; he is giving a practical standard for finding the truth in normal circumstances. The basis of this standard is the agreement which exists, in fact, between the Apostolic churches. Rome is singled out as the exemplar because of its inability to deviate from the truth. All the other Apostolic churches are thus, in fact, in agreement with Rome.

The ambiguity which occurs at the end of the passage does not

---

[1] Batiffol, *L'Église Naissante*, p. 252, and *Cathedra Petri*, p. 35.
[2] *Adv. Hæreses*, IV, 38, 3.
[3] *Adv. Hæreses*, IV, 26, 2.

actually effect the general sense of the paragraph. The words *in qua semper, ab his qui sunt undique, consevata est ea quae est ab apostolis traditio* [because in it the Apostolic tradition has always been preserved by the (faithful) of all places] could refer to two things. In the opinion of Harnack, Duchesne, and Funk the church implied is the universal church. Attention is thereby drawn to the fact that Rome is in agreement with the churches throughout the world, in which churches the Apostolic doctrine has been preserved. The theory entails certain grammatical difficulties, but it accords with the overall pattern of Irenaeus's thought. On the other hand, the grammar and the immediate context are more favourable to Batiffol's view, namely that Rome is implicitly designated.[1] On this assumption there is a parallelism with the beginning of the sentence which makes better sense for the whole, furthermore, unless Rome possessed the Apostolic tradition it would be useless as a norm of doctrine.

This famous passage from Irenaeus is the first clear statement about the superiority of the Roman church in matters of doctrine. It is not a complete analysis of the Roman primacy, yet the only possible basis for the supremacy which Irenaeus does accord to Rome is the peculiar authority possessed by the Bishop of Rome.

As the second century drew to a close the ecclesiastical world was troubled by a dispute whose principal interest now is the light which it throws on the authority of the Bishop of Rome. The cause of the disagreement was the oft-recurring problem of the date of Easter. It appears that by the middle of the second century the majority of the churches, including Rome, celebrated Easter on the Sunday which followed the fourteenth day of the Jewish month of Nisan. However, the churches of Asia observed the feast on the fourteenth day of Nisan, whether it happened to be a Sunday or not.[2] As early as the year 154 the aged Bishop Polycarp came from Asia to Rome, to confer with Anicetus with a view to establishing uniformity. The difficulty was that both practices had Apostolic warrant. Rome claimed to be following the institution of Saints Peter and Paul, whereas Asia traced its practice

---

[1] Batiffol, *L'Église Naissante*, p. 251, and Quasten, op. cit., I, p. 303. Also B. Botte (art. cit., p. 160) has suggested that in Rome the true tradition had been preserved from the contaminations of the heretics. An interesting explanation of the phrase '*ab his qui sunt undique*'.

[2] The problem is related to the question of deciding whether Christ himself celebrated the last Pasch on the same day as the majority of the Jews. Discoveries among the Dead Sea Scrolls may well elucidate this thorny problem, cf. A. Jaubert, *La Date de la Cène*, Paris, 1957.

back to the Apostle John. The discussions between Anicetus and Polycarp ended in an impasse and the latter returned to Asia still faithful to
his former practice.

Both parties were content to leave the matter as it stood until the
end of the century, when other factors had to be taken into account.
As a result of the heresies of the second century the ecclesiastical
discipline became more rigid with a view to establishing uniformity
in matters which hitherto had shown considerable diversity. One such
sphere was the liturgy. In addition to this the Asian usage of celebrating
Easter on the fourteenth day of Nisan had become associated with
Judaizing tendencies in theology. This had caused trouble in Rome
itself, among the numerous Asians resident in the city. It was most
probably this latter danger which inclined Pope Victor to intervene
vigorously. Unfortunately the records are fragmentary, yet it would
seem that Victor, who reigned from 189 to 199, acted in this affair in the
year 190.

Eusebius records that synods were held throughout the church and
he had before him letters from those which met at Caesarea in Palestine,
Pontus, Rome, Gaul, Osrhoene, and a letter from the Bishop of Corinth.[1]
Other documents which Eusebius had before him show that these
synods must have been universal. They were held at the same time and
all discussed the question of the date of Easter. It is unlikely that all
these synods would have met without some kind of central directive to
do so, and in fact one of the letters is quite clear on the point. Polycrates,
who presided over the synod of Asia, said in his letter to Victor: 'I could
also mention the bishops that were present, whom you requested to be
summoned by me, and whom I did call.[2] It is reasonable to deduce
from this indication that Victor had taken the initiative in arranging all
the synods, so that each local group of bishops could discuss the matter
of the date of Easter.[3]

The sense of universal responsibility displayed in this request for
synods is itself of relevance to the consideration of the power of the
Bishop of Rome. However, the dramatic sequel to these synods is still
more eloquent. Nearly all the churches declared that it had been their
practice to celebrate Easter according to the Roman custom. The
churches of Asia were the only champions of the other usage, and they

[1]Eusebius, H. E., V, 23.
[2]Quoted in Eusebius, H. E., V, 23.
[3]Batiffol, *L'Église Naissante*, p. 271.

refused to give it up, since they claimed to have inherited the practice from the Apostle John. Victor thereupon determined that he would excommunicate them. This decision provoked several protests from the bishops of other regions. Most noteworthy is that of Irenaeus, who pointed out in a respectful letter, which is recorded by Eusebius (H.E., V, 24), that the previous bishops of Rome had been prepared to tolerate the diversity of practice.

The sequel to this intervention is not altogether clear. Peace was restored, and later the whole church, as in so many matters, adopted the Roman usage. This was firmly established at the time of the council of Nicea, and then the only problem was to decide on what basis it should be computed. The key phrase of Eusebius, in which he records the action of Victor, could mean that he threatened excommunication but did not implement it, or that he passed the sentence and later withdrew it.[1] Other conclusions from the dispute emerge with greater clarity. The victims of Pope Victor's severity were not just the Asian parishes in Rome, but the Asian churches actually in Asia Minor.[2] The nature, too, of the excommunication must be understood accurately. It was not simply a dispute between Rome and Asia, but, as Harnack realized, it was a question of exclusion from the universal church. If Rome had enforced the sentence, then the churches of Asia would have been severed from the communion of the whole church.[3] This explains the intense interest which the matter aroused among the other bishops of the world.

Despite one or two obscurities, the incident is valuable for what it shows of the papal power at the end of the second century. In the first place, the initiative which impelled Victor to invite synods throughout the world is itself an indication of his consciousness of being in some way responsible for the universal church. Secondly his competence to inflict universally binding excommunication is accepted. It was the particular application of this power, not the right itself, which occasioned the disputes.[4] Finally this incident bears out the less conclusive evidence of the Epistle of Clement, that the bishop of Rome had a

---

[1] Eusebius, H. E., V, 24, 9. Ἀποτέμνειν τῆς κοινῆς ἑνώσεως πειρᾶται. Both interpretations are possible. cf. Fortescue, A., *The Early Papacy*, London, 1920, p. 36.
[2] Jalland, op. cit., pp. 120, 121, holds the view that it was merely parishes in Rome, against the majority opinion championed by Harnack, Duchesne, Batiffol, Lebreton and many others.
[3] Harnack, op. cit., Vol. II, pp. 160–1, Batiffol, *L'Église Naissante*, p. 272.
[4] Batiffol, *L'Église Naissante*, p. 274.

competence not only in matters of faith, but also in questions of discipline and church order. No contemporary record has survived expressing the theology of the papal power. As is natural, the exercise was ahead of the theory. Only at a later date, when their power had been challenged, did the bishops of Rome justify their rights. In Pope Victor's time the facts must be allowed to speak for themselves, and they indicate, in the words of the rationalist Renan, that 'the papacy was well and truly born'.[1]

The pontificate of St. Victor is a convenient point at which to close the study of the primitive papacy. In the third century the position of the Pope was already being complicated, so that his attitude to the various parts of the church was not quite the same. The emergence of the different zones of the papal power, which will be discussed in the following chapter, is an indication that the papacy had already passed through its infancy. It is not, therefore, untimely to allude to the question which was raised at the beginning of the chapter. Is it possible to account for the facts of the early papacy by reference to the forces of historical evolution? Or is it necessary to admit the presence of some other factor shaping the destiny of the papacy in a manner which is beyond the capabilities of human endeavours? A final answer to this problem must await a more complete study of the facts, yet already the verdict must begin to turn in favour of Newman's development rather than Harnack's evolution. Harnack considered that the papacy was establishing its position in the middle of the third century, not by a sudden seizure of power, but as the result of a process of evolution. This rate of progress would be quite reasonable if the human forces had been the only influences in operation, but the events of the second century are seriously at variance with such a chronology. It is hard to account for activity like that of Pope Victor without invoking the principle of Newman's theory of development. The Celestines and the Leos have not yet appeared on the scene; nevertheless the principles which were to govern their activity are seen to be operative already in a manner which is restricted, but in harmony with the subsequent developments.

[3] *La Papauté était née et bien née.* Quoted by Batiffol, *L'Église Naissante*, p. 271.

6

PAPAL POWER IN THE ITALIAN ZONE

THE proper understanding of the papacy demands the application of the principles of development, but as was indicated above, the papacy has the added complication that it both involves a doctrine and is an institution of government. This means that its development will be influenced by the factors governing the progress of ideas and also by the concrete situations which faced the bishops of Rome in the administration of ecclesiastical affairs. One of the most striking results of this latter consideration is the differentiation which is apparent in the various zones of papal power. Mgr. Batiffol drew attention to this situation,[1] but it is to be regretted that many standard works on the subject of the papacy do not take account of it adequately.

The power of the Bishop of Rome was exercised differently in three separate zones, Metropolitan Italy, the Western Empire, and the Eastern Empire. Each of these zones had a distinctive relationship with the see of Rome, and the nature of this relationship accounts for the number and the type of the interventions of the Pope in their affairs. This consideration provides, moreover, the only satisfactory answer to the statistical problem. From the numerical point of view, it would appear that the Pope had most contact with Italy, a little less with the West, and least contact with the Eastern church. A superficial examination of this situation might suggest that the Bishop of Rome was pope in Italy, patriarch in the West, and of little consequence in the East. Such a view would be grossly inaccurate, and Batiffol's theory of the three zones provides the most satisfactory method of understanding this differentiation, both numerical and qualitative.

The boundaries of the first zone varied somewhat in the course of its history, but for the present it will be sufficient to designate it as the region of Italy. Of the three zones, this one was the most closely united

[1]For instance, in *La Paix Constantinienne*, Paris, 1914, pp. 132–4, *Le Siège Apostolique*, Paris, 1924, pp. 150–70, and particularly in *Cathedra Petri*, Paris, 1938, pp. 41–59.

to Rome, and was subject to the Pope in a relationship of peculiar dependence. The first cause of this dependence was the fact that Rome was the mother church of all Italy. It is fairly certain that the evangelization of the whole of the Italian peninsula originated from Rome. In the primitive church this situation of mission churches and the parent body was the basis of the later metropolitan authority. It is easy to understand how naturally this liaison would arise, and it is not surprising that the mother church should be in a position of authority over the younger churches. This gives a partial explanation of the authority which Rome exercised over the whole of Italy, but it is not the complete account of the situation. The fact of having been the source of Christianity in Italy does not adequately differentiate the Italian zone from the Western zone, which was also evangelized from Rome, but which did not have the same close subjection to the Pope.

The ultimate factor which accounts for the situation in Italy is probably the late diffusion of episcopal authority. It would appear that the Bishop of Rome was the only bishop in Italy until the middle of the second century.[1] This would have led to an unusual degree of centralization, which was not the case in the rest of the Western church, which had its local bishops from the earliest times. It is not to be wondered at that this close dependence persisted even after the creation of other bishops in Italy in the latter half of the second century. The same situation is to be seen in Egypt, where Alexandria was for a long time the only episcopal see.[2] Precisely why Italy should have had only one bishop for so long, it is hard to say. It may possibly be connected with the fact that until the reorganization of the imperial provinces by Diocletian at the end of the third century there were no separate provinces in Italy. The weakness of this suggestion lies in the fact that it was not the custom at this early date in the West to arrange the ecclesiastical regions on the civil pattern.[3] On the other hand, the subsequent history of the Italian zone shows that its borders were coterminous with the administrative area known as the *regiones suburbicariae*. This would seem to suggest some deliberate imitation of the imperial divisions, and if such had been the case from the beginning, it would give a very cogent explanation of this concentration of the episcopal authority at Rome. Over and above these lesser ties there was, of course, the supreme power

---

[1] Zeiller, op. cit., I, p. 377.
[2] Duchesne, op. cit., I, p. 69.
[3] Duchesne, op. cit., I, p. 383.

of the papacy proper, which was wielded over Italy as well as over the rest of the church.

The situation in the other zones was less complicated. The Western part of the Empire was of course subject to the Bishop of Rome as Pope. In addition to this there was the added dependence of the mission churches on their church of origin. Rome enjoyed a position of special respect in the West, because it was the only Apostolic church there, and moreover it was the centre from which the whole of the West was ultimately evangelized. At a later date the metropolitan organization followed the civil pattern and each provincial capital was also a metropolitan see. Even then the traditional arrangement held sway to the extent that Rome was the super-metropolitan of the West. However, only in the time of Justinian was the title of patriarch applied to Rome in view of its relationship to the West.

Finally the Eastern zone presents the simplest situation of all. No part of the East was evangelized from Rome, nor was there any lack of Apostolic churches to give prestige to the Oriental empire. As a result, the Bishop of Rome intervened in the affairs of the Eastern church only with his full papal authority. This accounts for the comparative scarcity of such interventions and, as will be seen later, the momentous character of those incidents.

Although an attempt to summarize the situation is in danger of oversimplifying it, it is substantially true to say that in the East the Pope exercised only supreme authority, in the West he used both papal and metropolitan power, and in Italy he exercised these last two and the further power derived from the peculiar centralization within Italy. This classification gives a satisfactory explanation of the fact that the activity of the Pope was not perfectly uniform throughout the whole of the church.

The root causes of this situation were operative from the dawn of the church in Italy, but their effects were not clearly visible on the surface of ecclesiastical affairs until the third century. When the church obtained legal freedom under Constantine the divergences became more obvious, and after the Arian crisis the situation was further complicated by differences of a more disquieting nature.

The considerations outlined above indicate how it was that the Bishop of Rome came to have differing relationships with the East and the West. These factors of differentiation were rooted in the way in which the church expanded, and of themselves they would not have

caused any threat to ecclesiastical unity. However, at the same time as
these normal divergences were taking place, there was also a series of
influences in operation which could be called abnormal divergences.
These latter factors tended to divide the East from the West and their
constant presence was one of the principal circumstances favouring the
ultimate schism between Rome and Constantinople.

Since these latter influences were having their effect on the exercise
of papal authority at the same time as the factors of zonal differentiation,
it will be convenient to examine them briefly before studying the history
of the Italian zone.

Some of these differences were rooted simply in the natural divisions
of the Mediterranean world. Following the campaigns of Alexander
the Great the Greek language, and later its culture, were widely diffused
throughout the Eastern Mediterranean. However, although Greek was
spoken in Rome, the Hellenic influence in the West was negligible
compared with the prestige that it enjoyed in the East. This Greek
influence in the Eastern Empire was allied to its cultural superiority,
and the Western cities never attained the same intellectual reputation as,
for instance, Athens or Alexandria. In considering the secular differences between East and West, one must also recall certain political
events of the later Roman Empire. The transfer of the imperial capital
from Rome to Constantinople in the year 330 stressed the importance
of the East, which was further emphasized after the final collapse of
Roman power in the West in 476.

This political and cultural background had a considerable effect on
the church, but the ecclesiastical factors were still more influential. The
East was undeniably the older part of the church, and they were always
conscious of having been the source from which the West had received
Christianity. The state of learning in the East was, moreover, far
superior to that which the West enjoyed. In fact, though, it was not the
straightforward cultural superiority which tended to divide the two
parts of the church, but the differences in their attitudes to theology.

The Greek temperament and intellectual attitude shaped the Eastern
theology on a speculative pattern. They were intensely interested in the
theoretical as opposed to the practical and the 'other-worldly' as opposed
to the mundane. For the Greeks the visible institutions of religion were
of value principally in so far as they were images of the spiritual
realities. The predominating influence in their thought was Platonism
and its preoccupation with the invisible world rather than the human

world of shadows.[1] The Latins, on the other hand, were in a sense empiricists taking full cognizance of the earthly aspects of religion and having little taste for metaphysical speculation. This difference of approach is to be seen from the very first in their ecclesiology. The whole of the letter of Pope Clement to the Corinthians bears the imprint of the Roman concept of the rule of law, and the excellence of order and authority. It is conceived of, not merely as an administrative expedient, but as something commanding respect in its own right. A few years later the letters of Ignatius of Antioch reveal the Oriental attitude. He extols the ecclesiastical hierarchy, it is true, but principally because it is the incarnation of divine authority and the image oft the heavenly world. In the letter to the Trallians he describes the hierarchy thus: 'Let all respect the deacons as representing Jesus Christ, the bishop as a type of the Father, and the presbyters as God's high council and as the Apostolic college' (3:1).[2] A century later two contemporary writers can be cited showing a still greater divergence of attitude. For Tertullian the church is almost identified with the episcopal hierarchy,[3] but Clement of Alexandria viewed the hierarchy primarily as the representation of Heaven: 'According to my opinion the grades here in the church of bishops, priests and deacons are the imitations of the angelic glory . . . .'[4] In the third and fourth centuries the Greeks displayed little sense of legal correctness, and bishops of undeniable sanctity such as St. John Chrysostom would become involved in extra-territorial activities whose legal rectitude was, to say the least, questionable. Most serious of all was the fact that the Greeks did not develop an adequate theology of the institutional church. Legal and administrative business was little to their taste, and in practice it was attended to by the Christian emperors, who began to assume a quasi-sacerdotal role in the church.

It is probable that no other single factor did more harm to papal authority than this intrusion of civil government into church affairs. That it should have occurred is symptomatic of the root cause, namely an inadequate consciousness of the nature of the church's hierarchical government. When it did occur it proved expedient both for the emperors who wished to control everything in the realm, and for the

---

[1]Congar, M. J., *Divided Christendom*, London, 1939, p. 200 ff., being the translation by M. A. Bousfield of *Chrétiens Désunis*.

[2]The difference between the ecclesiology of Clement and Ignatius is discussed by Batiffol, *Église Naissante*, pp. 158–61.

[3]cf. *De Præscriptione Hæreticorum*, ch. 32, M.P.L., Vol. 2, cols. 44, 45.

[4]*Stromata*, 6, 13, 107, ed. Stählin, in G.C.S., Clement of Alexandria, Vol. 2, p. 486.

church's malcontents who would play off emperor against pope or synod for their own ends. This weakness of the Greek ecclesiology, manifested principally in the emperors' tendency to assume supreme authority in the church, was the underlying cause of that opposition to the papacy which occurred not infrequently in the East. Ultimately it led to the schism.

The same basic attitudes were responsible for another development in the East (which tended to weaken the papal authority in an analogous way), namely the growth of the Oriental patriarchates. Not only does it reveal their excessive dependence on the state, but their adverse effect on ecclesiastical unity can be seen even within the Eastern church.

The traditional grouping of the churches was based on the liaison between the mission churches and the mother church. This situation was always adhered to in the West, but in the East it gave way to a conformity with the civil pattern. When Diocletian reorganized the imperial provinces and grouped them together in the larger unit, the 'diocese', the ecclesiastical arrangement soon followed suit. In 325 the council of Nicea ratified the arrangement, but did not create it. The legislation of the council on this matter was comparativly slight, arranging that local councils should be on a provincial basis; but the principle of alignment with the state was already adopted.[1]

A further advance in the same direction was made at the First Council of Constantinople in 381. The principal task of this council was to repair the chaos which Arianism had left in the East. In the administrative sphere the ecclesiastical provinces were grouped according to the civil diocese in which they were situated. Thus the East imitated completely the imperial pattern without pausing to consider whether it would be suitable for the church. As a result, the Eastern church had five administrative regions corresponding to the five civil dioceses of Thrace, Asia, Pontus, the Orient, and Egypt. The patriarchs had not yet emerged in these regions,[2] but all the causes for their subsequent appearance had been prepared. Just as the metropolitan had come to resemble the civil governor of the province, the bishop of the diocesan capital would soon imitate the imperial *vicarius*.[3] In other words, the importance of the bishopric was becoming dependent on the civil

[1] Canons 4 and 5, Hefele-Leclerq, *Histoire des Conciles*, Paris, 1907, Vol. I, pp. 539, 584.
[2] Batiffol, *Siège Apostolique*, p. 131.
[3] Palanque, J. R., in Vol. III of *Histoire de L'Église*, ed. Fliche et Martin, p. 440.

status of the city rather than the Apostolic foundation of the church.

The final preparation for the fully-developed patriarchs was made at the Council of Chalcedon in 451. The redistribution of the provinces shows more regard for the ecclesiastical as opposed to the civil pattern, but the senior bishops concerned are given greater power. The provinces of Thrace, Asia, and Pontus were grouped in one region, and most significantly, put under the presidency of the Bishop of Constantinople. In a similar way the Bishop of Jerusalem obtained sway over the region of Palestine, and the Bishops of Alexandria and Antioch already possessed considerable personal authority in their respective regions. In the time of Justinian little more had to be done except to confer on these bishops the name of patriarch.

These differences between Eastern and Western ecclesiastical development had such an important bearing on the papacy that the history of Rome's authority cannot adequately be studied without taking full cognizance of them. The first set of influences which resulted in the three zones of papal power contained nothing which was prejudicial to the authority of the Pope. However, the other divergences between the East and West were of a different character. In times of tranquillity they caused a strain between the two halves of the church, but when heresy and other problems arose their influence was undeniably disruptive.

Having thus indicated something of the background, it is now time to resume the examination of the popes' activities from the end of the second century.

The papacy from St. Victor to St. Leo the Great does not lend itself to a straightforward study. The complexities are not overwhelming, but clarity demands that some kind of arrangement of matter be attempted. Perhaps the most convenient division is that of the three zones, since they are differentiated according to the local variations of papal authority. The simplest of these is the region of metropolitan Italy, and the relevant incidents in its history can be studied quite briefly. The Western zone is a little more developed, and last of all, the Eastern zone will demand the most thorough examination, since the events there are the most important of all.

One of the clearest indications of the peculiar status of the first zone of papal power is furnished by the council of Nicea. The sixth canon ratifies the hegemony of Alexandria and Rome in their respective localities. 'Let the ancient customs in Egypt, Libya and the Pentapolis prevail in such wise that the Bishop of Alexandria has authority over

them all, since this is also customary for the bishop in Rome.'[1] It is
generally agreed now that this is not a reference to the power which
Rome exercised over the West, but over Italy.[2] Nicea did not create this
situation, but accepted it as it was. At that time the region in question
comprised the whole of Italy and the adjacent islands; in fact, the whole
of Diocletian's diocese of Italy. These boundaries still appear to have
been the same in the year 343. In that year the council of Sardica met
and the synodal letter which it sent to Pope Julius contained the request
that he would arrange for the decisions of the council to be communicated to the Bishops of Sicily, Sardinia, and Italy.[3] It is reasonable to
deduce that the council knew of no administrative division of the
provinces of Italy, which indicates that Rome's region of peculiar dependence was still the whole of Italy.

The state of government there is indicated by a variety of events the
first of which is the deposition of the antipope Novatian in 251.
He was condemned in a council held at Rome, but what is unusual
is the fact that the bishops who attended this council came from all the
provinces of Italy. Still more remarkable is the action of Pope Cornelius
in deposing the three bishops who had consecrated Novatian and
appointing successors for them by virtue of his own authority.[4] Elsewhere this would have been done by a provincial council. Another
peculiarity of this zone was the way in which the Pope ordained the
bishops of the Italian provinces. It was the custom at this time for the
candidate to be elected locally and to receive episcopal consecration
from the bishops of the province. However, in Italy the Bishop of Rome
performed the consecration. This practice is indicated in the short biographies of the popes which are to be found in the *Liber Pontificalis*, and
thence in the Roman Breviary. Of the Pope St. Felix I it is said that 'he
held two ordinations in which he created nine priests, five deacons and
five bishops for various places'. The priests and deacons would have
been for the church of Rome, but the bishops were for the other regions
of Italy. The same kind of thing is recorded for the other popes, and it
is another indication of the peculiarly close subjection of the Italian
region to the Bishop of Rome.

The extent of this region was curtailed in the middle of the fourth
century, and when St. Ambrose was elected Bishop of Milan there was

[1]Text in Hefele-Leclerq, op. cit., I, p. 552.
[2]Batiffol, *Cathedra Petri*, p. 42.
[3]Hilary, *Hist. Fragmenta*, B II, 2 (i) in C.S.E.L., Vol. 65, p. 130.
[4]Eusebius, H. E., VI, 43, and Batiffol, *La Paix Constantinienne*, p. 132.

no consultation with Rome. The actual separation must have occurred at an earlier date, and the treatise of St. Athanasius, *Apologia pro Fuga sua*, is perhaps an indication that the north of Italy had been cut off by 357 (the date of its composition), since he addresses the Bishops of northern Italy separately. In seeking for a definite date for this dismemberment between 357 and 343 (the latest witness of the undivided region) one is inclined to favour the year 355. In 293 Milan became one of the imperial capitals and in the year 355 the Emperor Constantius II appointed the Arian Auxentius to be its bishop. It would seem most likely that on this occasion Rome gave up the direct supervision of the provinces of northern Italy (*Italia Annonaria*), whose capital was Milan.[1] Thenceforward Rome retained under its special supervision the provinces of the *regiones suburbicariae*, namely Tuscia and Umbria, Campania, Lucania and Brutium, Apulia and Calabria, Samnium, Picenum, Valeria, Sicilia, Sardinia, Corsica. There is no evidence that this reduction of the former region was resented in Rome, and as the papal authority as such was unlikely to suffer, the peaceful acquiescence is not to be wondered at.

In the time of Pope Siricius two relevant letters have survived dealing with the papal supervision of episcopal consecrations in Italy. The first of these, entitled *Cum in unum*, of January 6th, 386,[2] deals with a variety of matters relevant to ordinations. In particular the letter forbids anyone to perform an episcopal consecration without the intervention of the Apostolic See. The second of these letters is addressed to the 'orthodox believers in all the provinces',[3] which means actually the provinces of the *regiones suburbicariae*. The content of the letter is much the same as the previous one. The Pope insists on the qualities which must be exhibited by a candidate for the episcopate, and he urges the local bishops not to recommend those whose capabilities are judged on the record of their political achievements. In the course of this letter he makes it quite clear that he has the power to withhold consecration from a man whom he considers to be unworthy, despite the local recommendation.

A further practice which obtained only at Rome and Alexandria was the custom of restricting provincial councils. Each year the bishops of Italy used to come to Rome for the synod which was held on the anniversary of the Pope's accession. There is clear evidence of this practice

[1] Batiffol, *Siège Apostolique*, p. 154.
[2] Jaffé, n. 258.
[3] Jaffé, n. 263.

in the pontificate of Anastasius I (399–401), thanks to a letter of St. Paulinus of Nola.[1] Half a century later the sermons of St. Leo for his anniversary indicate that the occasion was celebrated in the presence not only of the clergy and laity of Rome, but also before a considerable number of bishops. Elsewhere in the church it was customary for each province to hold its own synod under the presidency of the metropolitan. In Italy, however, there is no evidence of synods other than those at Rome, until the tenth or twelfth century.[2]

The close supervision which Rome exercised over these churches of the *regiones suburbicariae* can also be judged by the matters on which the popes were consulted. The letter of Pope Innocent I to Decentius, Bishop of Gubbio,[3] contains directions on matters such as liturgy and ecclesiastical discipline. The Pope points out that it is correct for Decentius to seek his advice, since there must be a faithful observance of the Roman customs in the churches which Rome had founded. In legal proceedings, too, the Pope exercised, in this zone, the type of immediate supervision which elsewhere would have been the responsibility of a metropolitan. Several documents have been preserved recording disciplinary measures which were enforced by the Pope in seemingly insignificant cases. The letter *Multa in provincia* of Pope Innocent I[4] gives instructions to the bishops of Apulia for the degradation of a certain Modestus. Not only was this man a cleric, but he had been recommended for the episcopate. Since he had been guilty of certain crimes, Innocent commanded his punishment. The way in which the Pope appointed the judges and gave them instructions is indicative of the fact that they had no competence to deal with the matter on their own authority.

One can summarize the position of the Pope in this region by saying that 'the suburbican provinces possessed no provincial autonomy: they had neither councils nor metropolitans: the Bishop of Rome took the place of both council and metropolitan. On the death of its bishop each church elected the successor, but the candidate had to be approved and consecrated at Rome. The bishops of the suburbican region were obliged to come to Rome, at least once a year for the Pope's anniversary. They had to consult the Pope for the clarification of their doubts and the settling of their disputes. Disciplinary matters, too, had to be re-

---

[1] Paulinus, Letter XX, 2. ed. Hartel C.S.E.L., Vol. 29, p. 145.
[2] Batiffol, *Cathedra Petri*, p. 46.
[3] Jaffé, n. 311.
[4] Jaffé, n. 316.

ported to the Pope, and he delegated to the bishops of the province the mandate to proceed with the case if he did not judge the matter himself in council at Rome. For he was the judge of his suffragan bishops, and he deposed them when necessary: he governed them in a spirit of paternalism, without tyranny, but very firmly. He exercised over them an authority based on reasons which would justify his rule over a wider area than the suburbican region, since the principle in question is that his see is that of the Apostle Peter, "by whom, in Christ, there commenced the apostolate and the episcopate". On that account the Bishop of Rome, head and summit of the episcopate (*caput et apex episcopatus*), has the responsibility for all the churches (*omnium ecclesiarum curam*).'[1]

[1]Batiffol, *Siège Apostolique*, pp. 169–70.

7

PAPAL POWER IN THE WESTERN ZONE

IN his polemical treatise *Against Vigilantius* St. Jerome classifies the churches of the world thus: 'What will the churches of the East do? And those of Egypt? And those of the Apostolic See?'[1] In other words, the churches of the West were conceived of as being specially related to the see of Rome. The phrase from St. Jerome does not prove the existence of the Western zone of papal power, but it is an interesting contemporary observation of the situation. A detailed examination of region shows that such a division of East and West is amply warranted. The church of Rome was conscious of being the mother church of the West, but the area of this mission was so vast that the normal ties between an older church and the dependents could not persist.[2] Nevertheless this relationship of ultimate dependence, coupled with Rome's prestige as the only Apostolic church in the West, is the most satisfactory explanation of the frequent interventions of the popes in the affairs of the Western church. Compared with the East the appeals to Rome as a supreme court come with more frequency and less *éclat*. The subjects in dispute are seen to be of less importance. The straightforward consultations, too, relate to matters of secondary importance which the East would have dealt with locally. Thus in a variety of ways the Pope is seen to use an authority in the West which is often less than papal. His supreme authority as head of the universal church is invoked proportionately less frequently in the affairs of the Western church than in those of the East.

The boundaries of this zone were determined by circumstances which obtained long before the three regions began to show distinctive relationships with Rome. Originally it consisted of all the Western provinces of the empire excluding Italy. In the middle of the fourth century the north of Italy (*Italia Annonaria*) was assimilated when it ceased to form part of the Italian zone. The situation in Illyricum was unique. At the end of the third century Diocletian divided the empire into the Eastern and Western parts, and the whole of the Western

[1] Jerome, *Adversus Vigilantius*, ch. II, M.P.L., Vol. 23, col. 341.
[2] Batiffol, *Cathedra Petri*, p. 47.

empire tended to be identified with the Western zone of papal power, although the Balkans had not been evangelized from Rome. In 379 Gratian cut off the two civil dioceses of Dacia and Macedonia and transferred them to the Eastern Emperor Theodosius. In order to prevent their coming under the ecclesiastical influence of Constantinople, Pope Damasus and his successors gave these two dioceses a juridical status which was unique in the early church. The details of this situation will be examined further on, but for the present it is sufficient to observe that the action of Pope Damasus retained these regions in the sphere of influence of the Western zone.

From the very nature of the case it is not possible to isolate a particular year as revealing the emergence of the three zones. Nevertheless in the West there are numerous indications that the distinctive pattern had been achieved by the middle of the third century. Evidence for this is provided by the events of St. Cyprian's episcopate in Africa, and the contemporary incidents in Spain and Gaul which are known thanks to his letters. It is necessary, then, to examine the history of the Western zone, from the time of St. Cyprian until the period of St. Leo, in order to see whether there is evidence that the church accepted the Bishop of Rome as a superior. Furthermore some attention must be devoted to studying the nature of such an authority, should it exist, to see whether it was regarded as an innovation or as the legitimate inheritance of power from St. Peter.

St. Cyprian has made such a profound impression on the church by the force of his personality and sanctity that it is hard to realize that he was a Christian for only ten years. He was born at the beginning of the third century, probably at Carthage, in a wealthy and influential pagan family. He acquired great fame as a rhetorician and became a Christian shortly before the year 249. His conversion was prompted by the depravity of pagan life, and once converted he did not hesitate to fulfil the gospel injunction to be perfect. It speaks well for the balance of his character that in spite of his zeal he never adopted the rigorism which had been the downfall of the other great African, Tertullian. Soon after his baptism he was ordained priest, and without any notable delay he was elected to succeed Donatus as Bishop of Carthage, probably in the first months of 249. This rapid advancement had the disadvantage that his theological formation was sadly incomplete. According to St. Jerome,[1] he would read something from Tertullian every day. He was

[1]Jerome, *De Viribus Illustris*, 53.

evidently well versed in the Scriptures, but of the tradition of the church he seems to have been surprisingly ignorant. Newman, in fact, wrote of him: 'St. Cyprian does not treat of theology at all.'[1] Within a year of his consecration as bishop the persecution of Decius broke upon the church. During the persecution Cyprian was in hiding, not from cowardice, as his subsequent martyrdom shows, but because of the danger to the church if all her leaders were put to death. Fabian, Bishop of Rome, had just been killed, and the intensity of persecution was such that it was more than a year before a successor could be elected. Cyprian was able to return to Carthage in the spring of 251, and by that time two schisms had occurred—in Carthage under the leadership of Felicissimus and in Rome at the instigation of Novatian. Of the two, Novatian's was the more serious, not merely because it was at the centre of Christendom, but because of its extent; it soon spread beyond the church of Rome. It was principally the schism of Novatian that prompted the famous *De Unitate*, about which much has been said already, and it is not surprising that at this time Cyprian's relations with Pope Cornelius were very cordial. Later on this harmony with the Roman See was strained by the controversy as to the validity of heretical baptism. The dispute never ran its full course, since St. Cyprian was martyred before its conclusion, on September 14th, 258, in the persecution of Valerian.

In endeavouring to understand St. Cyprian and the disputes in which he was involved it is important to bear in mind that there was an unresolved conflict in his mind between two incompatible series of principles. One series he derived almost unconsciously from the habitual practice of the church, and the other he thought out for himself. The shortcomings of the latter were in a large measure due to his inadequate theological formation, and they resulted in several serious errors which will be discussed later.

The first of the events in Cyprian's career which are relevant to the position of Rome is the problem of the lapsed, or apostates, in the persecution of Decius. This persecution had several unusual features. It was preceded by a long period of calm during which the standards of the Christians had become lax, and then, for the first time, the penal laws affected all the church, even the rank and file. The number of those who apostatized was so great that their quest for readmission once the persecution was over presented a major problem to the church. In Africa, at the council of 251, Cyprian decided to admit the apostates to

[1] *Development of Christian Doctrine*, p. 17.

the ranks of the penitents with a view to their reconciliation after a time which varied according to the gravity of their fault. The same practice was adopted in Rome, and what is of more interest, throughout the whole church. The adoption of the Roman practice had the additional advantage that it curtailed, to a certain extent, the schism of Novatian, who had taken up a position of extreme rigorism with regard to the reconciliation of the apostates. A letter of Dionysius of Alexandria to Pope Stephen[1] enables one to infer how this uniformity came about. 'Now I wish you to understand, my brother, that all the churches throughout the east, and further, that were formerly divided, have been united again. All the bishops, also, are everywhere in harmony, rejoicing exceedingly at the peace which has been established beyond all expectation. These are, Demetrianus of Antioch, Theoctistus of Caesarea, Mazabanes of Aelia [i.e. Jerusalem] after the death of Alexander, Marinus of Tyre, Heliodorus of Laodicea after the decease of Thelymidres, Helenus of Tarsus, and all the churches of Cilicia, Firmilianus and all Cappadocia.' A familiar pattern is here seen in operation. After the paschal controversy the whole church adopted the Roman usage, under circumstances which are shrouded in obscurity. The same thing will happen after the dispute over the validity of heretical baptism. In the present instance, too, unanimity has been achieved. It is unlikely that this unification would have been realized had there been no centralizing cause influencing all the churches concerned. The letter quoted above contains a valuable indication of how this was achieved. 'All the provinces of Syria and Arabia, which at different times you supplied with necessaries, and to whom you have now written . . .' In other words, Rome was in communication with the churches of the East. This is far from being an apodictic proof that Rome had secured the unanimity of penitential discipline contrary to the Novatian practice, but it is a strong indication that such was the case.[2]

An illustration of Cyprian's attitude to the Pope in this period of his career is furnished by the Letter 59 which he wrote to Cornelius. Apparently Cyprian had given episcopal consecration to Fortunatus without first consulting Rome, and in writing to explain his conduct it is evident that he recognizes Rome's right to be notified on any matter of major importance: 'I did not write to you about it at once, dearest brother, for it was not a matter of enough importance or gravity to be

[1]Quoted in Eusebius, H. E., VII, 5, 1-2.
[2]cf. Batiffol, *Cathedra Petri*, p. 62.

reported to you in great haste. . . . Since I supposed that you were
aware of these facts and believed that you would certainly be guided by
your memory and sense of discipline, I did not consider it necessary to
notify you immediately and hurriedly of the heretics' antics. . . . And
I did not write to you of their performance because we despise all these
doings and I was soon to send you the names of the bishops who govern
the brethren soundly and correctly in the Catholic Church. It was the
judgement of us all in this region that I should send these names to
you.'[1] The last sentence indicates the source from which Cyprian has
learnt this manner of dealing with Rome. He is unconsciously in touch
with the tradition of the church and has not yet allowed his own theories
to guide his activity.

The year 254 reveals two incidents which are an interesting commentary on the conduct of church affairs. The surviving evidence is
fragmentary; in fact, they are recorded only in the letters of Cyprian,
but the essentials of the situations can be reconstructed from the indications which are furnished by the letters in question.

The first of these incidents concerns the Spanish bishops Basilides
and Martial. They had been deposed from their sees of Leon and Merida
by provincial synods, and it appears that they had appealed to Rome for
reinstatement.[2] Thereupon Sabinus and Felix, who had replaced them,
took alarm and wrote to Africa for 'consolation and aid'. The council of
Carthage held in 254 considered the matter and, as was always the case
in these African councils, merely voiced the opinion of Cyprian. In his
reply[3] Cyprian champions the cause of Sabinus and Felix, since he
considers that the two previous bishops had been guilty of serious
crimes. He alludes to the customary practice of admitting repentant
clergy to the ranks of the penitents, but never again to the functions of
the priesthood. In addition he mentions that the laity have the right to
secede from a bishop if he is a sinner, and should not take part in his
offering of the Mass, since it is now sacrilegious.[4] This is an unusual and
novel theory which finds no counterpart in the authentic tradition of the
church. It is one of the confused propositions of Cyprian's own specu-

[1]Letter 59:9, C.S.E.L., Vol. 3 (ii), pp. 676, 677.
[2]Batiffol considered that they were, in fact, reinstated (op. cit., p. 48, *L'Église
Naissante*, p. 451). Others are not so sure. cf. J. Lebreton in Fliche et Martin,
Histoire de L'Église, Vol. II, p. 198. What is of prime importance is the fact of the
appeal, the principle of which does not appear to have offended Cyprian or the
Spanish episcopate.
[3]Cyprian Letter 77.
[4]Letter 77:3.

lations. How the affair ended is impossible to say, but the details which have been recorded are not without interest for the history of the papacy. There is the fact of the appeal against the local sentence, and most probably a new judgement by the Pope.[1] The character of the communication to Africa is harder to determine. It does not appear to have been a juridical appeal as if the council of Carthage could reverse the sentence either of Spain or Rome. Rather it seems to have been a request that Carthage would support the Spanish decision and recognize the two bishops Sabinus and Felix.[2]

In the same year or possibly at the beginning of 255 a similar incident involved Marcian, the Bishop of Arles. Following the practice of Novatian rather than the Catholic bishops, he had been refusing to give his subjects the benefit of the milder penitential discipline. The bishops of Lyons and several other cities in the same province wrote to Rome and also to Carthage about the matter. In view of the principles that he enunciated in the case of the Spanish bishops, two courses were open to Cyprian. He could perhaps have advised the people of Arles to separate themselves from their bishop or advise the bishops of the province to attend to the matter themselves.[3] Instead he wrote to Rome, and in the clearest terms he urged Pope Stephen to settle the affair. 'Send letters to the province and to the laity of the church of Arles, in virtue of which, Marcian now set aside, another may be set in his place. Tell us clearly who replaces Marcian at Arles so that we may know to whom we should recommend our brethren and direct our letters.'[4]

The text does not say precisely who shall excommunicate Marcian, but from the circumstances it is clear that it must be Rome. In fact, this letter shows that Cyprian recognized Rome's power over Arles as being superior to that of the bishops of Gaul.[5] Here it is apparent that Cyprian is echoing the tradition of the church, namely in acquiescing in the right of appeal to Rome, and Rome's competence to excommunicate another bishop and decide who is the legitimate holder of the see.

Thus far Cyprian is, in the main, orthodox. His activities so far have been guided by the general practice of the church and they are in conformity with the usual customs. However, strange ideas are already to be seen in his thought, which are incompatible with his orthodox views.

[1]Batiffol, *Cathedra Petri*, p. 49.
[2]Batiffol, *Église Naissante*, p. 451.
[3]Batiffol, op. cit., 455.
[4]Cyprian, Letter 78:2 and 3.
[5]Admitted by Harnack and Sohm: quoted by Batiffol, op. cit., p. 456, n. 2.

Already there are indications that a conflict of principles is possible not
only within Cyprian's world of ideas, but in the affairs of the universal
church. The subsequent crisis of the baptismal controversy provided all
that was necessary to precipitate the latent conflicts in his ideas.

The dispute about the validity of heretical baptism which took place
during the pontificate of St. Stephen revealed a considerable divergence
of attitude in the church. Cyprian himself denied the validity of baptism
administered by a heretic as early as the period of his writing *De Unitate*.
This appears to have been the general sentiment in Africa and it was
shared by the church in Cappadocia. Syria and Phrygia also disputed
the validity of such baptism, but this seems to have been provoked by
the Montanists who altered the formula of baptism and conferred it
uniquely in the name of the Holy Spirit.[1] Rome, Egypt, and Palestine
upheld the validity of the sacrament regardless of the minister's allegiance. At this early date the details of sacramental theology had not
been thought out. There was no adequate distinction between schismatics and heretics whose intention, by latent principles, might invalidate the efficacy of a sacrament, nor did they have a full realization of
the comparative autonomy of the sacraments. The differences came to a
head after the Carthaginian councils of 255 and 256, in which the
African view was publicly declared. Pope Stephen asked for an explanation of the matter, thus provoking the dispute which resulted in
Cyprian's defending and acting upon his theory of the equality of all
bishops. Stephen's attitude is well known from his famous injunction
to stand by the tradition of the church. Cyprian then began to look
around for allies and found an able supporter in Firmilian, Bishop of
Caesarea in Cappadocia. The course of the dispute is not recorded in
detail, but one or two significant details have been preserved. Cyprian
felt justified in holding his opinion although Stephen decided otherwise.
Thereupon the Pope appears to have threatened to excommunicate the
dissidents. A letter from Firmilian to Cyprian provides an interesting
commentary on this excommunication, more by what it implies than
by what it says. 'What a terrible sin you will have laid upon yourself
[i.e. Stephen] when you have cut yourself off from so many of the flock.
Do not deceive yourself. You are cutting yourself off (and becoming a
schismatic), since the real schismatic is one who cuts himself off from
the communion and unity of the church. You think that you have power
to excommunicate the whole world: in fact, you will have cut off none

[1]Lebreton, op. cit., Vol. II, p. 199.

but yourself.'[1] Firmilian's protest amounts almost to the classical conditions for the argument from silence. Despite his anger there is no formal denial of Stephen's competence to excommunicate other bishops. Everything would seem to provoke such a denial if it had been possible. Instead he can say no more than that when Stephen has excommunicated everyone he will have severed himself from the whole of the church. By contrast there is no suggestion that Cyprian or Firmilian attempted to excommunicate Stephen. The persecution of Valerian put an end to this stage of the dispute, since both Stephen and Cyprian were martyred. At a later date the whole church, characteristically, followed the Roman tradition.

In order to assess the value of Cyprian's theory of the episcopate certain of his other theological positions should be borne in mind. Corresponding to his attitude to heretical baptism, he maintained that there was no true martyrdom outside the church,[2] nor indeed was salvation available except to the members of the visible church.[3] Somewhat analogous to these propositions is the notion that the laity should secede from their bishop if he is a sinner.[4] Connected with his views on the invalidity of heretical baptism were the two principles that the matter should be settled by reason rather than tradition,[5] and that bishops were entitled to adopt divergent attitudes as to the value of the heretic's sacrament.[6] The root cause of these difficulties was the fact that Cyprian was the first theologian to study the problem of schism as distinct from heresy,[7] and it must be admitted that his theological formation was unequal to the task. The recognition of these shortcomings in his general theology warrants an antecedent reserve in examining his ecclesiology.

The basic idea of Cyprian's scheme of church government was the equality of all bishops. This fact is now freely admitted by the majority of Catholic authors.[8] The counterpart of this equality was the ideal that the church would thence be ruled by their unanimous consent, as he

---

[1] Firmilian, among the letters of Cyprian, No. 75:2.
[2] *De Unitate*, ch. 18.
[3] *De Unitate*, ch. 19, and Letter 74:8.
[4] Letter 67:3.
[5] Letter 71:3.
[6] Letter 72:3.
[7] cf. art. of G. Klein, 'Die Hermeneutische Struktur des Kirchengedankens bei Cyprien', *Zeitschrift für Kirchengeschichte*, 1957, pp. 48–68.
[8] Among more recent authorities are to be included Batiffol, *Cathedra Petri*, p. 11; Bardy, *La Théologie de l'Église de S. Irénée au concile de Nicée*, pp. 195–6. Quasten, op. cit., II, pp. 376, 377; Bévenot, op. cit., p. 7.

states in the fourth chapter of *De Unitate*. How such unanimity was to be preserved he did not say, and as Chapman pointed out,[1] this notion could only have occurred to him as a result of his lack of experience of ecclesiastical affairs. The principle of unanimity is closely linked with Cyprian's insistence on the role of councils in the government of the church. Although it does not seem to have occurred to Cyprian, at least at the beginning of his career, the authority of a council is incompatible with the equality of bishops which he championed, and which he expressed so clearly at the council of Carthage in 256. 'None of us poses as the bishop of bishops; none tyrannizes his colleagues to force their assent, since every bishop is free to exercise his power as he thinks best; he can neither judge, nor be judged by, another bishop. We must all wait upon the judgement of Our Lord Jesus Christ, to whom alone it belongs to rule over us in the government of the church and to judge our conduct.'[2] In practice unanimity was ensured in the African councils by the force of Cyprian's own personality. If this unity were not forthcoming, Cyprian's theory had no remedy. Admittedly he approved of the excommunication of bishops, as in the case of Marcian of Arles, but this procedure was not consistent with his principles of the equality and autonomy of bishops. Basically he had no remedy for the disagreement of bishops, and it was a rude shock to him to realize that such a thing could happen. The dispute over the validity of heretical baptism exposed the inadequacy of Cyprian's theory; and in that time of crisis his ecclesiology broke down completely having no remedy to offer.

The gravity of the baptismal controversy has tended to focus undue attention on Cyprian's theory. In reality it was never widely held; Cyprian himself was the only early ecclesiastic who took it seriously.[3] It finds no echo in the authentic tradition of the church, and Batiffol did not hesitate to describe the idea of the autonomous bishop as a complete chimera.[4]

In the latter part of the third century the church had to endure two more persecutions after that of Valerian before the granting of religious freedom. The final persecution, that of Diocletian, was accompanied by an intensive search for the Christian records and documents. The wholesale destruction of Christian writings at this time explains the disparity

[1] *Studies in the Early Papacy*, p. 44.
[2] *Sententia*, 87, ed. Hartel in C.S.E.L., 3, (i), p. 436. Also consistently in his letters: cf. 30:1, 55:21, 59:14, 69:17, 72:3, 73:26.
[3] Chapman, op. cit., pp. 44, 45.
[4] Battiffol, *Cathedra Petri*, p. 11.

between the amount of information available about the church in the periods before and after Diocletian.

The religious freedom which was acquired under Constantine contained unsuspected dangers for the church, since it was closely connected with the conversion of the Emperor himself. The resultant circumstances of a Christian emperor and religious freedom constituted a situation of which the church had no previous experience. It is not to be wondered at that the church required a considerable time to adjust itself to the new conditions. In the West more than half a century was to elapse before a satisfactory settlement of the respective positions of the church and the Christian government was effected. In the East the church became the victim of *caesaropapism* before any such solution was arrived at.

The ecclesiastical policy of Constantine, like his conversion, cannot be summarized by any simple formula. It was a compound of several tendencies whose interrelation was not worked out clearly, since he too was experimenting with the unprecedented situation of the state toleration of Christianity. It would appear that he was sincere in his desire to promote the welfare of the church, but it was almost inseparable from his care for the welfare of the state.[1] The divisions caused by heresy were abhorrent to him, but one may well ask whether this care was prompted by doctrinal orthodoxy or the desire to promote political stability. From the very outset of his interest in ecclesiastical affairs the liberty of the church suffered. Frequently he took the initiative in religious matters, convoked councils himself, and in some cases actually presided over their deliberations. As might be expected the prestige of the papacy suffered. Constantine virtually ignored the popes, and although Melchiades handled the situation competently, his successor, Silvester, appears to have been unequal to the task. The long pontificate of the latter, which lasted more than twenty years, was devoid of constructive policy.

In the year 314, when Constantine was master of Italy and the western part of the empire, he summoned a council to meet at Arles. All the bishops of his provinces were notified, and when the council assembled it comprised representatives of forty-six episcopal sees from Italy, Spain, Gaul, and Britain. Pope Silvester was represented by two

[1]Palanque, J. R., in Vol. III of *Histoire de l'Église*, ed. Fliche & Martin, pp. 64, 65. His consciousness of possessing a divine vocation for guiding the church has been stressed by N. H. Baynes, *Constantine the Great and the Christian Church*, London, 1929, p. 29.

priests and two deacons. The business of the council concerned a variety of matters, such as Donatism, heretical baptism, and the arrangements for the publication of the date of Easter. The synodal letter was addressed to the Pope and it makes the request that he should notify the provinces of the West of the enactments of the council. In making this request an unusual phrase was employed: *Placuit etiam antea scribi ad te, qui majores dioceses tenes, et per te potissimum omnibus insinuari.*[1] Batiffol has suggested[2] that *antea* is a mistake for *omnia*, in which case the phrase would read: 'It pleased (the council) to write to you about all that was done, and through you especially the others may be informed, as you are in touch with the greater diocese.' The latter phrase 'in touch with the greater diocese' (*qui majores dioceses tenes*) has caused a fair amount of discussion on account of its obscurity. No altogether satisfactory explanation has been advanced, to elucidate the words. It was customary for the Pope to write to the churches of the West each year to inform them of the date of Easter, and on that account it would appear that the word diocese is used in its ecclesiastical sense and that the phrase is an allusion to the Pope's habit of writing to the churches of the West to ensure unity and discipline.[3] The deference which the council showed to the Pope is an indication of his superiority, though there is no explicit reference to anything more than a kind of patriarchal authority.

The principal event in the church's life during the fourth century was the rise and decline of Arianism. Indirectly the authority of the Bishop of Rome was involved to no small extent, but the great battleground both of Arianism and the Papal authority was in the East. The only situation which directly concerned the West was the council of Sardica, but it will be convenient to study the whole of the Arian crisis and its repercussions on the papacy in connexion with the affairs of the Eastern church.

In the time of Popes Liberius and Damasus orthodoxy returned to the Western church, and with it the re-establishment of normal ecclesiastical life. From this period important documents have survived which reveal this background of ecclesiastical reorganization. In the year 374 or thereabouts Pope Damasus wrote the famous letter *Ad Gallos Episcopos* (To the bishops of Gaul).[4] It is the reply to a series of inquiries of the bishops asking for guidance as to the law on a variety of matters

[1] Text in Mansi, II, col. 469.
[2] Batiffol, *La Paix Constantinienne*, p. 288.
[3] Batiffol, *Cathedra Petri*, p. 51.
[4] Text in M.P.L., Vol. 13, cols. 1181-1194.

of ecclesiastical discipline. The Pope expresses his pleasure that they should have had recourse to the 'Apostolic See' in such a matter, and then answers their queries in sixteen articles. These rulings concern matters such as the celibacy of priests and consecrated virgins, the need for a bishop to be consecrated by three other bishops, and with the consent of his metropolitan, and the prohibition against the subsequent advancement of a cleric who had ever been deposed.

The letter reveals the authority of the Pope by a variety of subtle indications. It appears from the text that the system of metropolitans with their suffragens was well established, but in spite of that Rome had to be consulted. Since the document is chiefly concerned with the clerics, it may have been felt that a higher authority was needed than that which the metropolitans possessed. It is to be noted, moreover, that the initiative came from the bishops of Gaul. That is to say, the mode of procedure was not pressed by the popes but was at least a natural course for them to adopt, if not even traditional. It is true that Pope Damasus does not invoke his own authority. He bases his decisions on the council of Nicea, possibly too Sardica, and the customs of the church of Rome. In spite of this absence of his own particular authority the prestige of Rome is indicated by the fact that no other see received similar inquiries about the law of the church.[1]

One is naturally led to inquire whether this was the first time that a pope gave laws to another part of the church. Certainly the letter *Ad Gallos Episcopos* is the earliest surviving record of such an enactment. However, it would be unwise to infer from that fact alone that there had been no other. The text itself indicates that it was by no means the first time that the Pope had dealt with such matters.[2]

During the same pontificate the Emperor Gratian promised considerable support to the Pope in the enforcement of ecclesiastical condemnations. Viewed in isolation it would appear that this was an innovation of major importance destined to revolutionize the position of the see of Rome. In reality, though, the principle of assistance by the secular arm had been known since the conversion of Constantine, and had been particularly prominent in the pontificate of Damasus.

The early days after the death of Liberius were unusually disturbed. Liberius died on September 24th, 366, and within a few days of his

---

[1]Batiffol, *Siège Apostolique*, p. 201.
[2]Section 5 of the letter: *Et jam quidem frequenter de his talibus sermo noster per plures manavit Ecclesias, maxime de sacerdotibus.*

burial two candidates were elected to succeed him. The minority part
led by seven priests and three deacons elected Ursinus and consecrate
him on the same day, while the majority of the Roman clergy electe
Damasus. For the next few weeks there was almost open warfar
between the two parties. Several battles took place, and when th
followers of Damasus captured the Liberian basilica 137 people wer
killed. It is not, therefore, to be wondered at that the prefect of the cit
intervened to restore order. Ursinus was banished and his followers wer
prevented from meeting in the city. The initiative in this series of inter
ventions was taken by the civil power and not by the Pope. Later in h
pontificate Damasus invoked the protection of the Emperor, and fe
much the same reasons. The situation in the city was far from tranqui
Many heretical groups flourished there and the party of the former ant
pope Felix was still a source of danger. In 371 Damasus was involved i
a civil lawsuit with the Jew Isaac, who accused him of murder. Th
charge was groundless, but the Pope had to be protected by the Em
peror. Valentinian's religious policy remained constant throughout a
these disturbances. He was unwilling to become involved in the affair
of the church, but he realized that he had the responsibility of preservin
public order. This was his sole motive in intervening,[1] and it show
a welcome improvement on the religious policy of Constantine, whic
held such potential dangers for the church.

This is the background against which one must consider the imperi
enactment alluded to above. The Roman synod of 378 addressed
letter to the emperor[2] (by then Gratian) requesting, among other thing
that if a bishop had been deposed by the Pope or the Roman syno
and still remained in his see, then he should be removed by the civ
authorities. Furthermore, it was asked that if a bishop was summone
to Rome for trial, and refused to come, he likewise should be compelle
to do so by the civil power. These two requests were received favourab
by the Emperor, and in the letter *Ordinariorum Sententias*[3] imperi
authority was promised to support the Roman decisions. In fact, t
Emperor offered to give more than had been asked. The council had
mind only Italy, but the decree envisaged the whole of the West.

Is it possible that this document was the origin of the juridic

---

[1]Duchesne, *Early History of the Church*, II, p. 365. Important rescripts of th
period are collected in the Collectio Avellana, Nos. 6, 7, 8, 9, 10, 11, 12, C.S.E.
Vol. 35, pp. 49–53.
[2]*Et hoc gloriae*, Mansi, III, cols. 624, 627.
[3]Collectio Avellana, No. 13, C.S.E.L., Vol. 35, pp. 54–58.

primacy of the Pope? Various non-catholic writers have thought so,[1] but in fact it is too facile a solution to account for the reality. In the first place it must be remembered that the principle of co-operation between the church and the state was well established, as can be seen from the other events of the pontificate of Damasus. Furthermore, it did not inaugurate a new type of papal policy. The prominence of the Roman See is evident before the date of the decree in question and it did not show any dramatic advance immediately afterwards. The right of appeal to the Pope was an established fact for which there is evidence since the time of Cornelius.[2] But more fundamental is Batiffol's criticism of the effectiveness of Gratian's decree.[3] If the decree were to have any marked effect on the status of the church of Rome, it would have required forceful implementation, yet it seems to have been ineffectual from the start. As early as 380 there is evidence that it was enforced neither by the Pope nor the Emperor. In effect the decree made no innovation in the conduct of church affairs. It merely re-echoed the principle, already understood, that the secular arm would give effect to the decisions of the church.[4]

During the pontificate of Damasus the life of the church was enhanced by one of the greatest ecclesiastics of all times. St. Ambrose, Bishop of Milan. Although his activity and writings had little direct bearing on the papacy, his indirect service of that institution was of the utmost importance. In contrast to the church of the East, the Latins possessed a well-developed notion of the theology of the church as an institution. St. Ambrose not only shared this outlook, but made a contribution of singular importance. He expounded in his writings, and put into practice a highly developed consciousness of the church's autonomy which extended to a measure of control over the civil government. Thus he contributed to the strength of the papal authority, by setting a barrier against the harmful procedure of appealing against the church authorities to the civil power. Freed from the danger of state interference, the church's own organs of government could reasonably be expected to function normally.

[1]Puller, op. cit., p. 151; Kidd, B. J., *History of the Church*, III, pp. 319, 358–9; and *Roman Primacy*, p. 60.
[2]Burn Murdoch, op. cit., p. 180, quite incorrectly speaks of the decree as making a provision of some novelty in giving bishops the right of appeal to the Bishop of Rome.
[3]Batiffol, *Siège Apostolique*, pp. 47, 48.
[4]Generally admitted by Catholic authors and by an increasing number of Anglicans, e.g. Jalland, op. cit., p. 247, with some reservations. Unhesitatingly by Giles, E., in *Documents Illustrating Papal Authority*, London, 1952, p. 129.

Ambrose was of Roman parentage, although his infancy was spent at Treves, where his father occupied the position of *praefectus* of the civil diocese of Gaul. After his father's death his education was completed at Rome, and he entered the imperial administration. His short and brilliant career in the service of the empire was terminated in 373, when, at the age of 34, he became Bishop of Milan, then the capital of the Western empire.

In propounding the doctrine of the independence of the church, Ambrose was not an innovator. The first thinker to treat of the matter was another Western bishop. St. Hilary of Poitiers, whose treatise *Contra Constantium* in 360 clearly set out the principles which St. Ambrose was to develop. Ambrose outshone his predecessor not only in the theoretical exposition of the question, but in the fact that he was able to put it into practice so forcefully. In this latter task Ambrose was fortunate in having been the tutor of the young Emperors, Gratian and Valentinian II. More important still was his dominating personality. Despite chronic frailty of body he possessed the qualities of leadership in the highest degree, so that he was able to influence not only his former pupils Gratian and Valentinian II, but also Theodosius, the greatest of the Christian emperors.

In the troubled days of his episcopate there occurred a series of incidents which gave him the opportunity not only to expound his views on the respective positions of church and state, but also to implement these principles in the politics of the day. The first of these concerned the Statue of Victory. The removal of this statue from the Senate aroused considerable bitterness among the pagans, who endeavoured to persuade Valentinian to restore it. In writing to the Emperor, Ambrose points out that since it is a matter of religion he, the bishop, is the only one competent to decide the issue. In 386 a crisis of a more serious nature was to provide the opportunity for a more ample exposition of the rights of the church. On this occasion the court party attempted to give freedom of worship to the Arians, and at the same time to bestow upon them one of the basilicas in Milan. The defence which Ambrose adopts is significant. He does not argue about the theological errors of Arianism, but maintains that since the matter is in the sphere of religion it is for the bishop to judge. He makes it clear that the civil power is fundamentally incompetent to decide such a question.[1] In the same crisis he preached the famous sermon against Auxentius in which he

[1] Ambrose, Letter 17:13 and Letter 21:2, M.P.L., Vol. 16, cols. 964, 1003.

defined the position of a Christian emperor. The famous adage *Imperator enim intra ecclesiam, non supra ecclesiam est*[1] sums up the whole of his attitude. In other words, even the emperor is a subject of the ecclesiastical authority where the affairs of religion are concerned. This conclusion was put into effect in a most dramatic fashion in 390. In that year the inhabitants of Thessalonika had rioted and in the course of the disturbances they put to death the Roman *magister militum*. To punish the city Theodosius ordered a general massacre. For this atrocious crime Ambrose excommunicated him, thus demonstrating the superior authority of the church in all matters which came into the religious sphere.

The fundamental principles on which Ambrose based his actions were the autonomy of the church and the civil power, and the immunity of the church from the direct control of the emperor. From these it followed that the Christian emperor was a subject of the church, that his authority in ecclesiastical matters was limited to their civil effects, and ultimately that the emperor could be punished by the authority of the church.[2] The importance of these principles cannot be exaggerated. It meant that the Western church had arrived at a solution to the problem of the position of the church in a Christian state. By way of anticipation it can be said that the Eastern church never devised a satisfactory solution to the same problem on account of their overall failure to arrive at an adequate ecclesiology of the organizational life of the church. From the time of Constantine the Great the church in the eastern empire was the victim of *caesaropapism* with the result that its autonomy was seriously compromised. The securing of immunity from imperial interference was a necessary prerequisite for the smooth functioning of papal authority.

Throughout the course of his episcopate Ambrose had cordial relations with the see of Rome. There was no major crisis in the West during that period which might have been expected to provoke opposition or support from the Bishop of Milan. However, his attitude to Rome can be judged accurately from certain incidents. In the funeral oration for his brother he declares that when he became a Christian he was careful to receive baptism from a bishop who was in communion with Rome.[3] He had in mind the schism of Lucifer of Calgari and the trend of his thought

[1]'The Emperor is within the church, not above it', *Sermon Against Auxentius*, section 36, M.P.L., Vol. 16, col. 1018.
[2]Batiffol, *Siège Apostolique*, pp. 78–81.
[3]*De excessu fratris Satyri*, I, 47, C.S.E.L., Vol. 73, p. 235.

is quite clear. If a bishop is to be in communion with the universal church, he must be in communion with Rome.

The same principle can be seen in the context of the council of Aquileia in 381. This was one of the many councils held during the period of the restoration of orthodoxy subsequent to the ravages of Arianism. The majority of the bishops present were from northern Italy, though a few came from Gaul and Illyricum. The personality of Ambrose dominated the whole council even though he did not preside, and the letter which was addressed from the council to the Emperor merely voices his opinions. He expresses joy at the thought that orthodoxy is now triumphant, but also warns the Emperor that the situation at Rome was dangerous on account of the activities of the antipope Ursinus. The reason why he drew attention to the internal condition of the city of Rome was the potential danger to the whole church, since Rome was its centre. *Tamen totius orbis Romani caput Romanam ecclesiam atque illam sacrosanctam apostolorum fidem ne turbari sineret obsecranda fuit clementia vestra, inde enim in omnes venerandae communionis iura dimanant.*[1] [Your Grace must be besought not to permit any disturbance of the Roman church, the head of the whole Roman world and of the most holy faith of the Apostles, for from thence flow out to all (churches) the bonds of sacred communion.]

The use of the expression *totius orbis Romani* (of the whole Roman world) indicates that he has in mind the church spread throughout the whole empire. In other words the Roman church is the senior in the universal church. He speaks, moreover, of the present communion of the churches which is assured by their being in communion with the church of Rome.[2] Although St. Ambrose recognized the pre-eminence of the see of Rome he did not present a highly developed theology of the primacy.[3] His major contribution to authority of the Pope was an indirect one; namely, his work for securing the independence of church government from civil encroachment.

Another of the Western fathers whose writings throw light upon the position of the Bishop of Rome is the redoubtable St. Jerome. He was a contemporary of St. Ambrose, and although he died in 419 his career is associated with the pontificate of St. Damasus, who commissioned him to translate the Scriptures into Latin. Though of a Roman family, he,

---

[1] Ambrose, Letter 11:4. M.P.L., Vol. 16, col. 946.
[2] Batiffol, op. cit., p. 26.
[3] cf. F. Homes Dudden, *St. Ambrose, His Life and Times*, Oxford, 1935, Vol. II, p. 640.

too, like St. Ambrose, was born outside the frontiers of Italy, actually in Pannonia, in the year 347 or thereabouts. He went to Rome for his literary studies, and thence his life divides into two almost equal periods; the first which lasted until 385 was one of study and travel, the second which was terminated by his death was spent mainly in Palestine.

Jerome has sometimes been understood as an antipapalist on account of his severe criticism of the Roman church. The fact of his strictures is undeniable, their precise import, though, can best be judged by studying them in the general context of his relations with the Roman church.

Jerome's first journey to the East took place when the church of Antioch was split by its notorious schism. Three men claimed to be the true bishop. Meletius, now recognized to have been the genuine claimant, was supported by the majority of the people, but Rome and Alexandria had granted communion to his rival Paulinus. The third party was that of Vitalis, a heretic of the school of Apollinaris. The situation was extremely confused, and in view of the obscurity it does not appear that Rome or Alexandria had formally excommunicated Meletius. When Jerome was confronted with the problem of deciding who was the true bishop his method of solution was simple (in principle). He wrote to Damasus to inquire which of the three claimants was in communion with Rome. His first letter of inquiry was written in 376 and a second followed a few months later. His letters bear witness not only to the state of the schism, but also to the Trinitarian heresies which had become involved in it. These latter questions of faith he also submits to the decision of Damasus.

In the first letter he comments on the divided state of the church and then explains his dilemma. 'I have considered that I ought to consult the chair of Peter, and the faith praised by the mouth of the Apostle . . . Following none in the first place but Christ, I am in communion with your beatitude, that is with the chair of Peter. On that rock I know the church is built. Whosoever shall eat the Lamb outside that house is profane . . . [He mentions the Trinitarian disputes] . . . Let three hypostases be no more mentioned if you please, and let one be held. . . . Or if you think fit that we should say three hypostases with the necessary explanations we do not refuse . . . Wherefore I beseech your holiness by the crucified salvation of the world, by the Trinity of one substance, that you will write and give me authority or refuse it to say three hypostases . . . At the same time let me know with whom to communicate at Antioch, for the Campenses [followers of Meletius] having joined with the Tharsenses desire nothing but to preach three hypostases in their old sense, supported by the authority of communion with you.'[1]

The reply was long in coming and Jerome wrote a second letter on the same problems a few months after the first. The theme is the same. He describes the situation of the schism: 'A church torn in three parts tries to seize me. The authority of ancient monks who dwell around rises against me. Meantime I cry aloud: If any is joined to the chair of Peter, he is mine. Meletius, Vitalis, and Paulinus say that they adhere to you. If one of them asserted it I could believe him. But now either two of them or all three are lying. Therefore I beseech your beatitude . . . if you will tell me by letter with whom I ought to communicate in Syria.'[2]

The essentials of Jerome's thought are quite straightforward, and they can be summarized as follows.[3] He regards the chair of Peter as the foundation of the whole church and the Bishop of Rome as the one who inherits this authority. Secondly, and as a result of the first consideration, the church of Rome is the centre of universal communion, even for an Eastern bishop.[4] Thirdly the Roman church must be in possession of the orthodox faith. It will be noticed that Jerome echoes the same idea as Ambrose when he insists that communion with Rome is essential for communion with the whole church. In addition he has a clear idea of the two powers of the Bishop of Rome, namely the competence to judge on matters of faith and to decide the question of juridical communion.

After his return to Rome, St. Jerome found that a considerable love of wealth was lowering the ideals of the Roman clergy, and the uncompromising nature of his opposition to such relaxations earned for him the hostility of the clergy, which forced him to leave for the East. At a later date it earned for him the reputation of being an opponent of the authority of the Roman church. Bishop Gore depicted him thus: 'In Jerome's earlier years his tone is papal, e.g. in his letters to Damasus from the East A.D. 375–380 (Ep. xv, xvi). Afterwards, disgusted with Roman manners and disappointed of the Roman episcopate, he broke with the church there, A.D. 385, and his abusive tone about the Roman clergy is subsequent to this date, e.g. Ep. lii ad Nepotian is after 393. His commentaries on the New Testament which contain the passages

---

[1]Jerome, Letter 15, C.S.E.L., Vol. 54, pp. 63–67.
[2]Jerome, Letter 16, C.S.E.L., Vol. 54, pp. 68–69.
[3]Chapman, op. cit., p. 114–16.
[4]Batiffol, op. cit., p. 33.

minimizing the episcopal office by comparison with the presbyterate, date A.D. 386–392. His letter to Evangelus (Ep. cxlvi) is marked by its hostile tone towards Rome to belong to the period subsequent at any rate to A.D. 385, and Ep. lxix ad Oceanum is about A.D. 400.'[1]

Chapman analysed the real situation of Jerome's departure from Rome and showed that it did not mean a denial of the authority of that church, although he criticized the clergy. The criticism of the clergy began before he left the city; in fact, it was the ultimate cause of his departure. His views on the episcopate expressed in the letter to Nepotian probably refer to the quarrel with John, the Bishop of Jerusalem, which engaged his attention then. It is, moreover, difficult to see how his minimizing of the episcopal office can be construed as an antipapal sentiment.[2]

Among the Roman clergy some of the principal victims of his attack were the deacons who tended to appropriate for themselves the honours which were due to the priesthood or episcopate. In order to remind them of the relative positions of the three orders Jerome points out that the pretensions of the Roman deacons are an exception to the general rule. He indicates that the deacons do not attempt to take precedence over the bishops and priests elsewhere in the church. Then he says: 'Wheresoever a bishop is, whether at Rome or at Engabium, at Constantinople or at Rhegium or at Alexandria or at Tanis, he is of the same worth, and also of the same priesthood' (*ejusdem meriti, ejusdem et sacerdotii*).[3] In this sentence there is a rebuttal of any implication that the Roman episcopate might be inferior to that elsewhere, and that the deacons were taking advantage of it to look down on the Bishop of Rome. When viewed in its proper context, it can be seen that he had in mind the relative positions of the three orders from the point of view of their sacramental not jurisdictional powers. Without, for the moment, considering Rome, St. Jerome could not have been ignorant of the lack of equality which existed between the Bishop of Alexandria and the other bishops of Egypt.

At the end of his life St. Jerome still upheld the authority of the Bishop of Rome, despite his criticisms of the clergy of the city. The letter to Demetrius which he wrote in 414 shows his attitude to Rome's decision on doctrinal matters. He speaks of the orthodoxy of Anastasius

---

[1]Gore, C., *The Church and the Ministry*, London, 5th ed., 1907, p. 158, n. 2.
[2]Chapman, op. cit., p. 119.
[3]Jerome, Letter 146 ad Evangelum, C.S.E.L., Vol. 56, pp. 310–11.

and then continues: 'I feel that I ought with the deepest affection to give you this advice, to hold the faith of the holy Innocent, who is the successor and son of that man [Anastasius] and of the Apostolic See, and not to receive any foreign doctrine, however prudent and clever you may think yourself to be.'[1]

In his virulent attacks on the Roman clergy St. Jerome had in mind the distinction between the office and the individuals, so that he could criticize without withdrawing his obedience. When this is borne in mind it must be admitted that Jerome is uncompromisingly propapal.

In addition to the theoretical expositions of the papal supremacy, the Western zone furnishes a wealth of evidence from its day-to-day conduct, and the presuppositions upon which that conduct was based. The phenomenon of appeals to the Bishop of Rome has been examined before, and indeed it is one of the constantly recurring elements of the life of the church in the West. The affair of the Priscillianists is of relevance for that very fact.

The founder of the movement, Priscillian, was born in Spain towards the middle of the fourth century of a wealthy and cultured family. Between the years 370 and 375 he propagated his doctrines on the question of asceticism. His divergence from the church was mainly one of practice, but his ascetic teaching was so extreme that it approached the Manichean type of asceticism based on the supposed intrinsically evil character of matter. His party and the doctrines which went with it, had considerable success in Spain and the south of Gaul. However, the divergences from the traditional Catholic attitude caused disquiet among the bishops, and in 380 the council of Saragossa condemned his teaching. Priscillian himself was not excommunicated, since he was not present to answer the charges against him. In order to avoid a stalemate, Ydatius, Bishop of Merida, obtained from the Emperor a decree banishing him from Spain. Priscillian took refuge in Gaul, but in 382 Delphinus, Bishop of Bordeaux, excluded him from his see. After this he decided to appeal to Damasus to vindicate him, and set off for Rome to make the appeal in person. Damasus refused to receive the request, and thereupon he appealed to Ambrose, unsuccessfully, and finally he sought refuge at the imperial court. There he was successful, and thanks to the good offices of Macedonius, the *magister officiorum*, whom he is alleged to have bribed, the decree of Gratian was annulled and he returned to Spain. His subsequent tragic death at the hands of Maximus,

[1] Jerome, Letter 130, C.S.E.L., Vol. 56, p. 196.

the rebel general who then held Gaul, lies outside the theological interest of the incident.

The fact of his appeals to the see of Milan and to the court would seem at first sight to diminish the significance of the appeal to Rome. It represents a tendency to extend appeals beyond the proper superior to any powerful refuge likely to prove helpful. The fact that he should appeal last of all to the imperial court suggests that in his anxiety he was trying every possible means to secure his exculpation. It is fortunate, though, for the proper understanding of the situation that he addressed a written memorandum to Damasus in which he states the grounds for his appeal. The document is valuable because it indicates the theological basis of Rome's authority in a manner which cannot be nullified by his subsequent appeals elsewhere. He declares that he has come to lodge his appeal. 'With thee, the senior of us all' (*apud te qui senior omnium nostrum es*). The seniority is, of course, the superior position of his see, and not any allusion to his age. This reference to his senior position is referred to again at the end of the document. 'Grant audience we beseech thee because thou art the first and senior to all. . . . We beseech thee to give letters to thy brethren the Spanish bishops' (*Praestes audientiam, deprecamur quia omnibus senior et primus es. . . . Des ad fratres tuos hispanienses episcopos litteras deprecamur*).[1] Although the bishops are brothers, there is one who is first and senior to the rest. Although Damasus declined to take up the affair, it is clear that a decision from him would have been sufficient to exculpate Priscillian.[2]

It is probable that the year of Priscillian's appeal to Rome, 382, is connected with another important piece of evidence in the history of the Roman primacy. In the preceding year the council of Constantinople had made the first claim that the Bishop of Constantinople should enjoy a special status, since his city was now the imperial capital. The third chapter of the *Decretum Gelasianum* defines the authority of Rome as depending on the Apostolicity of the see and not on conciliar decrees. Although the matter has been disputed, it now seems highly probable that these words came from the Roman synod of 382 as an answer to the pretentions of Constantinople.

Various manuscripts of the document now known as the *Decretum Gelasianum*[3] bear the names of Damasus, Gelasius or Hormidsas. It

---

[1]Priscillian Tract II, C.S.E.L., Vol. 18, pp. 34, 42, 43.
[2]Batiffol, *Cathedra Petri*, p. 57.
[3]Edited by Dobschütz in *Texte und Untersuchungen*, XXXVIII, 4.

appears to have been a private compilation, by a writer who had access to the official records, and it was not included in the official Roman compilations until the eighth century. The first three chapters bear the title *Concilium Urbis Romae sub Damaso Papa* (Council in the City of Rome under Pope Damasus). Thence arises the question as to the authenticity of these three chapters which claim to be of the time of Damasus. Dobschütz argued[1] that these first chapters were an integral part of the whole from the very beginning and therefore could not be as early as the time of Damasus since the rest of the document is certainly later than the fourth century. Although he was followed by Batiffol, the opinion is now generally discarded and the primitive character of the first three chapters is accepted by a variety of scholars. In the first place, the stylistic differences between the first three chapters and the rest make it difficult to attribute them to the same author. There is, moreover, a quotation from the third chapter in the preface to the Isidorian collection of the Nicene canons. Since this latter document was written soon after 418, the case for the authenticity of the first part of the *Decretum Gelasianum* seems to be very strong.[2]

The relevant parts of the third chapter are as follows: 'The holy Roman church is senior to the other churches [*ceteris ecclesiis praelata est*] not by virtue of any synodal decrees, but obtained the primacy [*primatum*] from our Lord and Saviour in the words of the Gospel, Thou art Peter and upon this rock . . . will be loosed in Heaven. . . . The first see of Peter the Apostle belongs to the Roman church, "having no spot nor wrinkle nor any such thing". And the second see was consecrated at Alexandria in the name of blessed Peter by Mark, his disciple and evangelist, and he after being sent forth by Peter the Apostle of Egypt, preached the word of truth and accomplished a glorious martyrdom. Moreover, the third see of the most blessed Apostle Peter at Antioch is held in honour because he dwelt there before he came to Rome, and there first of all the name of the new-born race of Christians had its origin.'[3] This document is important as being the first official definition of the papal claims which has survived. Nevertheless it is not an innovation.[4] In the second century the principle of Apostolic

---

[1]Dobschütz, op. cit., pp. 340–1.

[2]Chapman, op. cit., p. 20, n. 2. The authenticity is also accepted by Turner, Caspar, Kidd, Jalland, and others.

[3]*Decretum Gelasianum, III*, ed. cit., p. 32 ff.

[4]Kidd, *Roman Primacy*, pp. 68–72, stresses the novelty of expression rather than the continuity of thought with past declarations.

succession was thought out against the Gnostics and Marcionites, and since the third century the particular succession of the Roman see had been traced to the text 'Thou art Peter'. The principle there enunciated in 382 was the traditional thesis of the origin of ecclesiastical authority. At the particular time, though, it was important to reiterate it in view of the tendency in the East to associate ecclesiastical authority with the civil pre-eminence of the episcopal city. In other words, a clarification of this type, in response to particular circumstances, is almost a classical example of the development of a doctrine whose expression becomes more and more precise with the interplay of historical forces.

The last incident of the pontificate of Pope Damasus was a request addressed to him from Himerius, the Bishop of Tarragona, for guidance in the regulation of certain matters of ecclesiastical discipline which seem to have been seriously abused in Spain. Damasus died in December, 384, and the matter was attended to by his successor, Siricius, in the letter *Directa ad Decessorem* of February 10th, 385.[1] The document is a systematic exposition of the law concerning the problems in question, interspersed with parentheses justifying the decisions and indicating the Pope's consciousness of his authority.

In the preface Siricius declares that having succeeded to the authority of Damasus he is obliged to promote the welfare of the church with a zeal which is all the greater 'since he bears the burdens of all who are heavy laden; rather the blessed Peter bears them in us, since in all things he preserves and protects the heir of his administration'.

He then proceeds to answer the requests of Himerius. The Arians, he declares, are not to be rebaptized when they enter the church, they are to be reconciled by the imposition of hands and the prayer to the Holy Spirit. This rule, he says, is to be observed under pain of excommunication. The same penalty is threatened for those who depart from the customary practice of administering solemn baptism only at Easter and Pentecost. This time, however, the addition of the censure gives more information about the authority which declares it. 'The above-mentioned rule shall be observed by all priests who do not wish to be severed from union with the Apostolic rock upon which Christ established the universal church'.

In addition to ordering that Spain shall conform to the usual customs of the church, he also imposes regulations on his own authority. Concerning Christians who revert to idolatry, he says quite simply, 'We

[1] Jaffé, n. 255.

order that they be excommunicated' (*Iubemus abscindi*). The same tone is used of the clergy who have been guilty of incontinence. 'Let them know', he declares, 'that they are demoted by the authority of the Apostolic See, from any ecclesiastical dignity which they have dishonoured.' A further abuse which had been brought to his notice was that of the ordination of men who had been married more than once. Siricius recalls the instructions of St. Paul on that very matter, and adds: 'What is to be followed and what is to be avoided in the future by all the churches, we define by a general rule.'

In the final paragraph of the document he mentions that if Himerius consulted Damasus, it is because the Bishop of Rome is the head of the episcopal body. He extends the regulations to apply to the other provinces in Spain and adds that 'no priest of the Lord is free to ignore the regulations and pronouncements of his Apostolic See.'

This remarkable document reveals a consciousness of possessing extensive legislative power, since in addition to referring to the practice of the church, he commands certain measures on his own authority. Noteworthy, too, is the light which it throws on the nature of the papal office as it was then appreciated. Siricius declares that the whole church was established on Peter, and that he, as Bishop of Rome, inherits the powers of St. Peter. The continuity with St. Peter is also expressed, more poetically, as a permanent solicitude which St. Peter exercises through his successors.

It was once held that this was the first papal decretal. Compared with the letter *Ad Gallos Episcopos* of Damasus it shows an advance in so far as Siricius makes laws whereas his predecessor promulgated existing ones. Among the surviving decretals it is the oldest, but there is nothing in the text or the circumstances to suggest that it was an innovation. The fact that the initiative came from Spain would suggest that there was some precedent to motivate the request from Himerius. More conclusive, though, is a valuable phrase in the text itself. When dealing with the question of the Arians, he says that it is forbidden to rebaptize them, since such a practice was prohibited by the Apostle Paul, the canons, and 'by the general decrees sent to the provinces by my revered predecessor Liberius' (*Missa ad provincias a venerandae memoriae praedecessore meo Liberio generalia decreta prohibeant*). The Roman custom of making laws for other parts of the church, which became more and more common after this period, was not, therefore, an innovation, but, as Batiffol said, 'a new modality'[1] in the exercise of the existing powers of the Bishop of Rome.

As the fourth century drew to a close the authority of the Pope over the churches of the West was assured, and was maintained in a state of stability which would survive the collapse of the Roman political power. The last decades of that century are comparatively uneventful for the history of the Roman primacy, except for the unusual situation in Illyricum, where the Bishop of Thessalonika enjoyed the status of papal vicar. The origin of this arrangement is probably to be traced to the pontificate of Damasus. In 379, when Gratian was faced with the prospect of war on the Rhine and Danube, he transferred to his Eastern colleague Theodosius the dioceses of Dacia and Macedonia, which had been in the Western empire since the time of Diocletian's division. This transference created an immediate danger for the ecclesiastical hegemony, since it would tend to bring the church in Illyricum into the sphere of influence of Constantinople. The events of the Arian crisis and the subsequent problems of the East demonstrated the undesirability of such a situation, and for the next half-century the Popes were at pains to keep Illyricum in the Western zone of Roman influence. This was achieved, though not immediately, by making the Bishop of Thessalonika the vicar of the Pope and giving him exceptionally wide powers over the other metropolitans of Illyricum.

In the year 381 Constantinople was the scene of a council of the whole of the East, yet the bishops of Illyricum were absent, but for Acholius of Thessalonika. At a later date Pope Innocent I[2] speaks of the powers given to the bishops of Thessalonika by Damasus and Siricius. From these two pieces of evidence it is reasonable to infer that the special status of Thessalonika was inaugurated by Damasus very soon after the transfer of the two dioceses to the East.

During the pontificate of Damasus the relationship between Rome and Thessalonika was substantially the same as for any other Western metropolitan. The significant advance was made in the pontificate of Siricius, who gave to Anysius the right of controlling all episcopal ordinations in Illyricum.[3] When an episcopal see fell vacant the Bishop of Thessalonika was instructed to proceed to the place himself, or else

---

[1]Batiffol, *Cathedra Petri*, p. 57. E. Caspar, too (*Geschichte des Papsttums*, I, pp. 261–2), points out that the texts of these decretals contain nothing which would indicate that they were an innovation.

[2]Jaffé, n. 285.

[3]Jaffé, n. 259.

send letters to authorize the election and ordination of a suitable candidate. This letter marks the beginning of the unique powers of the papal vicar of Thessalonika.[1] One of the first acts of Pope Innocent I was to confirm the powers of Anysius, and another letter from the same Pope shows more clearly the nature of that authority.[2] The sphere of his influence is stated as being the dioceses of Dacia and Macedonia, whose provinces are mentioned by name. Both these provinces retained their own metropolitans, but Anysius has a supervisory power over them. In particular their business with Rome is to be transacted through Thessalonika.

Since this special power was a direct grant of authority from the Bishop of Rome, the influential position of Thessalonika did not tend to separate the region from the Western sphere of influence. In 414 Innocent wrote to Rufus of Thessalonika and the other bishops of Illyricum, answering a series of questions in a manner which is reminiscent of the *Ad Gallos Episcopos* of Damasus.[3] The decisions of the Pope refer to a variety of matters of ecclesiastical discipline, and to one case of a bishop of Illyricum who had been tried by Rome. This particular case is important, since it reveals that the Pope still acted as the supreme court of appeal, despite the extensive powers of the Bishop of Thessalonika. But for the close subjection of Thessalonika to Rome, the situation in Illyricum would have been similar to that in Egypt, where the see of Alexandria held sway over the other bishoprics. However, as the powers held by the Bishop of Thessalonika were delegated, the ecclesiastical affairs of Illyricum remained in substantial conformity with the rest of the Western zone.

The pontificate of Innocent I is chiefly remembered on account of his contemporary, St. Augustine of Hippo. It is only the latter part of his career which is strictly relevant to the present study. In 396 Augustine succeeded Valerian in the see of Hippo, and rapidly moved to the forefront of ecclesiastical affairs. In the second decade of the fifth century, when in controversy with the Pelagians, he became the dominant figure in the whole of the Western church.

The immediate background to the career of St. Augustine was provided by the Donatist controversy, and a certain measure of African juridical autonomy in relation to Rome. In the year 397 the Africans

[1]Batiffol, *Siège Apostolique*, pp. 247–8.
[2]Letter of June 17th, 412, Jaffé, n. 300.
[3]Jaffé, n. 303.

sought advice from Rome and Milan on the subject of admitting convert Donatists to Holy Orders. Only the reply from Rome has survived and the advice which it contained was politely but firmly rejected. It may appear strange that such an attitude should have been adopted, but it must be remembered that it was not a juridical appeal (Milan, too, was consulted), and their refusal to comply with the Roman reply was not resented by the Pope. Although the Africans felt at liberty to disagree on matters of discipline, they were well aware that communion with the see of Rome was essential if they were to be part of the universal church; Optatus stated the principle explicitly against the Donatists and it was repeated by St. Augustine.[1] More important still was the realization that Rome's judgement was supreme in questions which affected doctrine, as was shown in the Pelagian affair.

The heresy of Pelagius was the only truly theological dispute in the early history of the Western church. The movement, of which Pelagius was the figurehead more than the instigator, taught as its fundamental principle that divine grace was not absolutely necessary for the salvation of the soul. The movement was not confined to Africa, but it found there its most determined opponents. When the Donatists were no longer a peril, St. Augustine devoted the whole of his energies to writing and preaching against the Pelagians, and the rest of the African bishops were no less zealous for the defence of the traditional belief. In the year 416 two important councils were held at Milevis and Carthage, where the Pelagian doctrines were condemned. Both councils wrote to the Pope requesting that 'the impiety of Pelagius should also be condemned by the authority of the Apostolic See.'[2] At the same time Augustine, and four other bishops, addressed a further letter to the Pope dealing with the same matter. 'For we do not pour back our little stream for the purpose of replenishing your abundant source; but in the great temptation of these times . . . we wish to be reassured by you, whether our stream, though small, flows from the same head as your abundant river.'[3]

In seeking papal approval of their decisions the Africans were anxious that they should acquire the universal effectiveness which only the Roman See could give them.[4] In the following year the Pope replied

[1]Optatus, *De Schismate Donatistarum*, II, 2, 3, C.S.E.L., 26, p. 36. Augustine, Letter to Generosus, Letter 53, C.S.E.L., Vol. 34 (ii), pp. 153, 154.
[2]The documents are to be found among the letters of St. Augustine, Nos. 175, and 176, C.S.E.L., Vol. 44, pp. 665, 668.
[3]Augustine, Letter 177, C.S.E.L., Vol. 44, p. 688.
[4]Chapman, op. cit., p. 143.

to them by the three letters dated January 27th, 417.[1] The content of all three is much the same. The letter to Carthage contains an important digression on the authority of the Bishop of Rome, and it is here quoted in full, since it indicates the highly developed state of the papal theory at that date.

'In making inquiry with respect to those things that should be treated with all solicitude by bishops, and especially by a true and just and Catholic council, by preserving as you have done, the example of ancient tradition, and by being mindful of ecclesiastical discipline, you have truly strengthened the vigour of our religion, no less now in consulting us than before in passing sentence. For you decided that it was proper to refer to our judgement, knowing what is due to the Apostolic See, since all we who are set in this place desire to follow the Apostle from whom the very episcopate and whole authority of this name is derived. Following in his steps, we know how to condemn the evil and to approve the good. So also, you have by your sacerdotal office preserved the customs of the fathers, and have not spurned that which they decreed by a divine and not human sentence, that whatsoever is done, even though it be in distant provinces, should not be ended without being brought to the knowledge of this see, that by its authority the whole just pronouncement should be strengthened, and that from it all other churches (like waters flowing from their natal source and flowing through the different regions of the world, the pure streams of one incorrupt head), should receive what they ought to enjoin, whom they ought to wash, and whom that water, worthy of pure bodies, should avoid as defiled with uncleansable filth. I congratulate you, therefore, dearest brethren, that you have directed letters to us by our brother and fellow Julius, and that, while caring for the churches which you rule, you also show your solicitude for the well-being of all, and that you ask for a decree that shall profit all the churches of the world at once . . .'

After this dignified reminder of the papal authority, the letters go on to approve the decisions taken in Africa, and in particular Pelagius and his associate Celestius are excommunicated. Since the sentence was from Rome, its effect was universal and final.[2] A few months later St. Augustine preached a sermon which gave rise to the adage *Rome locuta est Causa finita est* (Rome has spoken, the matter is settled). What he

[1]To Carthage, Milevis, and Augustine and his companions. Jaffé, nn. 321 322, 323.
[2]Batiffol, *Le Catholicisme de Saint Augustin*, 5th ed., Paris, 1929, p. 401.

really said was: 'For by now two synodal letters have been sent on this dispute to the Apostolic See; from that see in turn replies have come. The matter is settled [*causa finita est*]: would that the error, too, might end at last.'[1]

In the eyes of the Africans the whole affair both of the doctrine and the actual excommunication of Pelagius had been satisfactorily concluded. The local councils had been given approval by Rome and the decisions had thus acquired universal force. It has been suggested that the settlement was regarded as the joint effort of both parties,[2] as if two equal partners were contributing to the final decision. The contemporary witnesses did not think so. A record of the affair was written by St. Prosper of Aquitaine, the disciple of St. Augustine: 'At that time the Pelagians, who had already been condemned by Pope Innocent, were being resisted by the vigour of the Africans and above all by the learning of Bishop Augustine.' Elsewhere he records the matter more poetically: 'They fell dead when Innocent of blessed memory struck the heads of the deadly error with the Apostolic sword.'[3] Marius Mercator records the matter in greater detail: 'Celestius and Pelagius were not then for the first time condemned by Zosimus of blessed memory, but by his predecessor Innocent of holy memory . . . [He refers to the examination of the books of Pelagius] . . . These books were sent together with the letters to the fathers and bishops in Africa, where the books were read at the three councils which were assembled. From thence reports [*relationes*] were sent to Rome, together with the books; the Apostolic sentence in reply to the councils followed, which deprived Pelagius and Celestius of ecclesiastical communion.'[4] It is clear that these fifth-century writers envisaged a subordination of authorities.

In the whole of the career of St. Augustine there is no other instance of his having recourse to Rome as he did in the Pelagian affair. In various of his writings he indicates several sources of guidance which are complementary rather than exclusive of each other. In his treatise on baptism he advises that if one were in doubt as to the procedure to follow (over rebaptizing) guidance should be sought from the practice of the universal church, whose attitude could ultimately be ascertained

[1]Augustine, Sermon 131 of September 23rd, 417, M.P.L., Vol. 38, col. 734.
[2]Kidd, *Roman Primacy*, p. 85.
[3]St. Prosper of Aquitaine, Chronicle ad ann. 416, and *De Ingratis*, Part I, M.P.L., Vol. 51, col. 592; M.P.L., Vol. 51, cols. 96–7; *Contra Collatorem* (21), M.P.L., Vol. 51, col. 271.
[4]Marius Mercator, *Commonitorium super nomine Coelestii*, III, 3, M.P.L., Vol. 48, col. 99.

from local or oecumenical councils.[1] He refers to the oecumenical council because he was under the impression that the rebaptismal controversy had, in fact, been settled by a general council. The apparent contradictions in his attitude have been clarified by Batiffol on the basis of his applying different criteria in different situations: 'Against the Donatists he preferred to invoke the authority of the universal church; for the question of baptism the authority of an oecumenical council. In the controversy against the Pelagians, Augustine regarded the Roman church as judge in matters of Faith.'[2] In the whole of Augustine's ecclesiology he manifests a preference for considering the church as a whole. However, this preference is not incompatible with the position of the papacy. In the last analysis communion with the universal church and communion with Rome have the same result. Augustine gives greater emphasis to the former, but the extent to which the two aspects harmonize can be judged from the letter to Gloriosus: 'Carthage . . . had a bishop of no mean authority, who could afford to ignore the hostile group of enemies, since he perceived himself to be joined by letters of communion, both to the Roman church, in which the authority of the Apostolic office [*apostolicae cathedrae principatus*] always persists, and to the other regions of the world whence the gospel came to Africa.'[3] In view of the fact that the Pelagian affair was the only truly theological heresy of his period, the infrequency of his appealing to Rome cannot rightly be regarded as an anomaly. What is truly significant and relevant in the Pelagian dispute is the spontaneous way in which the two councils, and Saint Augustine, referred to Rome for approval and confirmation.

There the matter should have ended but for the intrigues of the Pelagians and the impetuosity of Pope Zosimus. Zosimus succeeded Innocent in March, 417, and was soon approached by Pelagius and Celestius with the request that their case should be reopened. Without giving much thought to the matter, Zosimus declared his willingness to give them a hearing. Although the matter did not proceed very far, it is well to bear in mind that there was never a question of revising Innocent's doctrinal decision, but only of examining the justice of the personal sentences against Pelagius and Celestius.[4] Nevertheless the

[1]*De Baptismo*, II, 2; VII, 53; M.P.L., Vol. 43, cols. 128, 129, 242, 243.
[2]Batiffol, op. cit., p. 407.
[3]Augustine, Letter 43:7, C.S.E.L., Vol. 34 (i), p. 90. Cf. also: *Psalm Against the Donatists*, C.S.E.L., Vol. 51, p. 12.
[4]Batiffol, op. cit., p. 437; Butler, C., *The Church and Infallibility*, London, 1954, p. 182.

Africans took alarm, and a council at Carthage in November, 417, protested in favour of the previous decisions. Zosimus wrote to the Africans to calm their anxieties and also to affirm his competence in the matter. The first part of this letter, '*Quamvis patrum traditio*',[1] is, like that of Innocent to the Africans, a detailed statement of the nature of the papal authority. Since it emanates from the Pope, it is of value in showing how the papal function was understood:

'Although the tradition of the fathers has attributed to the Apostolic See so great authority that none would dare to contest its judgement, and has preserved this ever in its canons and rules, and current ecclesiastical discipline in its laws still pays the reverence which it ought to the name of Peter, from which it has itself its origin, for canonical antiquity willed that this apostle should have such power by the decisions of all; and by the promise of Christ our God, that he should loose the bound and bind the loosed, and an equal condition of power has been given to those who with his consent have received the heritage of his See. For he himself has care over all the churches, and above all of that in which he sat, nor does he suffer anything of its privileges or decisions to be shaken in any wind, since he established it on the foundation, firm and immovable, of his own name, which no one shall rashly attack but at his peril. Since, then, Peter is the head of so great authority, and has confirmed the suffrages of our forefathers since his time, so that the Roman church is confirmed by all laws and disciplines, divine or human; whose place we rule, and the power of whose name we inherit, as you are not ignorant, my brethren, but you know it well and as bishops you are bound to know it; yet, though such was our authority that none could reconsider our decision . . .'

Documents such as this letter and that of Innocent quoted above show how complete was the Roman appreciation of the papal power not only in practice but also in theory. The appeal to the Petrine text of Matthew had been characteristic of the Popes since St. Stephen, and expositions such as the present letter show how fully they had worked out the consequences of Peter's superiority being transmitted by succession.

In May, 418, two hundred African bishops met in Carthage and again championed the previous decision of Innocent. By the end of that month Zosimus, too, had reached the same decision, which he announced in the *Tractatoria*.[2] By then he had come to realize the

[1] Jaffé, n. 342.
[2] *Tractatoria* of Zosimus, Jaffé, n. 343.

insincerity of Pelagius, but it is undeniable that he was assisted in his decision by the firmness shown in Africa.

In addition to the affair of Pelagius, the year 418 is famous on account of the case of the African priest Apiarius. The event itself was of little consequence and the records are sadly incomplete, yet the question has become notorious, thanks to the interest which it aroused among the Gallicans.

It appears that the priest Apiarius was excommunicated by his bishop, Urbanus of Sicca, on account of certain crimes, and that he appealed to Rome for exculpation. In the same year the council of Carthage forbade appeals from Africa to higher courts 'across the sea' (*ad transmarina*).[1] It is not certain whether this was prompted by the appeal of Apiarius, but it would seem likely. The reference could possibly be an allusion to the journeys to seek support at the imperial court such as the Donatists were in the habit of making, but it seems more likely from the sequel that it was politely directed against Rome. Pope Zosimus reacted by sending legates to Africa to protest. This was an innovation in the practice of the Apostolic See, inspired no doubt by the imperial *executores*, but envisaged in theory as early as the council of Sardica. These legates upheld, among other matters, the right of bishops to appeal to Rome. Having declared the principle, they made the fundamental mistake of basing this right, not on the inherited prerogatives of St. Peter, nor on the tradition of the church, but on the authority of the council of Nicea. The reason for this claim was the fact that in Rome, at that date, the official records of the councils of Nicea and Sardica had become amalgamated, so that the canons of the latter were assumed to have emanated from Nicea. Hence the legates in Africa were unwillingly referring to the provisions which the council of Sardica had laid down with respect to the procedure of appeal to Rome. Aurelius, the Bishop of Carthage, was ignorant of such provisions in the acts of the council of Nicea, but he agreed to allow the appeals pending an examination of the Eastern collections of the canons of Nicea. This decision was adopted by the council of Carthage in May, 419, and for the moment the matter rested in this state of compromise.

Before very long the consultations with the major Eastern churches revealed that the council of Nicea had not been the origin of the canons in question. As a result of this discovery, it might have been expected that Africa would have put a stop to all appeals to Rome, yet in fact

[1]Hefele, II, p. 203.

nothing of the kind happened. Appeals still went from Africa to the Pope.[1] A well-known appeal of this period was that of Antonius of Fussala, which involved St. Augustine. It is clear that Augustine and his contemporaries did not object to the principle of appeal to Rome, and Augustine's letter on the subject indicates that it was a long-established practice.[2]

In 426 Apiarius again appears on the scene, once more excommunicated, and again he appealed, this time to Pope Celestine. As a result of this appeal the council of Carthage that year addressed to the Pope a long and dignified protest against the introduction of papal legates into Africa and the revision of an African sentence by the see of Rome.[3] It bears the signatures of many African bishops, but not that of St. Augustine.

The anomalies of this affair, and the fragmentary character of the evidence, have given rise to a variety of interpretations of the incidents. It can be asserted safely that Pope Celestine was satisfied with the outcome, since he did not excommunicate the Africans. It is unnecessary to insist that no question of faith was involved. The autonomous tendency was a novelty inasmuch as there was no African law against the appeals to Rome until the council of 418.[4] Augustine, in the letter referred to, says clearly that the right of appeal was an established practice.[5] It has been suggested that the letter *Optaremus* was no more than a protest against the alleged source which Zosimus had quoted to justify his action.[6] This would appear rather to underestimate the tone of the document. The evidence which has survived, though, is insufficient to warrant the unqualified claim that the African church enjoyed complete juridical autonomy.[7] What the long-term result would have been it is impossible to say. Before long Africa was overrun by the Vandals, and in the pontificate of Leo the close contact between Rome and Africa was resumed once again.

During the first half of the fifth century the Roman political power in the West was declining rapidly. The disorganization which resulted caused certain obstacles to the smooth functioning of the papal authority,

[1] Batiffol, op. cit., p. 468.
[2] Augustine, Letter 209, section 8, C.S.E.L., Vol. 57, p. 351, cf. Jalland, op. cit., p. 291; Batiffol, op. cit., p. 461, 462.
[3] Letter *Optaremus*, Mansi, IV, pp. 515, 516.
[4] Batiffol, op. cit., pp. 446, 447.
[5] The known cases are listed in Batiffol, op. cit., p. 462, n. 2.
[6] Chapman, op. cit., p. 204.
[7] cf. Sober judgment of Jalland, op. cit., p. 291.

though obviously it did not alter its nature in any way. There are indications in the correspondence of St. Leo that he was prepared to delegate to the provinces matters which his predecessors would have settled at Rome. The reason for this seems to have been the difficulty of keeping in touch with the local problems when communication with the more distant provinces had become so difficult. The essence of the papal power shows no marked changes during this half-century, and the pontificate of St. Leo, which is rightly regarded as the apogee of the early papacy, does not differ in type from that of his immediate predecessors. His actions are unquestionably those of a pope and are recognized as such. For that reason it is not necessary to discuss at length the incidents of his pontificate. His interventions in the government of the church are sufficiently clear to speak for themselves. What is distinctive of this pontificate is the cumulative effect of the various aspects of his work and person which have justly earned him the title of 'the Great'. He added nothing new to the theory of the papacy, except a precision and clarity of expression which surpassed the statements of all his predecessors. In the exercise of his power his dealings with the West differed only in quantity from those of earlier pontificates while in the East, as will be seen later, he was able to enforce the recognition of his authority more effectively than, for instance, Celestine. As far as theology was concerned he was the first Pope to be thoroughly conversant with the Christological disputes of the Greeks. In human qualities he was a Roman of the traditional pattern and similar to Ambrose in his bringing to the service of the church all that was finest in the Roman character. He was a veritable leader and a saint. This remarkable combination of qualities enabled him to fulfil the responsibilities of the papacy more effectively than all his predecessors and most of his successors.

According to the *Liber Pontificalis* he was a native of Tuscany. He must have entered the ranks of the Roman clergy at an early age, because by the year 430 he was already an influential personage. His consecration as Bishop of Rome took place on September 29th, 440. The anniversary of this event provided the occasion for the annual synod of the bishops of Italy, and the sermons which St. Leo preached on these occasions contain his teaching on the nature of the papacy. One of the clearest of these is the Third Sermon on the Anniversary of his Consecration:

'The firmness of the faith, which Christ praised in the prince of the

Apostles, is everlasting, and just as that which Peter believed of Christ is enduring, that which Christ instituted in Peter endures as well . . . The blessed Peter preserves the rock-like solidity which he has received and he does not abandon the government of the church which was entrusted to him. . . . Even at this time he fulfils his mission more completely and more powerfully; everything which pertains to his office and his responsibilities he discharges through the successor in whom and with whom he has been honoured. If anything is rightly done or decided by Us, if anything is obtained from the mercy of God by Our daily prayers', it is to be attributed to the labours and merits of him whose power and authority lives on in his See.'[1]

According to Leo's principles, St. Peter was in a unique position, since he had been entrusted with the care of the whole church. This was not merely a temporary function for the early days in Jerusalem, but it meant that he continued to exercise authority over all parts of the church.[2] This authority was merited by faith, but the transmission of the power did not depend on the merits of his successors; the short-comings of the Bishop of Rome could not minimize the dignity which was handed on.[3] In the opinion of Batiffol, this principle of succession is the very core of St. Leo's theology of the papacy.[4] In order to emphasize the permanence of the power which was entrusted to St. Peter he speaks of Peter living on in his see. In less poetical terms the precise powers of the Pope were conceived of as a responsibility for, and authority over, the whole church. Both these ideas are expressed succinctly in the letter which he sent to the Bishop of Thessalonika confirming his powers: 'We have entrusted to your charity the task of acting as our vicar, so that you may have a part of our responsibility without having the fullness of our authority.'[5] One practical consequence of this power was the fact that he realized his superiority over the other bishops.[6]

This theory found ample scope for application in the troubled times of his pontificate. The East was torn by heresy, and the West was being overrun by the barbarians. Both halves of the church were in need of the

[1]Leo, Sermon III, 2, 3, M.P.L., Vol. 54, col. 146.
[2]Leo, Sermon V, 4, M.P.L., Vol. 54, col. 155.
[3]*Cujus etiam dignitas in indigno herede non deficit,* Sermon III, 4, M.P.L., Vol. 54, col. 147.
[4]Batiffol, *Siège Apostolique*, p. 422.
[5]Leo, Letter to Vicar at Thessalonika, Jaffé, n. 411.
[6]Leo, Sermon III, 4, M.P.L., Vol. 54, col. 147.

strong central authority of the Pope and hardly a year passed without some evidence of the exercise of his universal power.

Roman Gaul had been reduced to a shadow of its former self. In the north-east the Burgundians were established on the West bank of the Rhine, and to the west the Goths controlled the region of Bordeaux. Arles was the centre of the diminishing region which still remained within the Roman sphere of influence, and it was the Bishop of Arles whom Leo had to hold in check. Pope Zosimus had been responsible for the thoughtless blunder of making the Bishop of Arles vicar of Gaul, with the same status as Thessalonika enjoyed in Illyricum. The scheme was totally unworkable and his successor Boniface restored the situation to the original pattern, reducing the Bishop of Arles to the position of an ordinary metropolitan. However, the memory of this promotion did not die out easily, and Hilary of Arles made no effort to confine his action to his own province. Various bishops appealed to the Pope, and in reply Leo addressed a letter to the bishops of Vienne curtailing the activities of Hilary.[1] He was forbidden to hold synods outside his own province, and debarred from interfering with episcopal elections. Finally the Pope reminded him that he was fortunate to be treated with such leniency.

The situation in Spain was more difficult than that in Gaul. By the time that Leo became Pope the whole country had been overrun by the Goths, who had adopted Arianism. In addition to these difficulties there was a revival of Priscillianism. In order to combat this latter danger Turribius, the Bishop of Astorga, wrote to Leo to solicit his advice and assistance. The Pope's reply was somewhat general in tone.[2] He condemned the errors of the Priscillianists, but for more immediate measures he advised the holding of a local council of the various provinces of Spain. In fact, the situation was so disorganized that it was not even possible for the bishops to meet. It is not surprising, therefore, that Leo confined himself merely to general directives.

Of all the regions of the Western empire the fate of Africa was the most tragic. By the year 455 all the Roman provinces there had been conquered by the Vandals. Christianity survived for some time, but its excessively Latin character was an obstacle once the Roman power had been expelled, and its total extinction was not long delayed. Amid the confusion of the period of conquest Rome had fairly frequent contact

[1]Jaffé, n. 407.
[2]Jaffé, n. 412.

with the African bishops. In 446 Leo was consulted about various abuses, particularly irregular ordinations. His reply[1] gives some definite decisions, but other matters he remits to local investigation. In the same letter he grants communion to the excommunicate priest Lupicinus, but refers his case to the examination of the African bishops.

The only part of the Western zone which remained unaffected by the barbarian invasions was Illyricum. There had been a time of crisis when Theodosius II had endeavoured to bring it under the influence of Constantinople. Pope Boniface resisted successfully, and when Leo became Pope it was only necessary to renew the delegation of power to the Bishop of Thessalonika. During his pontificate the situation there remained unchanged.

In examining the origins of the papacy it is superfluous to pursue the inquiry beyond St. Leo. The vast majority of non-Catholic scholars are prepared to admit that he was a pope in the modern sense of the word, even if they query the status of his predecessors. Before completing the inquiry by studying the Eastern attitude to Rome, it is possible to summarize the situation in the Western zone. The pontificate of Leo marks the culmination of a steady and consistent development in the consolidation of the authority of the Bishop of Rome. There are no revolutions, a few misunderstandings, inevitable modifications of policy with the change of circumstances, and all along an increasing precision in the theological expression of the status of the Bishop of Rome. The most fundamental principle is that communion with Rome is a necessary condition for communion with the universal church. In the maintenance of that communion Rome lays down the conditions. The practice at Rome is seen to be the norm for the church, whether it be for the date of Easter, the penitential reform or the question of rebaptizing heretics. Above all in matters of faith the Roman decision is final, ensuring uniformity of belief throughout the whole church. In matters of ecclesiastical law, there was naturally more regional independence than in later centuries when centralization became predominant. Even in this early period, though, Rome is seen to act as the supreme court of appeal, to declare the law and even to make laws for the other parts of the West. Theoretical pronouncements about the nature of the power wielded at Rome are of comparatively late emergence, and as with so many other doctrines, it was the occurrence of doubts and disputes that provoked the more detailed justification of the traditionally accepted positions. In the

[1]Jaffé, n. 410.

second century the principle of Apostolic succession was clarified to defend the episcopal authority against the Gnostics and Marcionites. In the third century this was taken one stage farther, linking St. Peter's superiority with his particular successor, the Bishop of Rome. From that time onward the text 'Thou art Peter' became the *locus classicus* for the vindication of the papal claims, and it was only to be expected that the clearest exposition of this principle should come from the popes themselves.

After the conversion of Constantine the emperors took no little interest in the affairs of the church. The Christian emperors even enforced the ecclesiastical decisions by means of their own authority. The effect of this intervention has frequently been exaggerated by Anglicans, influenced possibly by their experience of an established church. In particular cases it can be shown that the papal power was not created or extended by particular interventions of the state, but that the essence of the problem lies deeper. The possibility that the Emperor could alter, in any way, the nature of the church, or any of its essential institutions presupposes a measure of interdependence which did not exist in the early church. The Eastern church particularly made extensive use of the Emperor's power and influence, but they never formally incorporated him into the church's structure. The state interfered frequently in the affairs of the church, but it did not become part of the church. Although this interference caused considerable difficulties, it did not bring about any major changes within the church. The most striking demonstration of this was perhaps the latter part of the Arian crisis. Constantius II used every means in his power to impose religious uniformity on the basis of Arianism. Although at one time practically every orthodox bishop was either in prison or exile, the attempt failed, because even in the East the state was not part of the church and could not alter its intrinsic constitution.

In the Western zone imperial interference ceased to be a serious danger after the time of St. Ambrose. Heresies, too, were of less consequence than in the East. Even the barbarian invasions were survived, and despite this and other problems of his pontificate, St. Leo stands out in the history of the Western zone as the Pope who embodies most perfectly the characteristics of the papacy.

8

PAPAL POWER IN THE EASTERN ZONE

In his *History of Dogma*, Harnack embraces, with only minor reservations, the following statement from Döllinger: 'In the writings of the doctors of the Greek church, Eusebius, Athanasius, Basil the Great, the two Gregories, and Epiphanius not a word is to be found of peculiar prerogatives being assigned to a Roman bishop. Chrysostom, the most prolific of the Greek fathers, is absolutely silent on the point, and so also are the two Cyrils.'[1] Despite its air of authority, this estimate of the situation reveals only a part of the anomalies of the Greek attitude to the papacy. If the silence of the Greek fathers amounted to a negation of the Roman primacy, which is what Döllinger implied, then it is very difficult to understand why none of them denied the primacy explicitly. With the exception of Basil the Great, who resented bitterly the policy of Pope Damasus, not one of them wrote against the authority of the Roman bishop. In fact, their writings show an almost total lack of systematic ecclesiology. Apart from the theoretical considerations, it is important to judge their attitude to Rome by their conduct and dealings with the popes, since these practical indications will make up for the omissions in their writings.

It is against this background that the Eastern church's attitude to the papacy must be studied, and from the history of this region an attempt must be made to judge whether or not the Greek church accepted or rejected the papal authority.

By contrast with the Italian and Western zones the Eastern sphere of papal influence owes its distinctive character principally to the absence of the special ties which united the other two regions to Rome. No part of the East was evangelized from Rome, and the type of close dependence seen in Italy would have been impossible for more distant regions. The eastern churches had only one link with the Bishop of Rome, that of strictly papal power.

[1]Quoted in *History of Dogma*, Vol. III, p. 226, n. 2; from Döllinger's *Der Papst und das Konzil*, published at Leipzig in 1869 under the pseudonym of Janus.

Of the three zones, this latter was the scene of the most bitter struggles for the enforcement of the authority of the Pope. The difficulty was not caused by the absence of closer ties such as the West enjoyed, but by the abnormal factors of differentiation which tended to divide the East from the West. The differences of language, culture, and politics, have been indicated in Chapter 6, as well as the growing power of the Eastern patriarchs. The effect of these disruptive influences would have been considerable if they had operated alone. In fact they were overshadowed by the more serious peril of caesaropapism.

The inordinate influence of the Emperor in the affairs of the church (the Eastern church in particular) came about principally as the result of two series of causes. The first of these was the lack of a practical ecclesiology. Their preoccupation with the speculative questions of theology resulted in a serious neglect of the theory of church government. Added to this was a disinclination to attend to the practical details of organization. The natural result of this lack of practical policy was the occurrence of a kind of vacuum which the civil power was only too ready to fill.

The attitude of the state, or more particularly the Emperor, was the positive factor which so readily took advantage of the opening created by the ecclesiastical situation. The Eastern mind was well used to the idea of a king occupying a central place in the national religion. Usually this took the form of priestly office, but sometimes extended to the granting of divine honours to the sovereign. It is significant that it was in Egypt that Alexander the Great was first accorded divine honours, whereas Rome itself was one of the last places to admit the cult of the emperors. At the time of Constantine's conversion the Emperor was Pontifex Maximus, and the recipient of divine honours in religious cult. The Christian emperors were not at once willing to relinquish their religious prerogatives, and although they no longer aspired to divine honours it seemed most natural to them that they should transfer their religious responsibilities from paganism to Christianity.[1] Until the time of St. Ambrose the distinction of the two sovereignties was not clearly thought out, and in the East the theory was never implemented although it was appreciated in some quarters.

Even in the East the Emperor was never really taken into the church to form a part of its constitution, but the extensive use which was made of his influence made imperial authority one of the most important factors in the life of the church. Theoretically the history of the Eastern

[1] Scott, S. H., *The Eastern Churches and the Papacy*, London, 1928, p. 91.

church after the conversion of Constantine might well have been a straightforward struggle between the Emperor and the Pope for ascendancy in religious affairs. In reality the situation was complicated by the Trinitarian and Christological heresies as well as by very distasteful ecclesiastical politics. When the bishoprics had become sources of wealth and power, and when the Christian ideals had fallen from the high standard of the persecution period, the competition for ecclesiastical advancement not infrequently influenced the affairs of the church.

The main lines of papal policy are somewhat simpler than in the West. Fundamentally the Pope is seen to have the *sollicitudo* and *potestas* (responsibility and authority) over the East as he did over the West. The principal aim of this power is the preservation of the unity of the church on a basis of unity of belief. In the external communion of the churches it is seen that communion with Rome is necessary for communion with the universal church. In the maintenance of this communion Rome alone has the right to impose conditions, and this she does even though the condition may be the excommunication of one of the Eastern patriarchs. Furthermore, Rome is seen to be the final court of appeal in the juridical sphere, and the authority which gives approbation to the oecumenical councils. Although the East enjoyed considerable autonomy in juridical matters there is no difference between the two parts of the church in matters of belief. In questions of faith Rome is recognized as having final authority.

It is this latter principle of doctrinal authority which is revealed in the celebrated incident of Dionysius of Alexandria. The jurisdiction of the Bishop of Alexandria extended to the province of Cyrenaica, and it was in this region that the heresy of Sabellius was being propagated. Dionysius intervened and wrote to Pope Xystus about the matter in 257, expressing his concern and clearly anxious to keep the Pope abreast of the situation. The persecution of Valerian halted the events for the time being, but in the year 260, on his return from exile, Dionysius again took up the matter. In his zeal to refute the modalism of Sabellius it would appear that he overstressed the distinction of the three persons of the Trinity almost to the extent of making three Gods. Owing to the incompleteness of the records the extent of his deviation is hard to estimate. Athanasius, whose treatise *On the Opinions of Dionysius* is the principal source, is at pains to vindicate the orthodoxy of his predecessor. St. Basil, who had the relevant documents at his disposal, thought otherwise, and certainly the bishops Euphranor and Ammonius

accused their metropolitan of tritheism when they denounced him to
Rome. His namesake who had become Pope in 259 summoned a council
to deliberate on the matter. It appears that they prescinded from
judging the Bishop of Alexandria, but studied the doctrinal question on
its own.[1] Two documents were issued by the council: a personal letter
to Dionysius which has since perished, and a general statement of the
doctrine of the Trinity relative to the current heresies. The latter is of
interest for two reasons. It is the most important exposition of the
doctrine of the Trinity in the ante-Nicene period, and it also indicates
Rome's competence in questions of belief. Despite the prestige of
Dionysius and the see of Alexandria, Rome decides what is the true
tradition and there is no question of appealing against this decision.[2]

Dionysius wrote to the Pope protesting his orthodoxy and followed
up the letter by the four books of his *Accusation and Defence*. There is
no indication that he resented the action of Rome; on the contrary it is
evident that he was at pains to show that his doctrinal position was in
accord with the Roman teaching.[3]

Shortly after Dionysius had become Bishop of Rome, Paul of
Samosata was made Bishop of Antioch. He is generally regarded as the
father of Arianism on account of the subordinate position which he
attributed to the second person of the Trinity. For this unorthodox
opinion he was called to account by several synods at Antioch. It was
only at the third of these synods that he was condemned. The details of
the affair are very obscure. It is unusual, to say the least, that he should
have been tried in his own episcopal city by bishops who had no
ordinary power over him. Various influential bishops were in contact
with the synod, but none actually attended except those of the immediate vicinity. The bishops of Alexandria and Rome were not
represented. It has been suggested that Paul had already been delated
to Rome and that both Rome and Alexandria had severed relations with
him.[4] The hypothesis would explain much that is obscure, notably the
fact that the bishops of Rome and Alexandria are the only ones to be
named in the synodal letter, but it remains merely a hypothesis. After
the ecclesiastical sentence a deadlock threatened. Paul refused to relinquish the basilica and hand it over to Domnus, who had been elected
in his place. An appeal was made to the Emperor Aurelian and he

[1] Batiffol, *La Paix Constantinienne*, Paris, 1914 (1st ed.), p. 97.
[2] Lebreton, J., in Vol. II of Fliche & Martin, *Histoire de l'Église*, pp. 328, 329.
[3] Batiffol, *Cathedra Petri*, p. 64.
[4] Batiffol, *La Paix Constantinienne*, pp. 102, 106.

decided that the building should be handed over to the bishop who enjoyed the approval of the bishops of Rome and Italy.[1] This verdict is particularly interesting as it comes from a pagan, and is on that account a most valuable testimony to the principle of the universal communion of the churches and the role of the Roman church in that communion.[2]

The rest of the third century contains little that is relevant to the relationship of the Eastern church to the papacy. However, the period after Constantine's conversion contains much that is of vital concern to the authority of the Pope. The high promise of the Emperor's conversion and the cessation of the persecutions came to little, and before many years had passed the church had to endure one of the most serious crises of the whole of her history, the Arian controversy.

The theological details of this heresy are extremely intricate, but for the study of the papacy it is sufficient to examine only its outlines in order to understand how it affected the power of the popes. The heresiarch was a priest of Alexandria, where he was held in respect on account of his intellectual abilities. In reaction to what he considered to be the Sabellianism of his bishop, he taught that the Son was inferior to the Father, having been created in time. Alexander the bishop excommunicated him (probably in 323) for teaching this theory, and notified Pope Silvester of his action.[3] Thereupon Arius sought for allies among the bishops of the East and Alexander wrote to warn his fellow bishops of the danger. Under these circumstances the heresy spread rapidly, and at this early date Eusebius of Nicomedia, destined to be so prominent in the affair, already gave his support to Arius. By 325 the division of opinion in the East was so serious that Constantine summoned the bishops from all parts of the empire to meet at Nicea.[4] More than 200 attended and condemned Arius and his doctrine. The bishops upheld the eternal generation of the Son and declared that he was of the same nature as the Father. The word chosen was the non-scriptural term *homoousios*, which became subsequently the touchstone of orthodoxy.

[1] Eusebius, H. E., VII, 30.
[2] cf. Batiffol, op. cit., p. 109.
[3] Recorded by St. Hilary of Poitiers, *Collectanea Antiariana Parisina* (Frag. Hist.), A, VII, 4, C.S.E.L., Vol. 65, p. 91.
[4] The ecclesiastical policy of Constantine can best be understood if one subscribes to the highly probable view of N. H. Baynes that the Emperor was conscious of a divine mission to conserve the unity of the church, cf. *Constantine the Great and the Christian Church*, London, 1929, p. 29. It is doubtful whether he appreciated adequately the theological bases of the disputes, and certainly he viewed them as being subordinate to the overriding demands of unity.

A few years after the council Alexander died, and it was a foregone conclusion that he would be succeeded by Athanasius, who had been with him at Nicea. Athanasius was consecrated bishop on the 7th June, 328 and was destined to rule the church of Alexandria for 45 years. He is justly regarded as the champion of Nicene orthodoxy and in the defence of the *homoousios* he was five times exiled from his see.

The victory of the orthodox party at Nicea was more apparent than real, for half a century was to elapse before the Nicene faith would receive general acceptance in the East. In 328 the tide began to turn in favour of the Arians. In that year Constantine recalled Eusebius of Nicomedia from exile thereby setting aside the sentence of Nicea. None of the theories advanced to explain this decision is altogether satisfactory.[1] It is hard to see why Constantine should so soon undermine the enactments of the council. It is possible, though, that the Emperor acted on purely personal motives, since Eusebius was related to the imperial family and was very much in favour at court.[2]

Eusebius, now restored to his see, proceeded to depose various of his opponents on the pretext of ensuring peace and concord. It was not long before Athanasius became the object of his intrigues. Three attempts were made to convict him by accusations which were as ludicrous as they were malicious. At this stage Athanasius had little difficulty in proving his innocence. What is significant is that all the alleged crimes were offences against the civil law, hence he was charged and exculpated before the civil courts.[3] After these failures the Emperor was persuaded to summon the council of Tyre, which assembled in 335 allegedly to restore peace and concord in the East. The members of the council were carefully selected to make sure that only the Eusebians should be present; the Emperor was represented by the Count Dionysius. Athanasius was again charged with various improbable crimes, and seeing that he could hope for no justice in that assembly, he departed for Constantinople and was received by the Emperor. Constantine ordered the bishops of Tyre to come and accuse Athanasius in Constantinople. A deputation of five was sent and it was decided to charge him with attempting to stop the shipments of wheat from Egypt to the capital. Somehow they succeeded in convincing the Emperor, who ordered Athanasius to be exiled to Treves.

[1] Bardy, G., in Vol. III of Fliche & Martin, p. 100.
[2] Batiffol, *Cathedra Petri*, pp. 366, 367.
[3] Constantine had granted the clergy the privilege of trial before ecclesiastical courts, but it was not immediately put into effect throughout the whole empire.

Duchesne observed that Athanasius seemed to have no idea of appealing to Rome for justice.[1] In view of the sequel this may appear rather surprising, yet it must be remembered that the whole of the campaign against him had taken place in the sphere of civil law and the civil courts.[2] His opponents realized that it was useless to proceed against him on account of his fidelity to Nicea. The matter still appeared to be purely a process of civil law. Athanasius had not been deposed from the see of Alexandria nor was there any attempt to introduce another bishop into the see as if it were vacant. Furthermore, it does not appear that there was any known precedent of an appeal to the Pope against an Eastern council which might serve as an inspiration to Athanasius.

For the remainder of Constantine's life the situation remained unchanged. Athanasius was at Treves, Eusebius was all powerful, but the see of Alexandria remained vacant. Constantine died in 337 and after a brief struggle Constans I assumed control of the Western empire while Constantius II obtained the East. Their religious policy was not at first clear and the Arians underwent an initial setback when Athanasius was allowed to return to his see. The next incident in this rather intricate history is of exceptional importance and bears out what was stated above about the effect of caesaropapism in obstructing the authority of the popes. The Eusebian party was anxious to introduce into the see of Alexandria an excommunicated Arian by the name of Pistos, and accordingly they sent representatives to Rome to obtain for him the Pope's recognition. Indirectly, too, their aim was to secure recognition of the acts of the council of Tyre, thereby ensuring ratification of the displacement of Athanasius. The Bishop of Alexandria also sent representatives whose able defence of their pastor forced the Eusebian delegates to change their plans. They asked the Pope to summon a council and decide the matter himself.[3] This situation was the direct result of the apparent unconcern of the emperors and indicates how smoothly and easily the Eastern churches would have treated with Rome but for the interference of the civil power. As Batiffol remarked, 'In the absence of the imperial authority the affair followed the normal course, it finished at Rome.'[4]

[1]Duchesne, *Early History of the Church*, II, p. 521.
[2]cf. Scott, op. cit., p. 101, following Chapman.
[3]Contemporary accounts state explicitly that the initiative came from the Eusebian party. cf. Athanasius, *Apologia contra Arianos*, ch. 22, M.P.G., Vol. 25, col. 285. In modern times it has been agreed to by Harnack, *History of Dogma*, Vol. III, p. 224, n. 5.
[4]Batiffol, *La Paix Constantinienne*, p. 413.

When Pope Julius wrote to both parties summoning them to a council it seemed as if the affair was about to be settled once and for all. However, at that very moment Constantius II revealed his intentions by confirming the appointment to Alexandria of the candidate then favoured by the Eusebians, Gregory of Cappadocia. Gregory was introduced into the see under police protection, and Athanasius, after writing a dignified defence of his rights, fled to Rome. After various delays the Eusebian bishops wrote to the Pope refusing to attend the proposed council, denying his competence and threatening to excommunicate him.[1]

Despite the opposition of the Eusebians, Julius assembled the council in Rome in the autumn of 340. In addition to Athanasius a number of other Eastern bishops had come to seek justice after being expelled from their sees by Eusebius. The best known among them was Marcellus of Ancyra. He was joined by others from Thrace, Coelesyria, Phoenecia, and Palestine. After their cases had been heard they were all granted communion, and Julius addressed a letter to the Eusebian bishops announcing the decisions and justifying his action.[2]

As a vindication of the papal claims the letter itself leaves much to be desired. However, it must be understood in the context of the council. The very calling of the council was an unequivocal assertion of his superior jurisdiction, since it proclaimed the superiority of his council over the council of Tyre, and his competence to exculpate the Eastern bishops despite the previous condemnations. The letter which he sent announces these decisions and contains nothing which could weaken the stand which he had taken.[3] In view of the increasing tension between East and West he may well have considered it prudent to make no forceful statement of his claims for fear of aggravating an already delicate situation. The letter does, however, contain one passage which, though restrained, is a formal statement of his rights in the question of disciplinary troubles in the East:

'They [the bishops] should be judged in accord with the ecclesiastical law and not as has been done. All of us should have been notified, so that justice might thus be accomplished by all. . . . Are you ignorant that it is the custom that first of all we should be notified, and from here a just sentence should be decided. Surely if an accusation should be

---

[1] Text preserved in Sozomen, Ecclesiastical History, II, 15.
[2] Text preserved in Athanasius *Apologia*, chs. 21–33, M.P.G., Vol. 25, cols. 281–308.
[3] Batiffol, op. cit., pp. 427–8.

laid against the bishop of that city [i.e. Alexandria] notification ought to be sent to this church [i.e. Rome].'[1]

In reply to the action of Julius, the Eastern bishops, under the leadership of Constantius II and Eusebius, met in the autumn of 341 for the consecration of the basilica at Antioch and held a council there known ever since as the council *in Encaeniis*. This council represents the crystallization of the opposition to Rome. The assembled bishops confirmed Gregory in the possession of Alexandria and repudiated the bishops whom Julius had vindicated. In doctrinal matters they announced that they had granted communion to Arius, and in place of the Nicene creed they subscribed to the equivocal doctrinal formula attributed to Lucian of Antioch which made no mention of the keyword *homoousios*. There was, however, no explicit denial of the superiority of the Pope; that would come after Sardica.[2]

The council *in Encaeniis* marks the end of the first stage in the struggle for the recognition of the rights of Rome. The East had undergone many changes in less than half a century. Caesaropapism had appeared, Arianism was going from strength to strength, and opposition to the Pope was following in its train. By 341 the two parties have declared themselves. On the one hand there is Julius the Pope, Athanasius the champion of Nicene orthodoxy, and the bishops who have suffered for that orthodoxy at the hands of Eusebius. On the other hand there is the Arian Emperor Constantius II, the ambitious Eusebius now possessed of the see of Constantinople, and the Arian court party of the Eastern episcopate. The formal denial of the Roman claims was destined to occur after Sardica, and the high-water mark of Arianism would occur after 353, when Constantius II became master of the whole Roman world. The main course of the history of the papacy was thus to be set for the next century. Although generalizations are in danger of being inexact, it is substantially accurate to say that the latter half of the fourth century would see the restoration of Nicene orthodoxy, and the first half of the fifth century would witness the re-establishment of the Pope's authority. The third evil of the Eastern church, caesaropapism, was never remedied.

[1]Op. cit., section 35, M.P.G., Vol. 25, col. 308.
[2]Batiffol considered (*La Paix Constantinienne*, p. 446) that the fifteenth canon of the Council of Antioch (Hefele, I, p. 719) excluded the possibility of an appeal to Rome. However, it appears more probable that this interpretation of the fifteenth canon is not correct, and moreover that the Antiochene canons are to be attributed not to the council *in Encaeniis*, but to a synod held there in 330, cf. H. Hess, *The Canons of the Council of Sardica*, Oxford, 1958, pp. 112, 145–50.

Before proceeding to examine this series of events it is useful to pause and consider the legitimacy of the action of Athanasius. Although the document of Julius at the council of Rome in 340 seems to indicate, albeit in general terms, that the principle of appeal is not an innovation, it is nevertheless true that at the time of Athanasius there is no recorded instance of a strictly juridical appeal to Rome against an Eastern council. The situation confronting Athanasius is a classical example of the development of doctrine under the stress of circumstances. Athanasius had to decide whether in accepting Rome's offer to reinstate him he was acting in accord with the traditional principles or introducing an illegitimate deviation. It is clear that Athanasius considered that such an appeal to Rome was indeed in accord with the traditional principles; and he of all men cannot be accused of opportunism. Other witnesses, too, who wrote shortly after the events were of the same opinion. St. Ambrose, writing to the Emperor Theodosius, referred to the case of Athanasius and other Orientals who had recourse to Rome and the West, and the context of his letter shows that he considered it to be the correct and legitimate procedure.[1] In the following century the Eastern historian Socrates describes the appeal as if it were perfectly normal and adds the all-important reason: 'There each [of the accused bishops] laid his case before Julius, Bishop of Rome, who sent them back again into the East, restoring them to their respective sees by virtue of his letters, in the exercise of the Church of Rome's peculiar privilege.'[2]

In order to remedy the deadlock which ensued after the councils of Rome and Antioch, Pope Julius requested the Emperor Constans to negotiate with Constantius with a view to calling a council of both East and West. These preliminary negotiations were successful, and it was agreed that both parties should meet at Sardica (the modern Sophia), just inside the frontier of the Western empire.

The willingness of the Western bishops to reopen the case was a generous concession, since the judgement of Rome was considered as final. Regrettably there was no corresponding attitude on the part of the Eastern bishops. The council opened in the autumn of 343, and although the numbers are difficult to establish, it appears that there were approximately ninety Western and eighty Eastern bishops present. The Western party was led by Hosius of Cordoba, the veteran of Nicea; Julius was absent, but was represented by two priests. The Eastern

[1] Ambrose, Letter 13: 4, M.P.L., Vol. 16, col. 952.
[2] Socrates, *Ecclesiastical History*, II, 15.

party included some who were favourable to Athanasius, but the Eusebian party was in control and their decisions were operative. Before meeting in any formal session the Eastern party insisted that the condemnations of Athanasius and the rest should be considered as final. In the imposition of this condition their bad faith is manifest, since the council had been arranged precisely to reopen the whole matter. Hosius attempted every possible means of conciliation but the Eusebians were adamant. The Eastern bishops held a meeting of their own in which they reaffirmed the condemnations of Athanasius and the other bishops. They excommunicated Julius and the Western bishops who had accorded communion to their victims, and in an encyclical letter they upheld the principle, already implicit in their conduct, that the West (i.e. the Pope) could not revise the sentence of an Eastern council.[1]

The Western bishops do not appear to have been unduly disturbed by the departure of the others, and they proceeded to conduct the business of the council as it had been planned. The text of the letter which they sent to Egypt shows that they did not regard themselves merely as a localized council, but as one which had the competence to legislate for the whole church.[2] The council reaffirmed the innocence of Athanasius and the other Eastern bishops who had come to Rome and the intruders in their sees were excommunicated. The plans for the adoption of another Creed was successfully opposed by Athanasius, who held them to the creed of Nicea. Finally the canons of the council dealt with various duties and responsibilities of bishops and the all-important matter of appeal to Rome.

The actual words of the council are as follows:

'The Bishop Hosius said: If a bishop shall have been condemned and considers he has right on his side, so that a fresh sentence ought to be pronounced, let us honour, if it pleases you, the memory of the Apostle Peter; let those who have examined the case, or those who dwell in the neighbouring province, write to the Bishop of Rome, and he will furnish arbitrators. But if he cannot prove that his cause has need of a second judgement, let the first stand as valid.

'Bishop Gaudentius said: It is necessary, if it please you, to add to the decree full of charity which you have carried; if a bishop deposed by the judgement of the bishops of his region demand for himself a new

---

[1] cf. Synodal letter of the Eusebians at Sardica, preserved in Hilary, op. cit., A, VI, 24, 26, C.S.E.L., Vol. 65, pp. 63, 65.
[2] Batiffol, op. cit., p. 438, and *Cathedri Petri*, p. 227.

trial, let no successor be given to him before the Bishop of Rome, having decided the affair, has pronounced judgement.

'Bishop Hosius said: It has pleased us to add: if a bishop accused and deposed by the bishops of his district, in order to appeal about it takes refuge with the blessed Bishop of the Roman church to submit the matter to his decision, let the latter, if it seem right to him, proceed to a new examination of the case, let him be willing to write to the nearest bishops of his province to examine everything with care and exactitude and to decide according the truth.'[1]

The wording is somewhat discursive, but the provision is clear. The principle that the Pope is the final judge is upheld. In the execution of this function it is envisaged that the Pope will first decide whether another trial is warranted. If he should decide unfavourably at this stage, then the first decision is to be upheld. If, however, he should decide that a retrial is preferable he will designate the judges, and authorize a reopening of the case. This rather complicated machinery was never, in fact, utilized. In succeeding years the popes continued to receive appeals and to try them themselves.[2] The innovations of procedure are chiefly interesting as an indication of the spirit of conciliation which prompted them. The provision that the Pope should designate the judges of second instance, rather than hear the case himself, is a considerable concession which must have been made to placate the Eastern bishops.[3] There was no question of a new power, simply a new modality. Julius was explicit in holding the principle of appeal to have been traditional.[4] Finally the council addressed a synodal letter to Julius, who was saluted with the following words: 'For it will seem best and highly appropriate, if the Lord's bishops, each from his own province report to the head, that is to the see of Peter the Apostle.'[5]

The situation created by the events at Sardica represents the complete clarification of the two attitudes to the papacy. The parties which had been forming ever since the troubles of Athanasius began are now

[1]Text in Turner, C. H., *Ecclesiae Occidentalis Monumenta Juris Antiquissima*, Tome I, Vol. II, Fasicule iii, Oxford, 1930, p. 492, which is canon III in Turner's arrangement. The genuineness of these canons, once doubted, was vindicated conclusively by the same C. H. Turner in J.T.S., 1902, pp. 370–397.
[2]Duchesne, op. cit., II, p. 180.
[3]Bardy, G., op. cit., p. 129.
[4]Batiffol, op. cit., p. 447. The acknowledgement of Rome's superiority is undeniable, and it is not affected by the more intricate problem (still disputed) of the precise juridical status implied in that superiority, cf. Hess, op. cit., pp. 115–26.
[5]Hilary, op. cit., B, II, C.S.E.L., Vol. 65, p. 127.

seen to have adopted their definitive positions with regard to the principle at stake, namely the right of appeal to Rome, and indirectly the supremacy of the Pope. It is relevant at this point to inquire which party was in possession of the authentic tradition of the church. One party, that of the Eusebians under the protection of the Arian Emperor Constantius, denies the competence of the Pope to revise an Eastern sentence. The other party, that of Julius, Athanasius, the victims of the court bishops, and those who adhered to the faith of Nicea, uphold the Pope's competence. Merely to pose the question in these terms supplies the answer.

Although the opposition of the Arians was such that Julius seemed to have little success, his position was, in fact, stronger than it appeared. A century later the two Greek historians Socrates and Sozomen wrote about these very incidents and affirmed unquestioningly the rights of Rome. Their testimony is of considerable value, since it is generally recognized that they represent the general sentiment of their contemporaries.[1] In all the aspects of the struggle between Athanasius and the Eusebians they uphold the superior rights of Rome, but perhaps the most significant passage is the following extract from Socrates:

'On the receipt of these contradictory communications [i.e. reports of the innocence and guilt of Athanasius] Julius first replied to the bishops who had written to him from Antioch, complaining of the acrimonious feeling they had evinced in their letter, and charging them with a violation of the canons, in neglecting to request his attendance at the council, seeing that, by ecclesiastical law, no decisions of the churches are valid unless sanctioned by the Bishop of Rome.'[2]

The sources from which they derived their principles are not easy to discover. The account from which the above passage was taken contains certain errors which show that the writer was not relying solely on Athanasius.[3] The letter written by Julius on the occasion of the council of Rome was certainly known to them, but what they say goes beyond its scope. The reference to the 'ecclesiastical law' is not confirmed by any known legislation, and referred probably to the traditional unwritten customs of the church. Their testimony shows, in fact, how the power of the popes was received in the East despite the Arian opposition, and it

[1]Harnack, *History of Dogma*, Vol. III, p. 226, n. 2.
[2]Socrates, H. E., II, 17.
[3]Newman, *Development of Christian Doctrine*, edition of 1878, p. 159.

confirms that the attitude of the Eusebians was not the authentic tradition of the church.

After the council of Sardica the situation remained fairly static. The deadlock was almost complete and the only change to be observed was the steady increase of the power of the Arian party thanks to the favour of Constantius II. On January 18th, 350, Constans was assassinated and Magnentius assumed control in the West. As soon as Constantius had secured the Eastern frontier against the Persians, he embarked on an arduous campaign against his rival in the West. Magnentius was finally defeated in August, 353, after a long and bitter struggle, leaving the Arian Constantius sole master of the Roman world. Thereafter the situation deteriorated rapidly as far as the orthodox party was concerned. A bewildering series of synods and creeds followed in which the policy was directed against Athanasius rather than openly against Nicea. At the council of Milan all but four of the bishops capitulated to the pressure of the Emperor and condemned Athanasius. In 357, when even these had been deposed and Liberius, the Pope, was in exile, there was not one orthodox bishop left in any important see of the world. It appeared as if the Arian victory was complete.

Despite the appearances of the situation, the Arians were faced with many troubles of their own. The orthodox bishops had been removed, but the vast majority of the laity remained faithful to the creed of Nicea. What was perhaps more serious for the Arians was the extent of their own internal divisions. Although apparently united in their opposition to Nicea, they included within their ranks men whose attitudes to the Father and the Son ranged from theories of near equality to complete disparity. In fact, it was only the imperial backing which kept them in power, as the sequel was to show.

In the year 361 the new Emperor, Julian, reversed the policy of his predecessor by recalling the orthodox bishops from exile. Arianism was not immediately vanquished, but from that moment its fate was sealed. Several years were to pass before its extinction, even within the Roman world, but deprived of the imperial protection it could not survive. This dismal failure of the policy of Constantius is an indication of the limitations of the imperial power. The state could cause the utmost difficulty to the church from outside, but it was unable to alter the inner reality of the doctrinal system and constitution.

The next few years present another series of councils in which the faith of Nicea was asserted and an attempt was made to introduce order after the chaos of the Arian period. In the West the situation was relatively tranquil, owing to a succession of orthodox emperors. In the East, however, the short reign of the orthodox Jovian was followed by that of the semi-Arian Valens from 364 to 378, which threatened a recurrence of the policy of Constantius. Of the many synods of this period, that of Lampsaca is of interest on account of the evidence which it affords as to the state of papal authority. The synod met in 364 and among the legates who were sent to Rome to re-establish communion there was a certain Eustathius. This man had been elected Bishop of Sebaste in Lower Armenia in 356, but had been deposed by the Arians a few years later.[1] When the legates arrived at Rome, Liberius insisted that they should subscribe to the creed of Nicea. This they agreed to and they were granted communion. In order to protect them against the heretics who were still powerful in the East the Pope also assured them that if a charge should be brought against them they should appeal to him and he would appoint the judges who would hear the case.[2] As Batiffol remarks, this provision goes beyond the legislation of Sardica, since the Pope is here prepared to appoint even the judges of first instance.[3] The acceptance of this arrangement is a further indication that Sardica was acknowledged in the East more generally than its immediate sequel seemed to indicate.

Liberius also gave to Eustathius a document which appears to have been some kind of letter of reinstatement. Precisely what it was is uncertain, but when he presented it to the council of Tyana he was restored to his see. In the history of Oriental appeals to Rome this particular case has several unusual features, but the principle at stake is clear. What is of more interest is that St. Basil knew of the affair[4] and he seems to have regarded it as a regular method of procedure.[5]

One of the most serious difficulties alleged against the doctrine of the Roman primacy is the scant attention which it received in the teaching of the great Greek fathers. Odd remarks can be cited, such as the oft-quoted tributes of St. John Chrysostom and St. Gregory Nazianzen,[6]

[1] His own Trinitarian orthodoxy, both then and later, was decidedly questionable.
[2] Recorded by Socrates, H. E., IV, 12.
[3] Batiffol, *Siège Apostolique*, p. 11.
[4] Recorded in his letter No. 263, M.P.G., Vol. 32, col. 980.
[5] Batiffol, op. cit., p. 11.
[6] Chrysostom, *De. Sacerdotio*, II, 1, 'Why did Christ shed his blood? To purchase the sheep which he confided to Peter and those who came after him.' M.P.G., Vol. 48, col. 632. Gregory Nazianzen, *Carmina de Vita Sua*, vv. 568–72, describes Rome as the church which presides over all, preserving concord. M.P.G., Vol. 37, col. 1068.

but none of them has left a systematic study of the matter. A variety of reasons can be adduced to account for this. The Greek mind was little inclined to such an empirical matter as the theology of an organ of government. They were writing, moreover, at a time when the Roman power was to a certain extent obscured in the East, and when their energies were concerned with the more urgent danger of Arianism. It is always difficult to say how the fathers of the church would have answered had they been faced with questions which became actual only at a much later date, but in the problem of the Roman primacy an analogous solution is provided by the events of their lives. Had the career of St. Athanasius been one of unruffled peace it is doubtful whether he would have written about the right of appeal to Rome. Yet when faced with the opportunity of availing himself of this authority he decided that it was right to do so.

A similar situation arose in the life of St. Basil. He was elected to the see of Caesarea in Cappadocia in 370 and devoted the rest of his life to the restoration of orthodoxy and ecclesiastical communion in the East. The difficulties which faced him were immense. It is hard to appreciate the extent of the confusion wrought by the Arians and the Emperor Constantius. So many bishops had been deposed, exiled, and recalled that it was almost impossible to say who was orthodox or who was in communion with whom. This situation was aggravated by the tragic schism of the church of Antioch, where three bishops claimed to be the legitimate occupant of the see. Added to these difficulties was the attitude of the West, which was, at least in appearances, unsympathetic in the extreme. By this time the lack of understanding between East and West was growing acute. The language situation is an indication of the gradual drift apart. Greek had ceased to be the spoken language of Rome. In the middle of the third century Latin was adopted for the papal correspondence, and in the time of Pope Damasus the liturgy, too, abandoned Greek in favour of Latin. In the theological and practical sphere the West, with some justification, had tended to look on the whole of the East as heretical. What they expected of them was submission, not simply the resumption of communion.

St. Basil appreciated, almost from the outset of his work, that the East would be unable to recover from its plight without the assistance of the West. Accordingly he turned first to Athanasius as the most suitable intermediary, and asked him to solicit the sending of delegates from Rome.[1] On receiving encouragement from Athanasius, he wrote to

[1] Basil, Letter 69, 1, M.P.G., Vol. 32, col. 432.

Damasus with the same request, namely that representatives from the West should come and assist in the work of restoration.[1] Negotiations appeared to be going satisfactorily and Rome sent the priest Sabinus, who proceeded to Caesarea, where he was well received by the Eastern bishops. In spite of these auspicious beginnings, the Pope was wary of St. Basil on account of his being in communion with Meletius of Antioch, while Rome favoured his rival Paulinus. As a result, Sabinus departed for Rome equipped with yet more requests for assistance and sympathy, but no tangible results followed from the visit.

The persecution of the orthodox by Valens put an end to this first series of encounters, but when in 375, peace was restored to the church, Basil again wrote to the West for assistance. It does not seem that he was unduly optimistic about the outcome of his advances, for at the same period he wrote to Eusebius of Samosata lamenting the haughty disdain of Damasus and the Western church. He complained that they did not know the truth of the situation, nor would they condescend to find out.[2] A further blow to St. Basil was the granting of communion to Paulinus of Antioch by both Rome and Alexandria. In spite of all these setbacks Basil pursued his policy with a remarkable tenacity of purpose, and in 377 he wrote again to the West asking for the condemnation of Apollinaris for his heterodox Christological theory, and Eustathius of Sebaste because he denied the divinity of the Holy Ghost.[3] This letter was taken to Rome by Dorotheus, the emissary of Basil, and in response to the request Damasus summoned a council, among whose participants was Peter, the successor of St. Athanasius. Two fragments have survived which record the doctrinal decisions of the council condemning Apollinarianism and upholding the divinity of the Holy Ghost.[4] It is only by reference to another source that the personal condemnations can be ascertained. One of the letters of Damasus[5] which is difficult to date exactly, but which can be assigned to the period between 377 and 381, answers a request from a group of Easterns. It appears from the terms of the reply of Damasus that it was a request, from the priests of the church of Berytus that their bishop, Timothy, should be deposed because of his Apollinarianism. In reply to this appeal Damasus asks

[1]Basil, Letter 70, M.P.G., Vol. 32, col. 433, 436.
[2]Basil, Letter 239, M.P.G., Vol. 32, col. 893.
[3]Basil, Letter 263, M.P.G., Vol. 32, col. 980.
[4]The fragments known as 'Illud sane miramur' and 'Non nobis' are recorded in Coustant: *Pontificum Romanorum Epistolae*, Gottingen, 1796, Vol. I, pp. 334, 335.
[5]Jaffé, n. 234.

them why they keep asking about this matter, 'since he was deposed here, by a judgement of the Apostolic See, in the presence of Peter, Bishop of Alexandria, at the same time as his master Apollinaris'. This can hardly refer to anything but the Roman synod of 377 and provides reliable evidence that the accused bishops were condemned as well as their doctrines.[1] Since all this took place at the instigation of St. Basil, it serves as an indication that he recognized some measure of superiority for the see of Rome.[2]

In 379 St. Basil died, a few years before the council of Constantinople which achieved, in a large measure, what he had so long striven for. The bitter things which he said about the Pope do not amount to a denial of papal authority, but they show him to have inclined to the opinion widely accepted in the East at that date, that Rome was a source of final arbitration to be appealed to only when all else had failed. It was an attitude to the papacy which tended to regard it as something legitimate but extraordinary in the government of the church.

With the accession of the orthodox Theodosius in 379 the hopes of St. Basil appeared capable of realization. The Emperor's first preoccupation was to secure the Danubian frontier against the Goths. The achievement of this task left him free to turn his thoughts towards the welfare of the church. His orthodoxy was apparent from the first, since by the decree of February 28th, 380, he had commanded the acceptance of the faith which the Apostle Peter had preached to the Romans and which was upheld by Damasus and Peter of Alexandria.

Records of the council of Constantinople are fragmentary in the extreme. The details recorded by Socrates, Sozomen and Theodoret amount to no more than a list of participants, the canons, and the letter to Theodosius.[3] The Emperor summoned bishops from all parts of the Eastern empire. About 150 assembled in May, 381, representing all the Eastern provinces except Egypt. No Western bishop was present except Acholius of Thessalonika, who arrived after the opening of the council, as did two Egyptian bishops.

The purpose of the council was to restore Nicene orthodoxy to the East and to repair the confusion of the Arian period. In the practical

[1]Batiffol, op. cit., p. 107
[2]Batiffol, *Cathedra Petri*, p. 233. In fact, Basil's general attitude of applying to the West for help implies that there was some authority in the West which was capable of intervening in the East, and which did not have to await a general council.
[3]Mansi, III, cols. 557–60. Of the seven canons traditionally ascribed to the council, only the first four are genuine.

sphere the council provided a bishop for the see of Constantinople by electing first of all St. Gregory Nazianzen and after his resignation, Nectarius.

The legislation enacted is known only by the four canons. The first of these upholds the faith of Nicea and condemns the various Trinitarian heresies which were then troubling the East. Listed among them is the comparatively new heresy of the Macedonians who denied the divinity of the Holy Ghost. The second canon regulates the juridical affairs of the civil dioceses. The bishops of the various dioceses are forbidden to meddle in the affairs of other regions and the competence of each diocese for its own affairs is upheld. The importance of this canon in the development of the patriarchates has been discussed already,[1] and it should be noted that the individual patriarch is not yet envisaged. At this stage it was simply a question of safeguarding the regional autonomy, which was, of course, the prelude to an autonomous patriarch.

The best-known enactment of the council is the third canon, which states 'that the Bishop of Constantinople should enjoy prerogatives of honour after the Bishop of Rome because Constantinople is the new Rome'. The anti-papal interpretation of this canon has been considerably exaggerated, for, in fact, it is an indirect testimony to the traditional primacy of Rome.[2] The inadequacy, too, of Eastern ecclesiology is manifest. The notion that ecclesiastical authority should be based on the civil prestige of the city was altogether alien to the tradition of the church. Ever since the second century the principle of Apostolic origin had been the basis of a church's claim to pre-eminence. The formulation of this principle in the third canon represents the origin of Constantinople's challenge to Rome, a challenge which was void of justifiable foundation according to the traditional law of the church.

The fourth canon was merely a declaration of the invalidity of the ordination of Maximus, who had been intruded into the see of Constantinople some years previously. Of the rest of the council's deliberations practically nothing is known. The council held at Constantinople in the following year speaks of a longer dogmatic document whose text has not been preserved. It can be asserted safely that it was not the Creed which later bore the name of Constantinople. The intention of the council was against the production of another Creed and scholars

[1]See above, p. 138.
[2]Jalland, op. cit., p. 252.

are now agreed that the Nicene formula was accepted without modification.

After the closure of the council representatives were sent to Rome to obtain letters of communion for the newly elected Nectarius. The necessity of communion with Rome was recognized as being imperative. Until the schism of the eleventh century the bishops of Constantinople, Antioch and Alexandria would seek letters of communion from Rome on the occasion of their accession.[1] The letters of communion were duly given, but the Pope does not appear to have been acquainted with the *acta* of the council. At this date there was no question of its enjoying oecumenical status.

The effect of this council on the authority of Rome has been variously estimated. The opposition to the primacy is more apparent than real. What is perhaps more significant than the provisions of the third canon is the omission from the second. When limiting the spheres of influence of the Eastern bishops, the council made no mention of any limitation for Rome, although none of the participants could have been ignorant of the Pope's recent interventions.[2] It is true that it was an Eastern council, but Sardica had not hesitated to pronounce an excommunication against the Pope for his activities in the East. It is now fairly well agreed that the council was at pains to limit the authority not of Rome but of Alexandria.[3] However, it is important to retain a balanced opinion of the council. As Batiffol has pointed out its main purpose was not to oppose Alexandria but to restore orthodoxy to the East.[4] The basis of this restoration was the unity of faith guaranteed by the creed of Nicea. As a subsidiary means of preserving unity and concord the council attempted to set up a state of juridical autonomy which paid scant attention to the rights of Rome. Rome[5] was not blind to the dangers of this policy and the inherent threat of the third canon. In the following year Damasus held a synod at Rome which upheld the traditional principle of the Apostolicity of the older see.[6] The inadequacy of this system of church government was to be demonstrated dramatically by the tragic affair of St. John Chrysostom.

By the end of the fourth century the Eastern church had overcome

[1] Batiffol, *Cathedra Petri*, p. 75.
[2] Cayré, F., *Patrologie et Histoire de la Théologie*, 1953 ed., Vol. I, p. 466.
[3] Duchesne, op. cit., II, pp. 348–9; Caspar, op. cit., I, p. 234; Jalland, op. cit., p. 252; Bardy and Palanque in Fliche & Martin, III, p. 290.
[4] Batiffol, *Siège Apostolique*, p. 132.
[5] cf. Batiffol, *Cathedra Petri*, p. 73.
[6] See above, p. 165.

the first of its major difficulties, namely Arianism. The doctrinal orthodoxy proclaimed at Constantinople in 381 was secure, and Arianism survived only in isolated pockets of resistance. The second problem which remained to be rectified was the question of the authority of the Pope. The opposition of the Arians had recently caused it to be accorded little recognition in the East. The first stage towards a full exercise of the papal prerogatives was the policy of Innocent I in the affair of St. John Chrysostom.

Although attached to the church of Antioch, John was elected to the see of Constantinople on the death of Nectarius. According to Socrates he was consecrated bishop on February 26th, 398.[1] His predecessor, the aged Nectarius, had pursued a peaceful policy causing no trouble to anyone. By contrast St. John began at once to use his powerful eloquence to reform the many scandals and abuses in the Christian community, thereby earning himself many enemies. The hostility of this numerous group in the capital explains in part the ease with which he was later expelled from his see.

The first event in the process which culminated in his expulsion was the arrival of a group of Egyptian monks in the year 401. They had been excommunicated and expelled by Theophilus, the Bishop of Alexandria, and came to Constantinople seeking protection. Without trespassing on the rights of Alexandria, John wrote to Theophilus on their behalf. The reply which he received was the arrival of a group of delegates from Egypt who came with a wealth of alleged evidence against the fugitive monks. The monks retaliated by bringing legal action against their accusers, and also against Theophilus himself. So successful was this latter suit that the Emperor ordered Theophilus to come to Constantinople to answer the charges which had been laid against him. As it was primarily an ecclesiastical case, the Emperor appointed John as the judge in complete contravention of the council of 381. John rightly refused to do any such thing, since he had no jurisdiction over the see of Alexandria. Theophilus arrived in the summer of 403, not alone as he had been commanded, but accompanied by twenty-nine suffragens. Three weeks of intrigue followed, during which time he gained the confidence of the Emperor and rallied to his side the many enemies of St. John. Being assured of the imperial favour he held a council of his supporters in the imperial residence on the Bosphorus known as the palace of the Oak. John was summoned to present himself before this

[1]Socrates, H. E., VI, 2.

council, ever since known as the council of the Oak, but rightly he refused. In his absence he was charged with a variety of crimes, all of which were fictitious except, ironically, that of meddling in the affairs of another diocese. His condemnation was a foregone conclusion, and in spite of his protest against the illegality of the proceedings, the Emperor confirmed the sentence by a decree of banishment. In July, 403, John was exiled to Prenctos in Bithynia.

The Emperor's support, so easily given to Theophilus, was withdrawn with equal mobility, and John was permitted to return to Constantinople a few months after his expulsion. John, to his credit, did not seek to intrigue for the favour of the Emperor as a safeguard for the future, but continued his policy of moral reform as before. Theophilus, on the other hand, continued to intrigue against him from Alexandria, with such skill that in the spring of 404 the Emperor confirmed the previous sentence of banishment. On the eve of his departure John wrote to the Pope informing him of the situation and protesting against the illegality of the action.[1] The same letter was also addressed to the bishops of Milan and Aquileia. The same messenger also brought letters to Rome from the clergy of Constantinople and from a group of forty bishops who supported John. This batch of letters reached Rome three days after the letter of Theophilus, in which he had informed the Pope of the deposition of St. John. The contradictory statements of the two parties left the Pope somewhat confused, but before long he became acquainted with the true situation by a number of John's supporters who came to Rome on his behalf. At this stage in the case it is well to note that there was no question of an appeal in a strict juridical sense. The letter of St. John to Innocent makes no mention of the papal privileges.[2] Initially, at least, St. John was making a protest against the violation of the ruling of the council of Constantinople rather than an appeal of the type envisaged by Sardica.[3]

On the receipt of fuller information about the matter, Innocent decided to try and procure a general council which would decide the dispute. He suggested Thessalonika as the meeting-place, but the negotiations proceeded no further. The Eastern Emperor was unwilling to reopen the affair; Atticus, the new Bishop of Constantinople, was of the same mind, and Theophilus had no reason for wanting a review of

[1]Chrysostom, letter of April 404, reproduced in, Palladius, *Dialogue on the Life of St. John Chrysostom*, II, M.P.G., Vol. 47, cols. 5 ff.
[2]Batiffol, *Siège Apostolique*, p. 313.
[2]Caspar, op. cit., I, p. 316.

the case. As far as the matter concerned the rights of Rome and the council of 381 it is significant that none of the opposition was based on a claim of Eastern autonomy. St. John was agreeable to having the matter examined by a council as suggested by Rome, and it is hard to accuse him of motives of expediency.

The failure to secure a council did not deter the Pope. He wrote to John and assured him of his support and continuing communion,[1] thereby showing that Rome was not obliged to wait upon the decision of a council.[2] Next, he refused to give letters of communion to Atticus, and likewise he withdrew his communion from Porphyrios of Antioch, who had accorded his communion to Atticus, and from Theophilus the instigator of the crime. The death of St. John in Armenia on September 14th, 407, somewhat altered the affair. A council for his reinstatement was out of the question, so the Pope insisted that his name be reinserted in the diptychs. This may appear as a small point to hold out for, but the Pope could hope to obtain no more at that time.[3] It was, moreover, a subsequent acknowledgement of John's innocence and a tacit disavowal of the council of the Oak.

The first of the great Eastern sees to regain communion with Rome was that of Antioch. Alexander succeeded Porphyrios and on compliance with the Pope's condition he was accorded communion. Shortly afterwards Innocent wrote to him answering queries on various problems of ecclesiastical law.[4] The importance of this letter has been emphasized by Caspar, who points out that it marks the complete resumption of normal relations betwen Antioch and Rome.[5]

Theodoret declares that Atticus made several attempts to obtain the communion of Rome,[6] but Innocent insisted on reinsertion of John's name in the diptychs before he granted it. A letter which he addressed to Maximianus of Macedonia reveals his insistence on this condition, and throws light upon the role of the Roman church in this communion. 'Communion, once broken off, cannot be renewed until the person concerned gives proof that the reasons for which communion was broken off are no longer operative, and that what is imposed as a condition of peace has been fulfilled. We still await a declaration from Atticus giving

---

[1]Jaffé, n. 289.
[2]Batiffol, *Cathedra Petri*, p. 238.
[3]Batiffol, *Siège Apostolique*, p. 324.
[4]Jaffé, n. 310.
[5]Caspar, op. cit., I, p. 323.
[6]Theodoret, Ecclesiastical History, V, 34.

us assurance that all the conditions which at different times we have laid down have been fulfilled. We are willing to renew our communion with him when he makes fitting petition for it, and when he proves that he deserves it.'[1] Last of all Alexandria conformed to the required conditions and communion was granted to the successor of Theophilus, his nephew Cyril.

The successful conclusion of the affair was an important step towards the re-establishment of the rights of Rome which had been obscured to no small extent during the Arian crisis. It illustrates principally the necessity of communion with Rome and the right of the Pope to decide on the conditions for that communion.[2] Throughout the whole affair there was no suggestion that the Pope should keep out of the affairs of the East in compliance with the council of 381. In fact, the arrival at Rome of so many of John's supporters is a testimony to the superior status of Rome which they turned to for assistance.[3] The arrival of these advocates for John and the subsequent negotiations from Rome transformed the initial character of the affair. Originally there had been no question of an appeal, but in the end Rome was acting as the supreme court.[4]

The next major event in the East which involved the Pope was the Nestorian heresy, which culminated in the council of Ephesus. Although the council of Chalcedon is regarded as the high watermark of papal authority in the East, the council at Ephesus was, in fact, the decisive battle for the re-establishment of that authority. Needless to say, the question of the papal prerogatives was not on the agenda of the council. The authority of the Pope was incidental to the doctrinal debate and it must be understood against this background. Several complicating factors were also present to confuse the issue, and what should have been a straightforward examination of the official tradition of the church was unnecessarily complicated by the rivalries of the great Eastern sees, and the schools of Alexandria and Antioch, not to mention the imperial interference.

The heresiarch Nestorius, who had been trained in the theological tradition of the school of Antioch, became Bishop of Constantinople in 427. His zeal against the many heretics in the city was sincere, and it was partly in reaction to their tenets that he formulated his own theory

[1]Jaffé, n. 308.
[2]Batiffol, *Siège Apostolique*, p. 336.
[3]Scott, op. cit., p. 134.
[4]Batiffol, *Cathedra Petri*, p. 239.

on the natures of Jesus Christ. In order to safeguard the perfection of His humanity, Nestorius put forward the explanation that in Christ there were two persons, the divine and the human, united by a close moral bond. The theory is intrinsically possible and from the purely theoretical standpoint it had much to commend it. However, it did not accord with the facts of revelation which demanded a still closer union, in fact one person only. Although the intricacies of Christology had not been explored very deeply at that date, there was one fact which crystallized the dispute which was soon to arise. It was the status of the Virgin Mary. Traditionally the Greeks had accorded her the title *Theotokos* (God-bearer), because her son was truly divine. Nestorius, unwilling to admit the presence of only one person in Christ, considered that this title was theologically inaccurate.

The theory of Nestorius soon met with strong opposition in many quarters. In the capital itself it was ill received, especially by the monks, and more serious still was the hostility which it aroused in Egypt. Cyril of Alexandria kept himself fully informed of the affair and in 429 the two bishops exchanged correspondence on the subject. Undoubtedly the theological attitudes of their two schools contributed something to their differences, but Cyril realized, too, that the view of Nestorius was incompatible with the traditional teaching of the church. The first move towards Rome was made by Nestorius, who, realizing that trouble was brewing, wrote to the Pope to try and show that his Christology was acceptable. Pope Celestine made no decision then, but kept himself informed of the matter from sources other than Cyril.

In the following year the correspondence between Cyril and Nestorius became more heated, and by the Easter of 430 he decided to take action. He wrote first of all to the imperial court complaining of the unorthodoxy of Nestorius, and then wrote more fully to Celestine. The mere fact of this letter is an indication of the improved position of Rome in the eyes of the Eastern bishops. In similar circumstances Theophilus had not considered such a step necessary; evidently the affair of St. John Chrysostom had clarified the principle of diocesan autonomy which had been decided in 381. After acquainting the Pope with the heretical opinions of Nestorius, he asks whether communion should be broken off: 'God requires us to be vigilant in these matters and the ancient customs of the churches persuade that we should communicate with your Holiness in matters of this kind. . . . We do not openly and publicly break off communion with (Nestorius) before communicating these things to your Piety. Deign therefore to declare what seems to you right; and whether one must remain still in communication with him, or ought it to be proclaimed publicly that no one communicates with one who professes and teaches such errors.'[1] The letter formed part of a complete dossier of information relative to the case which Cyril sent to the Pope.

Celestine decided that the time had come for him to take action and he summoned a council of Italian bishops to meet at Rome in August. Unfortunately the acts of this council have not been preserved, but the decisions are abundantly clear, thanks to the letters which were issued at the close of it. The doctrine of Nestorius was judged to be heretical, the accuracy of the expression *Theotokos* was upheld and Nestorius was condemned. The circumstances of this condemnation are somewhat unusual. It is clear in the first place that the sentence had already been passed in Rome, and that it needed no more than to be put into effect.[2] The manner of executing the sentence was somewhat of an innovation. A letter from Celestine informs Cyril that he is commissioned to demand from Nestorius the retractation of his errors under pain of incurring the excommunication already decreed at Rome. If he does not comply within ten days Cyril is directed to depose him and arrange for the installation of a successor.[3] The key sentence is as follows: 'Wherefore, assuming to yourself the authority of our see and using our stead and place with power, you will deliver this sentence with the utmost severity. . . .' Dr. Kidd[4] declares that Cyril was told to 'join the authority of the Roman see to his own', deducing thereby that it was a joint endeavour. The inaccuracy of such a rendering has been pointed out by Scott,[5] who calls attention to the Greek συναφθείσης σοί, which accords perfectly with the immediate context, making it clear that Cyril is to act as Celestine's delegate. This interpretation is further confirmed by the letters which were sent to Antioch, Jerusalem, Thessalonika and Philippi.[6] Celestine speaks of the sentence 'pronounced by us', but makes no mention of Cyril. In making Cyril his executor he was imitating the imperial procedure; this particular practice had already been used in Africa.

[1]Cyril, Alex., Letter 9, M.P.G., Vol. 77, col. 37.
[2]Scott, op. cit., pp. 149, 150; Bardy, G., Fliche & Martin, Vol. IV, p. 173.
[3]Jaffé, n. 372. Greek and Latin texts in Mansi, IV, col. 1017.
[4]Kidd, op. cit., p. 106. This view is not uncommon among Anglicans.
[5]Scott, op. cit., p. 150.
[6]The text of each is the same. Jaffé, n. 373.

From then onwards the matter began to assume distressing complications. Cyril appears to have been in no hurry to act. He assembled a council at Alexandria in November to decide upon a plan of action. Four bishops were chosen to make the journey to Constantinople to demand the retractation of Nestorius. For the profession of orthodox faith which they would present to him Cyril put forward a formulary of his own, the famous twelve anathemas or propositions concerning the person of Christ. This document was so clearly the product of the school of Alexandria, and not exclusively the tradition of the church, that Cyril was acting outside his mandate in expecting Nestorius to subscribe to it.

The position of Nestorius was becoming more and more insecure. He wrote to the Pope again to try and make his theory seem acceptable,[1] but realizing that he could hope for little from that quarter, he had recourse to the expedient which had already caused so much trouble in the church—he appealed to the Emperor. The Emperor acceded to his request and summoned a general council which would meet at Ephesus on the feast of Pentecost, June 7th, 431. The four delegates from Egypt arrived after the council had been announced, and Nestorius, feeling somewhat more secure, refused to receive them. The canonical status of Nestorius was rather difficult to decide at this time, yet to judge from the letter which the Pope wrote to the Emperor acquiescing in the council, he considered the sentence as valid but still awaiting execution.[2]

The winter passed without further incident, and in the spring the various parties prepared for the council. In Rome three legates were nominated, the bishops Arcadius and Projectus, and the priest Philip. They were instructed to co-operate with Cyril, who would preside, and to ensure that the rights of the Roman see were safeguarded. They took with them a letter from Celestine to the council. The Emperor for his part acted, for the moment, with considerable prudence. The Count Candidian was sent to Ephesus to supervise the good order of the council and to ensure that the deliberations were conducted by the bishops alone. The first of the vitally interested parties to arrive at Ephesus was Nestorius, who was followed soon by Cyril, who came accompanied by fifty bishops and many other supporters. On June 12th Juvenal and the Palestinian bishops arrived, and shortly afterwards Memnon and the bishops of Asia. The official date for opening had

[1]The letter is included among those of Celestine, M.P.L., Vol. 50, col. 499.
[2]Jaffé, n. 380.

passed, but there was still no sign of the papal legates or John of Antioch and the bishops of the Orient. As each day passed the tension mounted. The bishops grouped around Nestorius and Cyril intrigued and schemed, while their supporters not infrequently came to blows in the streets.

On June 21st Cyril decided to wait no longer, and despite the protests of the Count Candidian, he summoned the bishops to meet in the principal church on the following day. The legitimacy of this action is even now debated. Whether he was anxious to start before the arrival of the pro-Nestorian Bishop of Antioch is not easy to say. However, this particular detail does not affect the position of Rome. If Cyril did act rightly it was in virtue of the authority that the Pope had given him. The first session comprised about 160 bishops from all the major groups in the town. Nestorius and his supporters refused to attend. Cyril ordered the reading of various documents relative to the case, including the famous twelve anathemas and his letters to Nestorius, and they were judged to be in accord with the faith of Nicea. The theory of Nestorius was next condemned as heretical and he himself was declared excommunicate and deposed. The text of this sentence is of importance not only for its reference to the Roman see but as evidence of the close link between the council and Rome. 'The Holy Synod said, since the most impious Nestorius will not obey our citation, and has not received the most holy and God-fearing bishops whom we sent unto him, we have necessarily betaken ourselves to the examination of his impieties, and having apprehended from his letters and his writings and from his recent sayings in this metropolis, which have been repeated, that his opinions and teachings are impious, we being necessarily impelled thereto by the canons and by the letter of our most holy Father and colleague Celestine, bishop of the Roman church, with many tears have arrived at the following sentence against him: Our Lord Jesus Christ, who has been blasphemed by him, defines by this present most holy Synod, that the same Nestorius is deprived of episcopal dignity and all sacerdotal intercourse.'[1] As Abbot Butler has pointed out,[2] the words 'necessarily impelled, etc.', rule out any idea of a semi-independent council as envisaged, for instance, by Jalland.[3] After this session both parties wrote to the Emperor, Cyril announcing the deposition and Nestorius protesting against the illegality of the proceedings.

[1]Mansi, IV, col. 1212.
[2]Butler, *The Church and Infallibility*, p. 174, n. 2.
[3]Jalland, op. cit., p. 299, n. 2.

On June 24th John of Antioch arrived with the bishops of the Orient. When they became acquainted with the situation they held their own council and excommunicated Cyril and Memnon. This decision, too, was communicated to the Emperor. Faced with conflicting missives, the Emperor adopted the expedient of repudiating all that had so far been decreed by any branch of the council. In the ensuing confusion the Roman legates arrived and from the start they succeeded in introducing a measure of order into the proceedings. Acting in accordance with their instructions, they associated with Cyril and presented the Pope's letter to the bishops. On the following day, July 11th, they asked to be acquainted with the proceedings of the previous session of June 22nd. The same documents were again read out, together with the sentence against Nestorius, and in the name of the Pope the legates confirmed what had been decided.[1] On this occasion the priest Philip made his celebrated speech expounding the papal authority: 'No one has any doubt, on the contrary it has been recognized in all ages, that the holy and most blessed Peter, chief and head of the Apostles, pillar of the faith, foundation of the Catholic Church, received from our Lord Jesus Christ, the Saviour and Redeemer of the human race, the keys of the kingdom, and that to him has been given power for the binding and loosing of sins: it is he who unto this day and without intermission both lives and judges in his successors. His successor and rightful representative, our most blessed Pope, Bishop Celestine, has sent us to this council, the assembly of which has been ordered by the most Christian Emperors, as substitutes for his appearance in person, in that he is ever mindful of the Catholic faith, and in preserving it safeguards the doctrines of the Apostles, as they have come down from your fathers and forebears.'[2] This statement is one of the clearest expositions of the doctrine of the papacy that is to be found in the early church. Its importance is enhanced, too, by its being enunciated in a general council. Although Philip spoke in Latin and few of his hearers would have understood it, the statement was translated into Greek and formed part of the official Greek text of the acts of the council. No protest was ever made, which can only mean that his statement was accepted by the fathers of the council.[3]

Two further sessions took place on the 16th and 17th of July. John of

[1]Mansi, IV, col. 1293.
[2]Mansi, IV, col. 1295.
[3]Scott, op. cit., p. 154.

Antioch, having been summoned, refused to attend and was excommunicated. Unlike Nestorius he was not deposed. In his case it was not a question of faith but of acknowledging the council's legitimacy. It has also been suggested by Duchesne that the Roman legates may have ensured this moderation.[1] Notifications of this were sent to the Emperor and the Pope, and the council came to an end after two more sessions.

The termination of the ecclesiastical deliberations did not at once put an end to the affair. The Emperor reversed his previous decision of repudiation and arrested all those who had been condemned by the earlier sessions. As a result Cyril and Memnon found themselves imprisoned as well as Nestorius. After much intrigue Cyril managed to procure the release of Memnon and himself. Nestorius, however, was banished. In other words the original plan of Celestine was at last put into effect. The Pope, in his reply to the synodal letter, confirmed all the enactments of the council with one exception. The excommunication of John of Antioch he reserved to his own competence, thereby annulling the sentence which the council had inflicted on him.[2] It was some time before John and Cyril made peace. Theodoret of Cyr acted as intermediary and induced John to accept the condemnation of Nestorius, while Cyril subscribed to an Antiochene formula on the natures of Christ.

The council of Ephesus has several features which are of singular interest in the history of the papacy. In the first place it is evident that the authority of Pope Celestine was the predominant influence, despite the important role played by Cyril. A few years later the council of Chalcedon spoke of Ephesus as being presided over by Cyril and Celestine, though they must have realized that Celestine had never left Rome.[3] Thanks to the discovery of an apologia of Nestorius himself, it is possible to ascertain his view on the role played by Celestine; he says as follows: 'The bishop of Rome who was exercising the direction of the plotting of the Council of Ephesus against me. . . .'[4] The effect of Celestine's intervention was decisive. It made possible the legitimate deposition of the Bishop of Constantinople. It can hardly be doubted that Cyril was ambitious to advance the influence of his see at the expense of that of Constantinople. Yet this does not account for the whole of the matter. He was sincerely concerned for the preservation of

[1]Duchesne, op. cit., III, p. 249.
[2]Section 8 of the letter to the bishops, Jaffé, n. 385.
[3]Mansi, VII, col. 29.
[4]Translated by F. Nau as *Le Livre d'Heraclide*, Paris, 1910, p. 327.

theological orthodoxy and in his activity he had to proceed within the framework of constitutional methods. The affair of St. John Chrysostom emphasized the fact that the Bishop of Alexandria had no legitimate power over his colleague at Constantinople. In the case of Nestorius, Cyril realized beforehand that he could not act alone. However the competence of Rome is undeniable. Celestine's action at this juncture represents perhaps the greatest single contribution to the reestablishment of the papal authority in the East. At this council the Emperor, the Pope and the bishops of Alexandria and Constantinople strove to uphold their legitimate or supposed authority. As Batiffol has remarked, Rome alone came out of the struggle in a stronger position.[1]

It is regrettable that the council did not entirely put an end to Nestorianism. Of the various manifestations of the heresy which persisted one is of peculiar interest to the present study, the appeal of two bishops of the East. After the settlement of 433 Eutherios of Tyana and Helladios of Tarsus wrote to Rome on behalf of a considerable number of bishops of Bithynia, Thessaly, Cappadocia, Cilicia, and Euphratasia. It appears that they were sympathetic to Nestorius and evidently believed the Pope to be of the same mind. In their letter to Pope Sixtus,[2] in which they liken him to a second Moses, they ask him to assist them against the new Pharao (Cyril) by making an inquiry into recent events, and bringing 'heavenly correction' to the injustices. The sequel to this request is not known, but the appeal itself is significant. It shows that these Eastern bishops were convinced that the Pope had the competence to do all that they asked.[3]

The climax of the history of the early papacy is to be seen in the council of Chalcedon. By the middle of the fifth century the authority of Rome was an accepted fact in the East,[4] and practically every incident of the council of Chalcedon illustrates this acknowledgement. Certain parallels can be traced between this affair and the council of Ephesus. Both were concerned with a Christological heresy; in fact, monophysism, which was condemned at Chalcedon, arose out of a reaction against Nestorianism. The author of this heresy was the aged Eutyches, superior over some three hundred monks, in one of the many monasteries of Constantinople. In order to compensate for the excessive divisions introduced into Christ by the dualism of Nestorius, he taught that the

[1]Batiffol, *Siège Apostolique*, p. 393.
[2]Text in Mansi, V, cols. 893–7.
[3]Batiffol, *Cathedra Petri*, p. 243.
[4]cf. Batiffol, op. cit., p. 17.

humanity of Christ was absorbed into the divinity like a drop of water falling into the ocean. The closeness of this fusion had the effect of transforming the humanity into something utterly unlike that which was possessed by other human beings. His excessive reliance on the authority of St. Cyril and the Alexandrian formulae soon brought him into conflict with the school of Antioch. His orthodoxy was attacked first of all by Domnus, the Bishop of Antioch, and then in 447 by Theodoret of Cyr. Eutyches does not appear to have been disturbed by this incipient opposition. His position was comparatively secure, thanks to his reputation for sanctity and the favour of the Emperor. The latter supported him fully on the first signs of opposition from the Orient, and Alexandria, too, ever ready to do battle with the school of Antioch, rallied to the cause of Eutyches. Presumably for greater security, lest the opposition should increase, Eutyches wrote to the Pope to seek his support also in what he alleged to be a stand against the Nestorians.

From the very beginning Flavian, the peace-loving Bishop of Constantinople, had endeavoured to keep himself from being involved. However, matters came to a head in the autumn of 488, when Eusebius of Doryleum startled the synod of Constantinople by formally accusing Eutyches of heresy. Flavian could no longer evade the issue and reluctantly summoned the accused monk to come before the council to answer for his orthodoxy. After many delays Eutyches came, accompanied by numerous supporters, among whom was the imperial functionary Florentius. After employing every stratagem that his subtlety could devise, he was obliged to state the core of his theory, and declared that there was only one nature in the incarnate Christ. The synod thereupon condemned him for heresy and deposed him from his position of authority.[1]

Eutyches then proceeded to seek assistance from many quarters. He wrote to all the most important Eastern sees with the exception of Antioch, and in the West he sought help from Ravenna and Rome. The text of his letter to Rome indicates what an Eastern monk considered the Pope to be capable of: 'I have recourse to you, you the defender of religion and the enemy of factions . . . and I ask you that, without regarding what has been intrigued against me, you will pronounce on the faith what you judge fit. Do not allow intriguers to pursue me with their calumnies, do not allow them to exclude from the number of

[1]Mansi, VI, col. 744.

Catholics him who has lived seventy years in continence and chastity.[1]
Even the Emperor wrote to the Pope on his behalf.[2] The reply of St.
Peter Chrysologus, Bishop of Ravenna, has been preserved among the
letters of St. Leo. He refers the whole question to the Pope, and in doing
so showed how clearly he understood the prerogatives of the Bishop of
Rome: 'We exhort you, honourable brother, to submit yourself in all
things to what has been written by the blessed Bishop of Rome, because
St. Peter, who lives and presides in his see, gives the true faith to those
who seek it. For our part, for the sake of peace and the good of the faith,
we cannot judge questions of doctrine without the consent of the Bishop
of Rome.'[3] St. Leo himself was, at that time, ill-informed of the situation
and replied with the utmost circumspection. Later, when he had become
acquainted with the facts, he upheld the judgement of Flavian.

By the time that Leo had arrived at this decision the situation in the
East had changed considerably in favour of Eutyches. The Emperor,
having summoned a council which was to meet at Ephesus in the summer, proceeded to arrange its personnel in advance. He appointed
Dioscorus of Alexandria as the president, excluded Theodoret because
of his known sympathies towards Flavian, and designated two high-
ranking court officials, Elpidius and Eulogius, to ensure that his own
interests were not neglected. Leo had practically no option but to
appoint legates who would represent him at the council, to ensure the
observance of justice and equity. It is not easy to decide whether the
biased composition of the council would have been readily discernible
in Rome at that time. The legates appointed were Julius, Bishop of
Puteoli, the priest Renatus, who died in the course of the journey, and
the deacon Hilary, destined later to become Pope. The many letters
which they took with them included the famous Tome of Leo in which
he expounded the orthodox tradition of Christ's two natures united
in one person.

The council opened on August the 8th 449 in the church of the Virgin
Mary which had been the scene of the council of 431. Although assembled allegedly for the examination of the trial of Eutyches, it was evident
from the start that the result was decided in advance. The effective
control within the council had been restricted to those who were known
to be sympathetic to Eutyches. The Roman legates had little influence

[1]Mansi, V, col. 1014.
[2]Batiffol, *Siège Apostolique*, p. 503.
[3]Among the letters of St. Leo, M.P.L., Vol. 54, col. 741.

and were brushed aside by Dioscorus. Admittedly they were ignorant of Greek, but their passivity cannot be excused thus easily. Eutyches was required to make a statement of belief which enabled him to evade the precise problem which lay at the heart of the affair. No accusation was allowed against him. Dioscorus next directed that the proceedings of the council at Constantinople should be read out, and after stormy scenes Eutyches was reinstated.[1] Under the direction of Dioscorus the council proceeded to the deposition of Flavian and Eusebius of Doryleum. At this suggestion there were protests from the deacon Hilary and various others. Dioscorus thereupon summoned the soldiers into the church, which was the signal for general confusion. The troops came in and with them the turbulent monks, Egyptian sailors, and other supporters of Dioscorus. Flavian was dragged from the altar where he had sought sanctuary, arrested, and carried off with such brutality that he died within three days. Eusebius and the deacon Hilary managed to escape to Rome. Meanwhile in the council Dioscorus and his supporters succeeded in compelling the bishops to consent to the deposition of Flavian and Eusebius.

The second session held on August 22nd disposed of more orthodox bishops. Sentence was pronounced against Ibas of Edessa, Theodoret of Cyr, Domnus of Antioch, and Irenaeus of Tyr. The victory of Dioscorus appeared to be complete. He had disposed of every influential opponent in the East, Flavian was dead, Eutyches was reinstated, and he remained secure, or so he thought, under the protection of the sympathetic Emperor Theodosius II. The situation might well have been a repetition of the council of the Oak had it not been for St. Leo, who was the one person who had the compeentce to rectify everything.

'The stage was being set for an ecclesiastical struggle on a titanic scale, in which questions of far greater importance than the prerogatives of bishops or of the precedence of sees were at stake. Amid scenes of equivocation, betrayal and tragedy, one figure stood out like a beacon light amongst the wreckage of the storm. We shall see how in the confusion of thought resulting from the cross-currents of imperial and ecclesiastical politics Leo, and he alone, offered to a distracted church security, order, and peace, in the recognition of the doctrinal *magisterium* of the Roman see.'[2]

[1] Mansi, VI, col. 839.
[2] Jalland, T. G., *The Life and Times of St. Leo the Great*, London, 1941, p. 253.

No sooner had the council dispersed than protests poured in to Rome from all sides. The deacon Hilary, who had succeeded in eluding the vigilance of Dioscorus, reached Rome and gave Leo a full report on the proceedings. In his anger Leo gave the council the title which it has retained to this day, the 'Brigandage of Ephesus'. Hilary brought back with him the appeal of Flavian which he had written shortly before his death. Although the fact of this appeal had always been known,[1] the actual text was only discovered in the capitular library of Novaro by Dom Amelli as recently as 1882.[2] The text does not reveal opportunism, but shows the appeal to be based on the theological foundations of the papacy: 'I appealed to the throne of the Apostolic See of Peter the Prince of the Apostles, and the universal blessed synod which is under your holiness . . . issue a decree which God will inform your mind to frame, so that a council of both East and West being held, a like faith may be everywhere preached, so that the statutes of the fathers may prevail, that all that has been done may be rendered void.'

Other appeals were received from victims of equal distinction and prestige in the Eastern church. Theodoret of Cyr, who, like so many Greek Fathers, composed no systematic treatise on the theory of the papacy, nevertheless expounds the essence of the doctrine in his eloquent appeal: 'The Apostles Saints Peter and Paul have rendered your throne most illustrious. This is the culminating point of your privileges. Further, their God has even now shed light on their throne, by placing in it your Holiness [who is now] shedding forth the rays of orthodoxy. . . . I have been condemned without being judged. But I await the sentence of Your Apostlic See, I pray, I beg Your Holiness, to whose just tribunal I make my appeal, to lend me your aid, to order me to come thither and give an account of my doctrine and to show that it is agreeable to that of the Apostles.'[3]

The third appeal to arrive at Rome was that of Eusebius of Doryleum. Like its two predecessors, it indicates the powers which Rome enjoyed and which were recognized in the East. In this appeal, moreover, the habitual character of the process of appeal is indicated: 'The Apostolic Throne has been wont from the beginning to defend those who are

[1] It is mentioned in the letters to Leo, Valentinian, and Pulcheria, Mansi, VI, cols. 7, 49, 52.
[2] Edited by Mommsen in *Neues Archiv.*, XI, pp. 362–4. The importance of this appeal, together with those of Theodoret and Eusebius of Doryleum, as evidence of Rome's status as court of appeal is admitted by T. G. Jalland, op. cit., p. 246.
[3] Theodoret, Letter 113, M.P.G., Vol. 83, col. 1313.

suffering injustice. . . . I entreat your Blessedness give me back the dignity of my episcopate and communion with yourself, by letters from you to my lowliness bestowing on me my rank and communion.'[1]

Leo, now fully informed about the council at Ephesus, refused to acknowledge its legitimacy and began at once to undo the harm which had been done. This repudiation by Leo is of capital importance, since it emphasizes the role of the papal consent in ratifying a council. Admittedly the irregularities were manifest, but this was not unknown in the East, and it must be borne in mind that a certain amount of 'brigandage' was not altogether absent from the oecumenical council of Ephesus! The Pope's first plan was to hold another council, and as that could not be carried out in practice without the Emperor's consent, he wrote to them, and to various others, protesting against the 'brigandage', and endeavouring to arrange for another council.[2]

Theodosius II was far from helpful. By consistent prevarication he opposed all Leo's attempts, so that the situation appeared to be a complete deadlock. This state of affairs was reversed overnight by the Emperor's sudden death after being thrown from his horse. His sister Pulcheria, now married to Marcian, set about reversing her brother's religious policy, and agreed to Leo's original plan for another council. By that time, though, the general situation in the East was so unfavourable to the council of 449 that Leo no longer considered another council necessary. However, the new Emperor was so determined to hold one that Leo acquiesced and appointed legates who would represent him at the council which had been summoned to meet at Nicea on September 1st, 451. This time five legates were nominated, the bishops Paschasinus, Lucentius and Julian of Cos,[3] and the priests Boniface and Basil.

The general council which resulted, named after the city of Chalcedon, which was its eventual meeting-place, is of importance chiefly in the history of Christology. Incidentally it provides evidence which is of value to the present inquiry, the examination of which entails a selective study of the proceedings of the council. By the beginning of September more than five hundred bishops, nearly all Eastern, had assembled at Nicea. While awaiting the arrival of the Emperor various

---

[1]Text in Schwartz, *Acta Conc. Oecum.*, Tome II, Vol. ii, part 1, p. 79. Its evidence as to the rights of Rome (not just flattery) is stressed by Harnack, *History of Dogma*, II, p. 168 n. 1.

[2]Letters dispatched in October, 449, Jaffé, n. 438–44.

[3]There are good reasons for thinking that the bishop traditionally referred to as Julian of Cos was, in fact, the Bishop of Cios in Bithynia, cf. Jalland, T. G., op. cit., pp. 235, 236.

administrative measures were arranged. It was agreed, in accordance with the wishes of St. Leo, that Paschasinus should preside. In the event it was the imperial functionaries who directed the procedure, although they did not vote. At the request of the Emperor the bishops moved to Chalcedon, and the first session took place on October 8th in the presence of over five hundred bishops and eighteen imperial functionaries. The first dramatic incident was the removal, at the insistence of Paschasinus, of Dioscorus from among the bishops and the introduction of Theodoret of Cyr because he had been reinstated by the Pope.[1] Dioscorus was placed among the accused, and the council proceeded to examine the acts of the synods of Constantinople and Ephesus. At Ephesus in 431 the presence of the Roman legates had enabled the approbation of the decisions of a previous session from which they had been absent. In this council it was their presence which permitted the revision of the previous councils' enactments. The reading of the injustices perpetrated against Flavian provoked many angry protests and amid stormy scenes his orthodoxy was vindicated.

The deposition of Dioscorus took place at the third session on October 13th. In pronouncing sentence against him the legate Paschasinus spoke in a manner which is reminiscent of the deposition of Nestorius: 'The most holy and blessed Archbishop of the great and ancient Rome, Leo, by us and by this very holy council along with the thrice blessed and glorious Apostle Peter, who is the rock and foundation of the Catholic Church, the foundation of the orthodox faith, has deprived Dioscorus of the episcopal dignity and of every episcopal function. Let the very holy and great council pronounce in regard to the said Dioscorus what is conformable with the canons.'[2]

The Pope had been unwilling that there should be any debate on the doctrinal questions. When the theological matters came under discussion at the fourth session the Tome of Leo was read out and was greeted by the well-known acclamations: 'This is the faith of the fathers, This is the faith of the Apostles. . . . Peter has spoken by the mouth of Leo.' The fifth session was taken up with more theological discussions, somewhat to the regret of the papal legates. However, in the doctrinal statement which resulted they insisted that Leo's precise formula 'in two natures' should be inserted. The council next turned its attention to the rearrangement of the ecclesiastical regions in the East. The most

[1]Mansi, VI, col. 589.
[2]Mansi, VI, col. 1048.
S.P.P.–H*

important change was the increase in the power of Constantinople whose bishop, acquired patriarchal powers over the civil diocese of Asia and Pontus in addition to Thrace, which was under his sway already.

After this had been agreed, the vexed question of the primacy of honour came to the fore again. On October 31st, in the absence of the papal legates and the imperial functionaries, a small number of the bishops approved the following canon:[1] 'The fathers rightly attribute to old Rome privileges which correspond to its political importance. And it is by a similar sentiment that the five hundred [*sic*] bishops have accorded to new Rome [i.e. Constantinople] equal privileges, rightly judging that, having both the Emperor and the senate, it ought to enjoy the same advantages, to have the same importance in ecclesiastical order and to keep in all things the second rank after old Rome.'[2] It is important to realize from the outset that this canon is not, as is sometimes supposed, a denial of the primacy of Rome. On the contrary, it is an acknowledgement of it, both in the text quoted and in the preface, which declared: 'We define first of all that the primacy and the eminent honour following the canons being safeguarded for the most holy Archbishop of ancient Rome . . .'[3] The idea expressed is erroneous in so far as it assumes the primacy to be based on the civil importance of the city.[4] Needless to say, the latent threat to Rome's position was very real. The Bishop of Constantinople was ultimately responsible, desiring for his see an influence in the East such as Rome enjoyed in the West.[5]

It is only to be expected that Rome opposed the canon from the beginning. In the council itself the papal legates protested vigorously when they learned what had been enacted in their absence. Leo in his turn refused to ratify such a dangerous principle. His official notification of the events of the council, as well as the somewhat naive request to approve the twenty-eighth canon, came to him in the form of the synodal letter addressed to him by the bishops before they dispersed. Like other incidents in this council, it is a remarkable testimony to the authority of the Pope as it was then understood in the East. The Pope is addressed in the following terms: 'You have been for us the interpreter of the voice

[1]Scott, op. cit., p. 193, points out that only eighty-four bishops signed it.
[2]Text in Hefele, op. cit., II, ii, pp. 815–18.
[3]cf. Scott, op. cit., p. 194.
[4]Bardy, op. cit., p. 238, n. 2.
[5]Batiffol, *Siège Apostolique*, p. 557.

of the blessed Peter, and you have bestowed on us all the blessing of his faith. . . . We were about five hundred and twenty bishops whom you led as the head leads the members.'[1] The contents of the letter indicate clearly the papal power of approving the enactments of the council: 'We bring to your notice the fact that we have decreed several other matters [i.e. the twenty-eighth canon] in the interests of peace and good order in ecclesiastical affairs, and in confirmation of the statutes of the church, knowing that Your Holiness will confirm and approve them. In particular we have confirmed the ancient custom in virtue of which the Bishop of Constantinople has ordained the metropolitans of the diocese of Asia, Pontus, and Thrace. . . . We beg you therefore to honour our decrees with your approbation; and just as we have adhered to your decree [on doctrine], may Your Eminence do what is fitting for his children.' The title of 'head' is evidently applied to him as head of the church. To use it only in view of his presiding over the council would be an anomaly, particularly in view of the fact that the 'chair' was taken by the imperial functionaries.

Leo was profoundly concerned by the twenty-eighth canon and for that reason delayed several years before giving approbation to the council. When at last on March 21st, 453, he did reply officially to the synodal letter, he gave approbation to the doctrinal decisions, but refused his assent to the offending canon.[2] The letter which Anatolios of Constantinople wrote to regain Leo's favour serves further to confirm the council's need of papal approbation. After disavowing all thought of personal ambition, he points out that all the council's enactments required the Pope's confirmation.[3]

The council's main tasks had been to depose Dioscorus and to ensure that the Eastern episcopate was in accord with the definition of doctrine already pronounced by St. Leo.[4] These alone furnish considerable evidence for the papal authority. In addition three other relevant points emerge. The expressions of loyalty on the part of the bishops are too consistent and spontaneous to be set aside as sycophancy or Oriental obsequiousness. Secondly the importance of the papal approbation is seen in this council more clearly than in any previous one and its need is admitted even by an historian as little biased towards Rome as Dr.

[1] Text among the letters of St. Leo, No. 98. M.P.L., Vol. 54, cols. 951–60.
[2] Jaffé, n. 490.
[3] Text among the letters of St. Leo, No. 132, of April, 445, M.P.L., Vol. 54, col. 1082.
[4] Scott, op. cit., p. 201.

Kidd.[1] Thirdly the authority of Pope Leo, represented by his legates, enabled the legitimate deposition of Dioscorus and the repudiation of the 'Brigandage' which could have been a second 'Oak'.

The sequel to Chalcedon was much the same as that of Ephesus. The doctrinal problem was settled for good, and, in fact, the title 'orthodox' which certain Eastern churches use to this day dates from their loyalty to Chalcedon which differentiated them from the Monophysites. The old animosities of the great Eastern sees continued in a somewhat subdued form, but ready to erupt again if provoked. Just as certain of the Nestorians broke with the church after Ephesus, so also on this occasion a large section of the Monophysites, notably the Egyptian church, refused to accept the decision of the council. The divisions of the Eastern churches which persist to the present day took their origin in this century in defiance of the ruling of the various oecumenical councils.

The council of Chalcedon is a convenient point to terminate the study of the early papacy in its dealings with the Eastern church. In St. Leo the papal powers are seen to be fully developed, and indeed formally acknowledged by the Eastern church. The causes of the subsequent schism lie outside the scope of this study, but they could not invalidate the attitude of the early church. The foregoing historical inquiry makes possible an analysis of the Pope's powers in the East in the period when the Eastern zone had assumed its distinctive characteristics. In marked contrast with the Western church, the Pope is seen to exercise little influence on the day-to-day organization of the Eastern zone. His sphere of action is concerned almost exclusively with the matters of major importance. In particular it is clear that an Eastern patriarch needed communion with Rome if he was to be in communion with the universal church. In the maintenance of this communion Rome alone had the right to impose conditions, and thence to sever the bond if they were not complied with. Allied to this was the power to excommunicate and bring about the deposition of even the most important Eastern bishops, and conversely to reinstate them even in spite of their having been condemned by an Eastern council. The papal power over councils was similarly decisive, extending to the ratification or nullifying of those which were of oecumenical status. Finally in questions of belief which concerned the whole church the authority of the Pope is seen to be superior to that of any other bishop, to the extent that he did not have

[1]Kidd, op. cit., p. 147.

to await the decision of a general council before giving definitive pronouncement. The importance of these powers need not be stressed any further: they speak for themselves. As a result the Eastern zone, though sometimes regarded as a weakness in any exposition of a papal authority, furnishes in fact its strongest evidence, as will be seen in the final analysis of the evidence.

9

CONCLUSION

THE pontificate of St. Leo the Great is a convenient point at which to halt an investigation of the history of the early popes. From St. Leo to the present the papacy has changed so little that an inquirer whose experience was confined to the modern popes would have no difficulty in seeing that Leo held the same office in the church as, for instance, Pius XI. An examination of his pontificate shows that he possessed all the characteristics which are now recognized as being of the essence of the papacy. Mgr. Batiffol remarked that he was not, as has been alleged, the first pope, but he was fully a pope.[1] In his pontificate the institution of the papacy can be said to have achieved its term of normal development. It is necessary now to reflect on the history of that institution from Peter to Leo in order to propose a theory which will explain adequately all the relevant facts. In particular it is necessary to account for the prominent position of St. Peter, followed by an apparent regression, and then swift rise to pre-eminence by those who claimed to be his successors.

Four main theories have been suggested to explain the phenomenon. The theories of the usurpation of a power which was never given by Christ, the acquisition of pre-eminence by reason of the civil importance of the imperial capital, straightforward historical evolution, and finally institution by Christ together with the normal development which has attended all Christian doctrines.

The theory of usurpation has in its favour the undeniable fact that this kind of thing was not unknown in the early church. It was this type of ambition which prompted the depositions of Chrysostom and Flavian at the hands of Theophilus and Dioscorus. Similarly the ambitions of the bishops of Constantinople motivated their endeavours to secure for their see the primacy of honour. It is, however, important to bear in mind that the rivalry between the great sees of the church, which was

[1] D.T.C., art. 'Leon I', Vol. IX (i), col. 300, cf. In substance, T. G. Jalland, in *The Life and Times of St. Leo the Great*, p. 422, who stresses the importance of his predecessors.

pursued so unscrupulously, was a characteristic which appeared fairly late upon the ecclesiastical scene. The bishoprics were sought by the unscrupulous, and their power was augmented only in the period when they had become sources of wealth and influence. The special authority of Rome is seen to have been a reality before that era. It was during the persecutions, in the time of heroic and unworldly bishops, that the church of Rome occupied the position which at a later date many other churches would have liked to possess. By the end of the persecutions, when the sees became desirable to the worldly, and when the great Eastern bishops strove to increase their power, the Bishop of Rome was already in possession of his peculiar authority. In fact, a close examination of the activities of the early Roman bishops yields no satisfactory evidence to substantiate the charge of usurpation. It is principally on account of this lack of historical realism that the theory of usurpation has generally been abandoned at the present time.

The second theory, that of the advancement of the Bishop of Rome thanks to the civil importance of the city, has been popular for a longer period than the suggestion of usurpation. Like its predecessor it has in its favour the fact that it is intrinsically possible. The political influence of Rome could indeed have promoted its ecclesiastical importance, but on one condition: namely, if there had been any close link between the two institutions. In the East an adequate connexion between church and state did exist after the conversion of the emperor. The sovereigns thenceforward took no small interest in the affairs of the church, thus promoting the cause of the bishop of the capital city. The result for Constantinople was almost unbelievable. In the year 300 there was no thought even of building such a city, yet by the end of the century its bishop was so powerful that his only serious rival in the East was the patriarch of Alexandria. All this, it must be remembered arose as a result of the very real link between the emperor and the bishop of his city. On the other hand, the absence of such a connexion was equally effective in determining the opposite kind of result. In the Middle Ages, when the authority of the popes was secure, Rome might well have been expected to have become the centre of the intellectual life of the church. In fact, no such thing happened. Paris, Bologna and other university cities saw the flowering of the sciences, while Rome remained the administrative centre. At first sight this situation might appear somewhat unusual. However, in view of the fact that there is no necessary connexion between the centre of authority and the centre of learning, there is no reason why Rome should have been prominent intellectually.

The contention that the Bishop of Rome benefited from the civil importance of the city stands or falls by the strength of the bonds which united emperor and pope and in the formative period of the latter's authority. During the Apostolic era the church was not sufficiently developed to have anything like official relations with the civil government. By the time she had become in any way established the mutual attitudes had been determined by the legislation of the state. Persecution was the official policy and the two systems were destined to be estranged from each other for the first three centuries. This state of mutual hostility was further aggravated by the spiritual reaction against paganism and everything that it stood for. In the fervour of their conversion the early Christians developed an attitude of loathing and contempt for the pagan religions, morals, customs, and even the culture which had been bred by non-Christian society. They did not at once separate the good from the bad in pagan civilization, but classed it all as evil. The persecution merely strengthened this hostility, and on Rome, the centre of it all, they bestowed the most derogatory title at their disposal—Babylon, the symbol of all that is abominable in the eyes of God.[1] Early in the third century the school of Alexandria began the task of sifting out what was good in the culture of the pagans with a view to using it in the service of God. In the West, however, the old hostility persisted, so much so that Tertullian did not hesitate to brand civil government as the enemy of God.[2] Although there were degrees of animosity, it is true to say that a state of hostility was the normal attitude of the Church to the government during the period of the persecutions. For this early period it is clear that the Bishop of Rome would gain nothing in the eyes of Christians from his proximity to the seat of the Imperial organization. As a recent writer has expressed it, 'There is no single positive piece of evidence from the first three centuries to prove that the respect or submission which Christians showed to Rome, and which the Bishop of Rome frequently presumed upon, was connected with the civil importance of the imperial capital.'[3] It should also be noted that no other religion looked to Rome as its centre, not even those which

[1] In the canonical scriptures it is used of Rome in I Pet. 5:13; Apoc. 14:18, 16:19, 17:15, etc.
[2] *De Idolatria*, 18, C.S.E.L., Vol. 20, p. 53.
[3] Hastings, A., art. 'The Papacy and Rome's Civil Greatness' in the *Downside Review*, 1957, p. 366.

might have been expected to be the most closely allied to the city. Rome did not provide a spiritual centre for Judaism after the fall of Jerusalem, nor for Mithraism, nor, most surprisingly, did it become the focus of the cult of the emperor.[1]

The period of official toleration could have benefited Rome, had the circumstances been other than they were. By the time that Constantine had become actively interested in the affairs of the church Rome had ceased to be the imperial capital. From the time of Diocletian's transference of the authority to Milan the north of Italy became the centre of gravity of the Western empire. For the next half-century, during the reigns of Constantine and his son Constantius II, the Eastern empire overshadowed the West, and Constantinople, not Rome, became the most important city in the world. Moreover, in the religious policy of these two emperors there was no room for a pope. The Bishop of Constantinople acquired great power it is true, but only as the servant of the emperors, and the sovereigns themselves wielded much of the universal control which should have been the popes'. The policy of these Christian emperors, together with other factors described elsewhere, had the effect of obscuring the papal authority in the East until the fifth century.

In the West considerable attention has been focused on the imperial rescripts which gave support to the sentences of the Pope's tribunal. Their effectiveness was confined to giving civil recognition to an already established ecclesiastical authority.[2] They came too late to influence the growth of the papal power. In the West the Pope's position had been long since acknowledged, while the East being, already in a state of political separation, would take little heed of such provisions in favour of a Western bishop. Their effectiveness, too, was severely limited. The emperors who issued them, mere shadows of their former glory, were not long destined to hold sway in the West. Before long the Roman power would be swept away, leaving the popes strong in the possession of their spiritual authority.

The theory of the Pope's deriving influence from being in the imperial capital is, in fact, no more able to explain the papal authority than the previous charge of usurpation. The third theory, that of evolution, is the one which has the greatest intrinsic merits, and, at the present time, the greatest measure of support outside Catholic circles.

[1]Jalland, *The Church and the Papacy*, p. 106.
[2]Hastings, art. cit., p. 376.

It has, moreover, the distinction of being exemplified in at least one department of papal history, that of the temporal power. The acquisition of political and military power by the mediaeval popes does not stem from the essence of the church as instituted by Christ. It came about, according to the most satisfactory theory to be advanced,[1] by an evolutionary process according to simple historical factors. Whether the same can be said of the spiritual authority is a different matter altogether. The best-known champion of the evolutionary explanation was the distinguished German scholar Harnack, who attempted to account for the authority of the Roman bishops without reference to the institution of that power by Christ. However, a close examination of the history of the early papacy reveals that a purely evolutionary theory creates greater difficulties than it solves.

In the first place it is difficult to account for the apparent regression of the Roman authority in the transition from St. Peter to the early popes if the only forces in operation were those of progressive evolution. The theory is equally out of accord with the explanations given by the early witnesses. Many popes (who were in the best position to know the truth), and other writers, state clearly that the popes inherited power from St. Peter. On the other hand, no early writer suggested that there had been a gradual assumption of power by the once quite ordinary bishops of Rome. It is possible that all these witnesses were ignorant, or liars, but it remains difficult to accept such a view. A more serious difficulty for the school of evolution is the rate of progress which is to be seen in the rise to power of the papacy. Although Harnack ascribed the 'papal era' to the fifth century, he had to admit that pre-eminence had been achieved by about the middle of the third, and its causes were ready before the end of the second.[2] Thus in the primitive history of the church the superiority of the Roman church appears on the scene so early that it must have risen by means of revolution if the explanation is to be confined to the interplay of merely human influences between erstwhile equal-ranking bishops. It is, moreover, alleged that the Roman church was able to supply a norm and a service of centralization. One is naturally led to ask why it should have fallen to the Roman church to provide such a service for the whole church. Any one of a dozen

[1]The thesis is developed by J. Lecler in *The Two Sovereignties*, London, 1952.
[2]Harnack, *History of Dogma*, Excursus Catholic and Roman, Vol. II, p. 149. Also *The Constitution and Law of the Church in the first Two Centuries*, London, 1910, p. 168, n. 1 (being F. C. Pogson's trans. of *Entstehung und Entwickelung der Kirchenverfassung und Kirchenrechts in den zwei ersten Jahrhunderten*).

Eastern sees was better able to take the lead in ecclesiastical affairs. Jerusalem, as the parent community, had an unequalled prestige in the infant church. Antioch, too, had a unique distinction in being the cradle of gentile Christianity. Throughout the whole of the infancy of the church the East was superior in numerical strength, intellectual development and ecclesiastical organization. If it were simply a question of the rise to power of one church on its acquired merits, it is certain that one of the Eastern sees would have assumed the leadership.

Two more characteristics of the early church's progress are relevant to the present considerations and their import is even more decisive than the preceding observations. The first of these concerns the general organizational trend of the fifth century, which far from being conducive to the production of a papacy, was, in fact, a tendency towards regional autonomy. In the East it was the time of the definitive emergence of the patriarchates and the establishment of the heretical Nestorian and Monophysite churches. In the West, too, though less developed than in the East, this same tendency was at work, most notably in the case of Africa, which possessed a considerable amount of local autonomy. It is wellnigh impossible to concede that these same forces of evolution should have produced at the same time just the opposite effect, namely a unifying movement culminating in a centralized authority. The second characteristic of the fifth century, this time the nature of the popes' interventions, also tells decisively against the theory of the evolution of the papacy. The events of the fifth century present the remarkable enigma of an authority whose power had been obscured in the East for almost a century regaining recognition by intervening only in matter of the utmost importance. If the popes had proceeded from lesser to greater matters there might be some ground for alleging a purely human acquisition of power. In fact, though, they are seen to concern themselves almost exclusively with such questions as the deposition of patriarchs or the approbation of general councils. All this was carried out at a time when the Eastern bishops were employing every possible means to further the interests of their own sees. Such a situation cannot be explained by the laws of historical evolution, but demands the activity of some decisive influence shaping the destiny of the papacy independently of the normal pattern which historical evolution would demand.

The identification of this influence entails the adoption of the fourth and last theory as the only adequate explanation of the papal power. All the facts which have been discussed in the course of this brief study are adequately explained by attributing to Christ the origin of the peculiar status of the Bishop of Rome. The authority thus vested in St. Peter was transferred to his successors in Rome, and the subsequent history of the institution, in common with all Christian doctrines, underwent the normal process of development. Such a theory does justice to all that the Scriptures teach about St. Peter without necessitating any minimization of his position. The apparent regression which followed on St. Peter's death is explained satisfactorily only by this theory, since alone of all the hypotheses this one takes into account the difference between the primary sources of Christian revelation and the subsequent studies of the writers of the early church. The ensuing development in this, as in all doctrines, owes its characteristic rapidity to the fact that it is not merely the human progress in ideas but the gradual appreciation of all that was contained in a body of truths which was already known.

Undoubtedly there are difficulties which this theory must face. The frequent opposition which was so strong might well seem to militate against the alleged institution by Christ himself. This fact could be a serious difficulty, it is true, but it depends almost entirely on the nature, not merely the fact, of the opposition in question. St. Paul had frequently to defend his authority, but no one would suggest that he was an impostor for having had to vindicate his apostleship. Similarly it is necessary to examine the nature of the opposition which faced the popes, to see whether it constituted a valid argument against the rights of their office. Setting aside the question of St. Cyprian, whose attitude is an anomaly in the early church, the first serious opposition to the papacy came from the Eusebian party in the Arian crisis. The reasons which prompted their hostility are not hard to estimate, since they represent a recurring pattern of Eastern affairs. It came as a shock to John Henry Newman to realize that the anti-papalists of the early church were at the same time the Arians, Nestorians, and Monophysites, while the champions of orthodoxy, like Athanasius and Cyril, were also the papalists. It is unlikely, to use no stronger term, that the heretics would have preserved the authentic tradition concerning the papacy any more than they had preserved it in their Trinitarian or Christological theories.

The later opposition arose out of the pretensions of the see of Constantinople. This series of incidents points more clearly than the former to the ultimate source of the difficulty. The claims to pre-eminence advanced on behalf of the see of Constantinople rested solely on the civic importance of the city. Such a principle had never been admitted in the church. Although it resulted in a real obstacle to the authority of the popes, its basis cannot be regarded as valid either in favour of the see of Constantinople or as a legitimate argument against the Roman supremacy.

The root cause of so much difficulty in church government is indicated by the nature of the claim of Constantinople. It was the defective character of the Greek ecclesiology.[1] They did not appreciate the nature of the church as an organization. This failure is to be seen even among the saints of the Eastern episcopate.

Whether it was legally correct for St. Gregory Nazianzen and St. John Chrysostom to occupy the see of Constantinople is not altogether certain. If, indeed, they were justified in acquiescing in their respective elections, it is a striking indication of how easily the Eastern church (and its saints) could abandon the provisions of Nicea, which strictly forbade such translations. Worse still was the failure to appreciate the dependence which the local church owed to the universal, resulting in the secession of large sections of the East in defiance of the councils of Ephesus and Chalcedon. At the root of it all lay their willingness to allow the civil power to administer the affairs of the church. This was the most serious failure of the Eastern church and it was the ultimate cause of their hostility to the papacy, as well as various other problems.

Caesaropapism, which came upon the church after the conversion of Constantine, was never eradicated from the East, even when orthodoxy had replaced Arianism and the rights of Rome had been re-established. When this Erastian tendency became firmly implanted it was obvious that the papal authority would suffer, since the system was incompatible with a supra-national authority. In consequence every more recent division of political authority in the East has been followed by a corresponding division of ecclesiastical authority resulting in a sovereign hierarchy in each sovereign state. Under such circumstances it has not been possible for them even to envisage a general council, although they have always acknowledged the authority of those which were held in the past. The Greek schism of the eleventh century was almost inevitable because caesaropapism was never eradicated.

The two phenomena of opposition to the papacy and caesaropapism do not constitute a valid objection against the rights of the Pope,

[1] Batiffol, *Siège Apostolique*, p. 615; Harnack, History of Dogma, III pp. 233–5.

although they presented many obstacles to the exercise of his authority. Since they are explained by defects in the Eastern church, they cannot seriously weaken the theory of Christ's institution of the papacy.

One further consequence follows, concerning the papal authority, which is frequently overlooked by Anglicans, even though they are prepared to admit a fair degree of legitimacy to the papal prerogatives in the early church. If indeed the papal authority is to be traced back to the institution by Christ of St. Peter's special status, then it follows that it is of the unchangeable essence of the church. As a result neither the Christian church, nor any part of it, has the right to change this arrangement. In purely human affairs nations may legitimately adopt one form of government in place of some other. If, for instance, it would serve the interests of the nation to be governed by a democracy rather than an oligarchy, then such a transition would be legitimate. God has not predetermined any specific form of government for civil society. In the church it is otherwise.

In concluding this survey of the early papacy two general principles can be isolated which are of supreme importance in the right understanding of the whole question. The first of these is the role of caesaropapism in the Eastern church. But for this, it is probable that there would have been no schism in the eleventh century. In the West the same peril could have menaced the ecclesiastical authority, but thanks to a better understanding of the nature of the institutional church, the danger was permanently averted. So much for the order of realities. In the comprehension of the early papacy another principle must be invoked—that of development, in the sense which Newman expounded. All the doctrines of the church have undergone this process of development, the papacy more than most. The authority derived from St. Peter is both a doctrine and an institution in whose development the forces of history have played a considerable role. As a result the correct understanding of this doctrine, more, perhaps, than any other, demands that it be studied in the light of the principles governing the development of Christian doctrine.

ALPHABETICAL INDEX OF NAMES AND SUBJECTS